The American Ways

The American Ways

AN INTRODUCTION TO AMERICAN CULTURE

SECOND EDITION

Maryanne Kearny Datesman *Georgetown University*

JoAnn Crandall *University of Maryland Baltimore County*

Edward N. Kearny *Western Kentucky University*

Longman

Datesman, Maryanne Kearny.
 The American ways : an introduction to American culture / Maryanne
Kearny Datesman. JoAnn Crandall, Edward N. Kearny. — 2nd ed.
  p. cm.
 Edward N. Kearny's name appears first on the earlier ed.
 Rev. ed. of: The American way, c1984.
 Includes bibliographical references and index.
 ISBN 0-13-342015-9
 1. English language—Textbooks for foreign speakers. 2. United States—
Civilization—Problems, exercises, etc. 3. Readers—United States. I. Crandall,
JoAnn. II. Kearny, Edward N. III. Kearny, Edward N. American way. IV. Title.
 PE1128.D347 1996
 428.6'æÆ4—dc21   96-44476   CIP

Publisher: *Mary Jane Peluso*
Editor: *Sheryl Olinsky*
Development Editor: *Barbara Barysh*
Permissions and Photo Research: *Vivian García*
Electronic Production Editor: *Steven D. Greydanus*
Manufacturing Manager: *Ray Keating*

Electronic Image Production Supervisor: *Todd Ware*
Electronic Image Production/Scanning: *Marita Froimson*
Art Director: *Merle Krumper*
Interior Design: *Merle Krumper/Steven D. Greydanus*
Cover Design: *Wanda España*

© 1997 by PRENTICE HALL REGENTS
A Pearson Education Company
Pearson Education
10 Bank Street
White Plains NY 10606

Printed in the United States of America

10

ISBN   0-13-342015-9

Contents

To the Teacher

What is "culture"? There are many definitions. Some would define it as the art, literature, and music of a people, their architecture, history, religion, their traditions. Others might focus more on the customs and specific behavior of the people. We choose to use a sociological definition of *culture* as *the way of life of a group of people, developed over time and passed down from generation to generation*. This broad definition includes every aspect of human life and interaction. It would be impossible to cover every facet of American culture in a single book. We have, therefore, chosen to take a values approach to our discussion, focusing on the traditional mainstream values that have attracted people to the United States for over 200 years. After explaining how these traditional values developed, we will trace how they affect various aspects of American life.

Why a book on American culture? There are many reasons. Those of us who have worked with foreign students in American universities or who have taught English to students both here and overseas are repeatedly confronted by questions about life in the United States. Students who are preparing to come to the United States to study, or who are already enrolled in English as a Second Language or other programs in American universities, frequently are confused or even mystified about the values, attitudes, and cultural patterns that surround them. Even those students who have mastered enough English to take courses in an American university may find that they have not adequately mastered the cultural rules that are required for them to be successful American students. Many of these rules can be understood only within the broader context of American cultural patterns in general.

It is not only students who need information of the kind presented here. Foreign business people, visiting scholars or government officials, and even tourists would find their time spent in the United States more satisfying if they were able to understand more of the values underlying American behavior patterns and institutions. Newly arrived immigrants or refugees, as well, would find adaptation to their new home easier if they had a systematic introduction to their new country and its inhabitants.

Thus, *The American Ways* is suitable for a variety of students. It has been used as a text in a number of programs for foreign students, including intensive ESL or EFL programs, short summer courses in the United States for foreign high school and college students, both quarter and semester courses at American universities, government programs for foreign visitors, and classes for immigrants. It has also been used in many different settings outside the United States, both as a text for students and as a reference guide — for American Peace Corps volunteers, for example, and others who are teaching American culture to ESL or EFL students.

What do we really learn when we study about other cultures? First and foremost, we learn about our own. Until we are confronted by a different way of doing things, we assume that everyone does things the same way that we do, and thus our own culture — our values, attitudes, behavior — is largely hidden from our view. When we spend some time analyzing another culture, however, we begin to see our own more clearly and to understand some of the subtleties that motivate our behavior and our opinions. Therefore, students using this book cannot help but begin to understand themselves and their own cultures better as a result. To enhance this understanding, we have followed each of the chapters with a series of exercises, some of them specifically designed to encourage students to think about their own values or patterns of behavior and to compare these with what they are learning about or experiencing in American settings. We have also included a number of exercises that are intended to encourage foreign students to interact with and talk with Americans. In these exercises, we have provided a set of carefully structured questions that students can ask Americans. This information will help students get a composite picture of American beliefs and practices as they relate to education, business, government, sports, recreation, and so on.

Some of the chapter exercises will provide students with an opportunity to explore more fully an idea that has been presented or to discuss these ideas with other students. You may wish to assign different exercises to different students or small groups of students and then ask them to share their findings and opinions with the rest of the class. If possible, small groups should include students from different countries so that in addition to learning about American culture and their own, they are also learning about others.

Perhaps this is the real goal of a culture course: to help us become more sensitive to cultural differences and more accepting of them. However, there will always be things about another culture that we do not "like," no matter how much we might understand it. Thus, the objective of this book is not to persuade others to approve of all facets of life in the United States but rather to help them understand it more fully and be able to adapt, even if only temporarily, whenever it is desirable to do so. There are always opportunities for exploiting one's "foreignness," but there are also times when being from a different culture can be a real liability. The ultimate choice is up to the individual, but we hope that this introduction and cultural overview will enable people working or studying with Americans to make more informed choices.

■ ■ ■ ■

About the Second Edition . . .

We have tried to change this book as little as possible, concentrating on updating events that have occurred since its original publication in 1984. If you have previously used the text, however, there are some changes that you should watch for. Perhaps the most significant difference is the addition of material on multiculturalism. We believe that this issue deserves special attention because the United States has become much more culturally diverse since the early 1980s. It is now even more difficult to describe "the American culture" than it was then. In fact, we modified the title of the book to *The American Ways* to reflect this multiculturalism. The basic conceptual framework of values is the same, but now these values are referred to as *traditional*, basic values. The first and last chapters have undergone extensive revision; the material on television has been moved from Chapter 5 *The Heritage of Abundance* to Chapter 10 *Leisure Time: Organized Sports, Recreation, and Television*. Also, Chapter 11 *The American Family* has new information about nontraditional families, reflecting changing American lifestyles. For each chapter, we have added a list of movies that may be used to illustrate ideas or themes presented in the chapter. You may choose segments, or show a whole film, depending on your class. Please be sure to preview all films because some segments are *likely* to contain material that may offend or be totally inappropriate for your students.

We have been delighted to hear from many teachers about creative ways they have used *The American Way* — not only to introduce American culture, but also in cross-cultural communication, listening/speaking, reading/writing, academic preparation, and even literature courses. Teachers have used the values framework to design courses where students could explore ways in which the values appear in American literature or current events, for example, focusing on materials the teacher developed from other sources and presented in addition to the text.

Originally, we envisioned this book primarily in ESL/EFL courses, preparing students to study in American universities. Because we believe that these students need experience presenting information and voicing their own personal opinions to others, they should be encouraged to make oral reports and participate in debates and formal discussions. We have written many exercises that suggest appropriate topics and activities. The first edition also included other exercises that could be used to help the student become more effective in an American university. For example, the outlining exercises provided instruction on how to organize information into main ideas and supporting details. For the second edition, however, we have eliminated the outlining and the skimming exercises to make room for more pair work and small group discussion activities of general interest. But the outlining work is not lost! New outlines for the second edition have been done and are published in the *Teachers' Resource Manual* that accompanies *The American Ways*. In this manual you will find the exercises from the first edition, as well as answer keys, lesson plans, and graphic organizers — all presented as reproducible masters. The manual includes many other ideas for listening/speaking activities using movies and videos available commercially.

The Book at a Glance

Purpose
To increase students' awareness and understanding of the cultural values of the United States, their own country, and, we hope, other countries.

To provide interesting cross-cultural activities for small group and class discussions, and topics for oral presentations, research, and writing projects.

Level
High intermediate to advanced. The vocabulary level is in the range of 3,000 to 4,000 words. Grammatical structures are not controlled, although an effort has been made to avoid overly complex patterns. (The level of the second edition is somewhat higher than the first.)

Content
Information about the traditional basic American values, where they came from, and how these values affect various institutions and aspects of life in the United States: religion, business, government, race relations, education, recreation, and the family.

Types of Exercises
Vocabulary practice, comprehension check, questions for discussion, cloze summary paragraphs, values clarification, questions for Americans, suggestions for research and oral reports, suggestions for writing, debate topics, proverbs, people watching, understanding the media, suggestions for further reading, recommended movies, pair and small group activities, and experiments.

Use of Text
- To orient students to American culture
- To foster cross-cultural communication
- To promote reading, discussion, and composition
- To encourage conversation
- To serve as a conceptual framework and accompany other materials focusing on literature, the media, current events, and so on.

Acknowledgments

Our great appreciation goes to Elizabeth Coppolino, Gwen Blase, and Vivian García for helping us with research, photos and permissions. Our thanks also to Sheryl Olinsky, Barbara Barysh, Todd Ware, Marita Froimson, and Steven Greydanus at Prentice Hall Regents. We wish to acknowledge the comments and encouragement we have received from many colleagues who have used this book in a wide range of settings all over the world. We would also like to thank the numbers of foreign students we have worked with over the years for sharing their insights and perceptions of the United States with us, and in the process, for helping us to better understand our own American culture.

M. K. D.
J. A. C.
E. N. K.

Dedicated to Lisa Kearny and Joseph Keyerleber

American mosaic: Beyond the "melting pot"   **Steve Schapiro**

CHAPTER 1

Introduction

> Culture hides much more than it reveals, and strangely enough what it hides, it hides most effectively from its own participants. Years of study have convinced me that the real job is not to understand foreign culture but to understand our own.

> **Edward T. Hall**

Before You Read

1. What is "culture"?
2. What do you know about the **ethnic diversity** of the American population? Where did the people originally come from?
3. How have patterns of immigration to the United States changed over the years?
4. Do you think it is possible to make **generalizations** about Americans?

Life in the United States

People are naturally curious about each other, and when they meet people from different countries, they want to know about them:

- What is life like in their country?
- What kind of houses do they live in?
- What kind of food do they eat?
- What are their customs?

If we visit their country, we can observe the people and how they live, and we can answer some of these questions. But the most interesting questions are often the hardest to answer:

- What do the people believe in?
- What do they value most in life?
- What **motivates** them?
- Why do they behave the way they do?

In trying to answer these questions about Americans, we must remember two things: (1) the immense size of the United States, and (2) its great ethnic diversity. It is difficult to comprehend the size of the country until you have tried to travel from one city to another. If you got in a car in New York and drove to Los Angeles, stopping only to get gas, eat, and sleep, it would take you four or five days. It takes two full days to drive from New York to Florida. On a typical winter day, it might be raining in Washington, D.C., and snowing in New York and Chicago, while it is warm enough to swim in Los Angeles and Miami. It is not difficult to imagine how different daily life might be in such different climates, or how **lifestyles** could vary in cities and towns so far apart.

ROB ROGERS reprinted by permission of United Feature Syndicate, Inc.

The other significant **factor** influencing American life, ethnic diversity, is probably even more important. Aside from the Native Americans who were living on the North American continent when the first European settlers arrived, all Americans came from foreign countries, or their ancestors did. (Incidentally, some of the Native Americans are themselves members of separate and distinct Indian nations, each with its own language, culture, traditions, and even government.) From the 1600s to the birth of the new nation in 1776, most immigrants were from northern Europe, and the majority were from England. It was these people who shaped the values and traditions that became the **dominant** culture of the United States.

A Nation of Immigrants

In 1815, the population of the United States was 8.4 million. Over the next 100 years, the country took in about 35 million immigrants, with the greatest numbers coming in the late 1800s and the early 1900s. In 1882, 40,000 Chinese arrived, and between 1900 and 1907, there were more than 30,000 Japanese immigrants. But by far the largest numbers of the "new immigrants" were from central, eastern, and southern Europe. The "new immigrants" brought different languages and different cultures to the United States. Gradually most of them **assimilated** to the dominant American culture they found here.

In 1908, a year when a million new immigrants arrived in the United States, Israel Zangwill wrote in a play:

> America is God's **Crucible**, the great Melting-Pot where all the races of Europe are melting and re-forming.... Germans and Frenchmen, Irishmen and Englishmen, Jews and Russians—into the Crucible with you all! God is making the American!

Since Zangwill first used the term *melting pot* to describe the United States, the concept has been debated. In Chapter 8 we will consider this issue in more detail, and we will trace the history of African-Americans, as well. Two things are certain: the dominant American culture has survived and it has more or less successfully absorbed vast numbers of immigrants at various points in its history. Some years during the first two decades of the 20th century, there were as many as one million new immigrants per year, an astonishing 1 percent of the total population of the United States.

In 1921, however, the country began to limit immigration, and the Immigration Act of 1924 virtually closed the door. The total number of immigrants admitted per year dropped from as many as a million to only 150,000. A **quota** system was established that specified the number of immigrants that could come from each country. It heavily favored immigrants from northern and western Europe and severely limited everyone else. This system remained in effect until 1965.

After World War II, several exceptions were made to the quota system to allow groups of refugees into the United States:

1940s	600,000	"displaced persons" (refugees)
1950s	40,000	Hungarians
1960s	675,000	Cubans
1975	100,000	Vietnamese and Cambodians
1980	100,000	Cubans

The immigration laws began to change in 1965, and the yearly totals began to rise again—from about 300,000 per year in the 1960s to over a million per year in the 1990s. The United States now admits more immigrants than all the other industrialized countries combined. Changes in the laws that were intended to help family **reunifications** have resulted in large numbers of non-Europeans. In the late 1990s, 90 percent of the immigrants were coming from Latin America, the Caribbean, and Asia. In addition to the legal immigration, illegal immigration was adding an additional estimated 500,000 per year.

Immigration in the 1990s is the largest in almost 100 years and accounts for one-third of the yearly growth in total population. The present population is 25 percent nonwhite (black, Hispanic and Asian), and if present trends in immigration patterns and birth rates continue, these minority groups will make up 41 percent of the population by 2040. Already there are areas of the country where the majority of students in the schools are from minority groups, many of whom are recent immigrants who do not speak English well. In Miami,

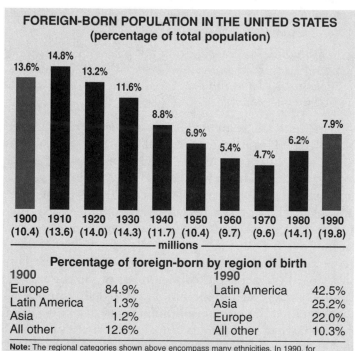

FOREIGN-BORN POPULATION IN THE UNITED STATES
(percentage of total population)

1900	1910	1920	1930	1940	1950	1960	1970	1980	1990
13.6%	14.8%	13.2%	11.6%	8.8%	6.9%	5.4%	4.7%	6.2%	7.9%
(10.4)	(13.6)	(14.0)	(14.3)	(11.7)	(10.4)	(9.7)	(9.6)	(14.1)	(19.8)

———— millions ————

Percentage of foreign-born by region of birth

1900		1990	
Europe	84.9%	Latin America	42.5%
Latin America	1.3%	Asia	25.2%
Asia	1.2%	Europe	22.0%
All other	12.6%	All other	10.3%

Note: The regional categories shown above encompass many ethnicities. In 1990, for example, more than 80 ethnic divisions comprise "Europe."
Source: U.S. Department of Commerce. Bureau of the Census, *We the American Foreign Born*, Sept. 1993.

Reprinted by permission from *The American Enterprise*, a Washington-based magazine of politics, business, and culture (1-800-596-2319)

three-fourths of the population speak a language other than English at home, and 67 percent of these people say they do not speak English well. Contrast this, however, with a state like South Dakota, where only 6.5 percent of the people were born in another country. Across the United States, 9 percent of the total population is "foreign-born," almost one in ten.

The vast majority of new immigrants choose to live in seven states: California, Texas, New York, Florida, Illinois, New Jersey, and Arizona. Seventy-nine percent of all new immigrants settle in one of these states. The accompanying chart shows the distribution. Note that California alone takes in 40 percent of the total number of legal immigrants coming to the United States.

America's Legal Immigrants: Who They Are and Where They Go

The United States accepts more immigrants than all other industrialized nations combined. In fiscal 1991 the United States government granted 1,827,167 people legal permanent residence. Seventy-nine percent of these legal immigrants, looking for everything from freedom to financial opportunity, chose the seven states below as their new homes.

Newsweek, August 9, Julie Shaver, Immigration and Naturalization Service. © 1993 Newsweek, Inc. All rights reserved. Reprinted by permission.

[Percentages are of total legal 1991 U.S. immigrants.]

ILLINOIS
More Poles live in Chicago than any other city in the world except Warsaw. The Polish community continues to draw new immigrants to the Windy City.

- Mexico 54%
- Poland 9%
- India 5%
- Philippines 4%
- Former USSR 4%
- Others 24%

NEW YORK
Ellis Island closed as a port of entry in 1954, but New York City still lures more immigrants than any other U.S. city.

- Dom. Republic 12%
- Former USSR 10%
- Jamaica 6%
- China 5%
- India 5%
- Others 62%

NEW YORK 188,104 (10%)

ILLINOIS 73,388 (4%)

NEW JERSEY 56,164 (3%)

CALIFORNIA 735,732 (40%)

ARIZONA 40,624 (2%)

TEXAS 212,600 (12%)

FLORIDA 141,068 (8%)

NEW JERSEY
Asian Indians, one of the fastest-growing immigrant groups in New Jersey, speak as many as 20 different languages.

- India 9%
- Dom. Republic 7%
- Colombia 6%
- Mexico 5%
- Peru 5%
- Others 68%

CALIFORNIA
When Los Angeles erupted in rioting in 1993, tensions grew between the black community and immigrants; roughly 2,000 Korean-owned businesses were among those looted or damaged by fire.

- Mexico 69%
- Philippines 4%
- El Salvador 3%
- Vietnam 3%
- China 2%
- Others 19%

ARIZONA
Although many are just passing through in search of opportunities, Arizona's Mexican immigrants often feel at home amid the state's Hispanic heritage.

- Mexico 86%
- Vietnam 2%
- Others 12%

TEXAS
Texas and Mexico share some 1,200 miles of porous border, along which the INS has apprehended about 380,000 illegal aliens so far this year.

- Mexico 80%
- El Salvador 4%
- Vietnam 2%
- Other 14%

FLORIDA
Fleeing Haitians are the latest wave of immigrants to Miami, but record numbers of Cubans continue to cross the 90-mile stretch on makeshift rafts.

- Mexico 30%
- Haiti 21%
- Cuba 6%
- Jamaica 4%
- Colombia 4%
- Others 35%

Cultural Pluralism in the United States

One of the critical questions facing the United States today is what role the new immigrants will play in their new country. How much will they choose to take on the traditional American values and culture? How much will they try to maintain their own language and cultural traditions? Will they create an entirely new culture based on some combination of their values and those of the traditional American culture?

Historically, although the children of immigrants may have grown up **bilingual** and **bicultural**, many did not pass on much of their parents' language or culture to their own children. Thus, many grandchildren of immigrants do not speak the language of the old country and are "American" by culture. However, in some parts of the country with established communities that share a common language or culture, bilingualism and biculturalism continue. This is particularly true in communities where new immigrants are still arriving. In general, **cultural pluralism** is more accepted in the United States today than it was in the first half of the 20th century, and many of the school systems have developed bilingual programs and multicultural curricula. We will discuss this more in Chapter 9.

At the close of the 20th century, there seems to be a rise in the consciousness of ethnic groups around the world, and a sense of pride in what makes them unique. This occurs in the United States among many different groups, and in some cases it has resulted in new names to symbolize each group's identity. In the United States, people have become very sensitive to the language used to describe these groups, and they try to be "politically correct" (P.C.). For example, many black Americans, particularly young people, prefer the term

Immigrants arriving at Ellis Island, New York City   **Library of Congress**

African-American instead of *black*, to identify with their African **heritage**. Some Spanish speakers prefer to be called *Latinos* (referring to Latin America) instead of *Hispanics*, while others prefer to be identified by their country of origin (Cuban-American or Cuban, *Chicano*, Mexican-American or Mexican, and so on). Most of the **census data** continues to use the terms *black* and *Hispanic*, so we will generally use these terms, along with *African-American* and *Latino*.

In spite of some very important differences, however, there is still a tie that binds Americans together. That tie is a sense of national identity—of "being an American." Incidentally, when citizens of the United States refer to themselves as *Americans*, they have no intention of excluding people from Latin American countries. There is no word such as *United Statesians* in the English language, so people call themselves *Americans*. Thus, what is really a language problem has sometimes caused misunderstandings. Although citizens of Latin American countries may call the people in the United States *North Americans*, to most people in the United States this makes no sense either, because the term *North American* refers to Canadians and Mexicans as well as citizens of the United States. (NAFTA, the North American Free Trade Agreement, for example, is a trade agreement among Canada, the United States, and Mexico.) The word *American*, then, will be used in this text as the adjective and nationality for the people who live in the United States of America.

Making Generalizations about American Beliefs

What, then, can we say about these Americans? What holds them together and makes them feel American? Is it possible to make generalizations about what they believe? It is, but we must be cautious about generalizations. As we talk about basic American beliefs, we must remember that not all Americans hold these beliefs, nor do all Americans believe these things to the same degree. The way in which some Americans practice their beliefs may also differ, resulting in a great variety of lifestyles. What we will attempt to do here is to define and explain the traditional, dominant cultural values that have for so many years attracted immigrants to the United States.

Throughout this book we will be drawing on the wisdom of a famous observer of the American scene, Alexis de Tocqueville. De Tocqueville came to the United States as a young Frenchman in 1831 to study the American form of democracy and what it might mean to the rest of the world. After a visit of only nine months, he wrote a **remarkable** book called *Democracy in America*, which is a "classic study of the American way of life." De Tocqueville had unusual powers of observation. He described not only the democratic system of government and how it operated but also its effect on how Americans think, feel, and act. Many **scholars** believe that he had a deeper understanding of traditional American beliefs and values than anyone else who has written about the United States. What is so remarkable is that many of these **traits** of the American character, which he observed nearly 200 years ago, are still visible and meaningful today.

Pioneer life in 1892 **Library of Congress**

Another reason why de Tocqueville's observations of the American character are important is the time when he visited the United States. He came in the 1830s, before America was industrialized. This was the **era** of the small farmer, the small businessman, and the settling of the western frontier. It was the period of history when the traditional values of the new country were newly established. In just a generation, some 40 years since the adoption of the U.S. Constitution, the new form of government had already produced a society of people with unique values. The character traits that de Tocqueville describes are the same ones that many Americans still take pride in today. He, however, was a **neutral** observer and saw both the good and the bad sides of these qualities.

This is a book about those traditional basic American beliefs, values, and character traits. It is not a book of cold facts about American behavior or institutions, but rather it is about the motivating forces behind the people and their institutions. It is about how these traditional basic beliefs and values affect important aspects of American life: religion, business, work and play, politics, the family, and education.

We invite you to participate in this book. We will describe what many Americans think and believe, but you will have an opportunity to test these descriptions by making your own observations. As you read about these traditional basic values, think of them as working hypotheses that you can test on Americans, on people of other nations, and on people of your nationality. Compare them with your own values and beliefs and with what is most important in your life. Through this process, you should emerge with a better understanding not only of Americans but also of your own culture and yourself. It is by studying others that we learn about ourselves.

■ ■ ■ ■

New Words

ethnic diversity people of many different races and nationalities

generalization a statement that is generally true

motivate to cause someone to do something or act in a certain way (a motive is an idea or feeling that causes someone to act)

lifestyle the way people live: their clothes, their homes, their jobs, their leisure activities

factor point; ideas or elements that cause a result

dominant ruling, most powerful and important

assimilate to become part of a country, or a group

crucible a large pot used for melting metal

quota a specific number or amount; a limit on numbers; the maximum (or minimum) number permitted

reunification the process of reuniting or bringing together again

bilingual speaking two languages (the prefix *bi* means two—"bicultural" means having two cultures)

cultural pluralism accepting more than one culture

heritage conditions of life or culture that come to us from the past

census data the information learned in the census (the official count of the population) taken every ten years in the United States

remarkable surprisingly good

scholar someone who studies a subject thoroughly

trait characteristic

era time, period of time in history

neutral not taking one side or the other; seeing both sides (the good and the bad)

A. Vocabulary Check

Complete the sentences using words or phrases from the New Words list.

1. The immigrants who came from England established the _____ culture in the United States.

2. The United States gets _____ _____ at the beginning of each decade (1980, 1990, 2000).

3. If you want to discuss the characteristics of someone's personality, you can speak of that person's personality _____.

4. Something that is surprisingly good is _____.

5. If two countries are at war and a third country chooses not to take sides, the third country may declare itself _____.

6. For the past several decades, the U.S. immigration law has favored family _____.

7. Someone who lives and works on a farm has a different _____ from someone who lives in the city and works in an office.

8. Unlike some other countries that do not have people of many different races and nationalities, the United States has great _____ _____.

9. If more people in the world were _____ and _____, communication would be a lot easier.

10. If we want to understand why people think and act the way they do, we must understand what _____ them.

11. A person who has studied a subject thoroughly, such as a "historian" who has studied history, is called a _____.

12. As immigrant families adjust to life in their new country, learn the language, and become comfortable with the culture, we say that they _____.

13. For a period of time in the 1930s and 1940s, big bands were very popular in the United States. It was the big band _____.

14. If the economy of a country suddenly improves, there may be many reasons or _____ that have caused the change.

15. If I state something that is generally true—such as, "Most Americans are proud of their freedom"—I am making a _____.

16. A _____ is used in the process of making steel.

17. There is more _____ _____ and less prejudice in the United States now than there was a generation ago.

18. In 1924, the United States set _____ establishing the number of immigrants permitted from each country.

19. In order to identify with their ethnic _____, some people refer to themselves as African-Americans, Mexican-Americans, Irish-Catholics, and so on.

B. Comprehension Check

Write T *if the statement is true and* F *if it is false according to the information in the chapter.*

_____ 1. One factor affecting lifestyles in the United States is the different climates.

_____ 2. Native American Indians all speak the same language.

_____ 3. The dominant American culture was established by immigrants who came from southern Europe.

_____ 4. Throughout the history of the United States, more immigrants have come from English-speaking countries than any others.

_____ 5 Zangwill believed that immigrants would lose their native cultures and become something different when they came to the United States.

_____ 6. All immigrants want to assimilate to the U.S. culture completely; they have no desire to maintain their own culture.

_____ 7. U.S. immigration policy has stayed the same for the last 100 years.

_____ 8. The English language has no adjective for United States and therefore uses the term *American* to refer to its people.

_____ 9. It is not possible to make generalizations about what Americans believe because they are so different.

_____ 10. Many of the characteristics of Americans that Alexis de Tocqueville observed in the 1830s are still true today.

 C. Questions for Discussion

1. What effect does the geography of a country have on its people? Does your country have different climates? What effect does climate have on the lifestyles of the people in your country? How is life in a small country different from life in a large one?

2. What different ethnic groups are there in your country? Where do they live? How are they different from the majority of people in your country: language? clothing? food? music? customs? What effect do different ethnic groups have on a country?

3. What is your country's policy on immigration? Are there quotas for how many people are allowed to come from each country? Can immigrants become citizens? Are there "guest workers" (people who work there temporarily) in your country? How do people in your country feel about foreigners?

4. Do you think it is possible to describe the average person in your country and what he or she believes? How would you describe the traits of the people in your country? Do you think people all over the world are basically the same or basically very different? How are Americans different from people in your country?

D. Cloze Summary Paragraph

This paragraph summarizes the chapter. Fill in each blank with any word that makes sense.

In describing the beliefs of _____*the*_____ average American, it is important _____ consider the great size of _____ United States and its enormous _____ diversity. Except for the Native _____ Indians, all Americans, or their _____, came from another country. The _____ numbers of immigrants came in _____ late 1880s and early 1900s. _____ 1924 until the 1960s, the _____ States severely limited immigration. However, _____ the end of the 1900s, _____ United States was accepting more _____ than all the other industrialized _____ combined. In spite of their _____, Americans have a sense of _____ identity. They share many basic _____, although their lifestyles may vary. _____ the 1830s, a Frenchman named _____ described American life and basic _____. Many of his observations are _____ true today.

 ## E. Ask Yourself

What do you think Americans are like? Write an X to show which characteristics Americans have compared with the people in your country. The closer to the word you put your X, the stronger your feeling that this word describes Americans.

tall __*X*__ _____ _____ _____ _____ short
This answer shows that you think Americans are much taller than people in your country.

tall _____ _____ __*X*__ _____ _____ short
This answer shows that you think they are about the same—neither taller, nor shorter.

tall _____ _____ _____ __*X*__ _____ short
This answer shows that you think Americans are a little shorter than people in your country.

1. friendly   ___ ___ ___ ___ ___   unfriendly
2. unhappy   ___ ___ ___ ___ ___   happy
3. helpful   ___ ___ ___ ___ ___   not helpful
4. shy   ___ ___ ___ ___ ___   outgoing
5. thin   ___ ___ ___ ___ ___   fat
6. poor   ___ ___ ___ ___ ___   rich
7. quiet   ___ ___ ___ ___ ___   loud
8. cooperative   ___ ___ ___ ___ ___   competitive
9. active   ___ ___ ___ ___ ___   passive
10. lazy   ___ ___ ___ ___ ___   hard-working
11. well dressed   ___ ___ ___ ___ ___   poorly dressed
12. dirty   ___ ___ ___ ___ ___   clean
13. positive   ___ ___ ___ ___ ___   negative
14. hostile   ___ ___ ___ ___ ___   loving
15. satisfied   ___ ___ ___ ___ ___   dissatisfied
16. attractive   ___ ___ ___ ___ ___   unattractive
17. relaxed   ___ ___ ___ ___ ___   busy
18. loyal   ___ ___ ___ ___ ___   disloyal
19. selfish   ___ ___ ___ ___ ___   concerned for others
20. patient   ___ ___ ___ ___ ___   impatient

Decide whether each characteristic listed above is positive or negative. If it is positive, give a score of +1 or +2. If it is negative, give a score of -1 or -2.

	+2	+1	0	-1	-2	
positive	___	___	___	___	___	negative
	-2	-1	0	+1	+2	
negative	___	___	___	___	___	positive

Add up the scores for each pair and compare scores with those of other students. If you mark the center blank, count the pair as 0. What stereotypes do you have about Americans? What about people from your country?

 F. Think, Pair, Share

Think about the following questions, and write down your answers. Discuss your answers with a partner. Then share your answers with another pair of students.

1. How would you define "culture"? Look at several dictionaries to find definitions, and read the first paragraph of the preface to this book. What do you think is the most important aspect of your native culture?

2. Complete the statements in Exercise J about your own country and share your answers. For example: People from my country are _____.

G. Suggestions for Writing or Making an Oral Report

Michael J. Weiss has written a book called *Latitudes & Attitudes: An Atlas of American Tastes, Trends, Politics, and Passions*. Weiss maps 211 consumer markets, geographical regions where people share similar lifestyles, attitudes, and shopping habits. Some of the biggest differences are between the coastal metropolitan areas and the "heartland" interior. In mapping political liberals and conservatives, for example, Washington, D.C., New York, Boston, Chicago, Miami, Houston, San Francisco, and Los Angeles have more people who identify themselves as liberals than the national average of 20 percent.

However, in contrast to liberals, conservatives are more scattered across the country, with the highest concentrations in the South and Midwest. Nation-wide, 34 percent of Americans identify themselves as political conservatives. Weiss notes that there are several types of conservative people:

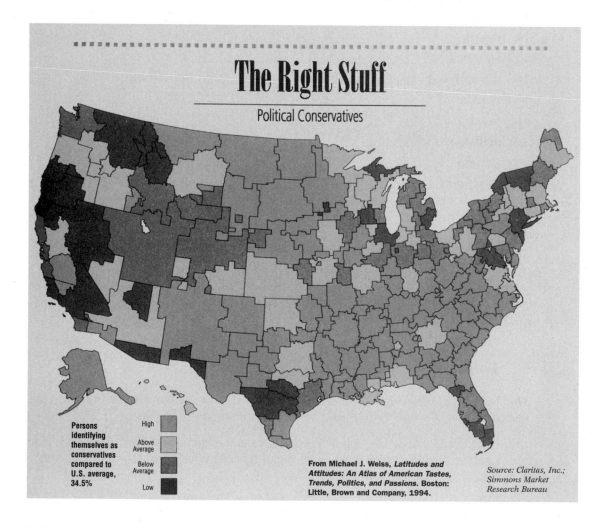

The Right Stuff

Political Conservatives

Persons identifying themselves as conservatives compared to U.S. average, 34.5%

High
Above Average
Below Average
Low

From Michael J. Weiss, *Latitudes and Attitudes: An Atlas of American Tastes, Trends, Politics, and Passions*. Boston: Little, Brown and Company, 1994.

Source: Claritas, Inc.; Simmons Market Research Bureau

- Upscale, metropolitan couples who are pro-business and anti-government.
- Young suburban families whose overriding concern is economics.
- Older, downscale, small-town, and rural voters who believe in hard work, family stability, and religious values.

How do the lifestyles of liberals and conservatives differ? Because many conservatives live in the heartland, they tend to have traditional roles and interests. Weiss says:

> *They're more likely than average Americans to hunt, fish, camp, and drive a pickup truck. Around the house, the men enjoy woodworking, the women gardening, and everyone snuggles into their recliners to watch TV.... It's no surprise that these voters believe in God, country, and respect for their elders—Ronald Reagan especially. On the issues, they're for school prayer, family values, and the death penalty, pro-life [anti-abortion], and against gun control.*

While these characteristics do not apply to all conservatives, they do lead to some interesting observations. What are liberals and conservatives (or people with strong traditional values) like in your country?

Write a comparison/contrast essay or give an oral report on one of these topics:

1. Liberals and conservatives in my country
2. Lifestyles of people who live in cities vs. small towns or rural areas
3. Two regions (or cities) in my country that are very different

 ## H. Small Group Discussion

As mentioned in this chapter, Americans in recent years have become aware of how language may reinforce cultural or gender stereotypes—that girls and women are "emotional" and "dependent" by nature, for example, while men are the "strong," "independent leaders" and "achievers" of the society. The result is that writers and speakers look for neutral language that refers to an ethnic group by the term that group prefers, or language that does not carry a gender bias. For example, instead of saying "fireman" (implying that all those who fight fires are men), it would be "politically correct" to say "fire fighters," since in fact there are American women who fight fires.

James Finn Garner has taken a humorous look at political correctness in a little book called *Politically Correct Bedtime Stories: Modern Tales for Our Life & Times*. The book cover explains that the fairy tales were written by middle-aged white males and "reflected the way in which these men lived and saw their world: that is, the stories were sexist, discriminatory, unfair, [and] culturally biased...." Garner has rewritten the stories so that they are now politically correct.

Here is an excerpt from Garner's version of "Little Red Riding Hood." The phrases that are underlined show changes that he made in the story.

> There once was <u>a young person</u> named Red Riding Hood who lived with her mother on the edge of a large wood. One day her mother asked her to take a basket of <u>fresh fruit and mineral water</u> to her grandmother's house—<u>not because this was womyn's work</u>, mind you, but because the deed was generous and helped engender <u>a feeling of community</u>. Furthermore, her <u>grandmother was not sick</u>, but rather was <u>in full physical and mental health</u> and was <u>fully capable of taking care of herself as a mature adult</u>....

Read the traditional version of "Little Red Riding Hood," and then compare it with the excerpt above. Why has the author made these changes in order to be politically correct? For example, *women* is spelled *womyn* to avoid having *men* in the word.

Divide the class so that the females and the males are working in separate groups. Each group should have a large sheet of paper with a line drawn down the middle of it. On one side of the paper, each group should write all the stereotypes about women that they can think of; on the other side, they should write all the stereotypes about men. (Dictionaries are permitted.) When the lists are completed, compare what females and males have said about gender stereotypes.

Choose a folk tale from your culture, and retell it in English. Are there any stereotypes that you would consider "politically incorrect"?

 ## I.   Understanding Polls

Conducting opinion polls is very popular in the United States. A newspaper, a magazine, a TV station, or a professional polling organization asks a representative group of Americans several questions to determine what their opinions are about a given topic. The people chosen for the poll are supposed to represent a broad cross-section of the American population; that is, the pollsters choose men and women of different ages, occupations, and races in the same proportion that these groups are found in the population. Sometimes, however, a *random* sample is taken, which means picking people by chance. Both methods are designed to learn what the average person, sometimes called "the man in the street," believes.

Polls are especially popular around election time because everyone wants to know which candidate is ahead in the race and what the voters are thinking about the key issues of the campaign. Many politicians have their own polling organizations to keep them in constant touch with public opinion. There are three well-known polling organizations that measure public opinion on a variety of topics: Louis Harris and Associates, the Roper Organization, and Gallup International Research Institutes. A poll conducted by these groups is popularly referred to as "a Harris poll," "a Roper poll," or "a Gallup poll."

The following polls were conducted by the Gallup organization. The first two polls deal with what terms people prefer to be called: *black* or *African-American*, *Hispanic* or *Latino*. Which terms are preferred? What percent say it doesn't matter? In the next poll, blacks, Hispanics, and Asians are asked about their interest in news stories that deal with issues related to their ethnic group. Which group is most interested in stories about their group? Which group is least interested?

The Gallup Poll Monthly, September 1994

(Asked of blacks) Some people prefer the term *African-American* while others prefer the term *black*. Which term do you prefer— *African-American* or *black*?

Preferred appellation

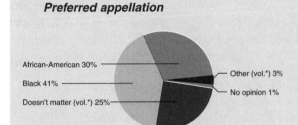

African-American 30%
Black 41%
Doesn't matter (vol.*) 25%
Other (vol.*) 3%
No opinion 1%

(Asked of Hispanics) Some people prefer the term *Hispanic* while others prefer the term *Latino*. Which term do you prefer— *Hispanic* or *Latino*?

Preferred appellation

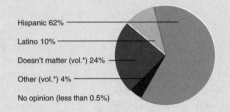

Hispanic 62%
Latino 10%
Doesn't matter (vol.*) 24%
Other (vol.*) 4%
No opinion (less than 0.5%)

*Vol. = Response was volunteered by respondent in place of the choices offered in the poll.

How interested are you in news stories that deal with issues related to your own ethnic group... very interested, somewhat interested, not too interested or not at all interested?

Stories About Our Own Ethnic Group

	Blacks	Hispanics	Asians
Very interested	70%	39%	46%
Somewhat	21	43	37%
Not too	6	11	10
Not at all	1	5	7
No opinion	2	2	*
	100%	100%	100%

*Less than 0.5%.

J.   Ask Americans

Interview several Americans of different ages, and ask them to complete the following statements.

1. Americans are _____.
2. They like _____.
3. They don't really _____.
4. Most Americans feel _____.
5. They act _____.
6. Most Americans believe in _____.
7. The United States is a country where _____.
8. The average American is _____.
9. Americans today are worried about _____.
10. The most important thing in life to most Americans is _____.

 K.   People Watching

Different countries have different rules for "personal space"—that is, when people touch, how close they stand when they are speaking to one another, how close they sit, how they behave on elevators, and so on. The rules for personal space sometimes differ according to how well people know each other. People are usually not consciously aware of these rules, but they become very uncomfortable if the rules are broken and "their space" is entered without permission. You can discover the rules by observing people interacting and also by testing or breaking the rules to see how other people respond.

Perform the following experiments. Record in a journal the reactions of the people involved as well as other observations you make while "people watching." Work in pairs: One person tests the rules while the other observes and records what happens. If you are not in the United States and do not have an opportunity to observe Americans, you may still learn from these experiments by observing people in your own country.

Rule: Americans have a bubble of space around their bodies that is about an inch thick. This bubble of space must not be broken by a stranger. If American strangers touch each other accidentally, they mutter an apology such as "Pardon me," "Excuse me," "Oh, I'm sorry," or just "Sorry."

Observation: Watch people in a crowd, standing in line, waiting in a group, or passing on a street or in a hallway. Who is touching whom? What does their relationship appear to be? What happens when people touch accidentally? How does the person touched respond? What does the one who has broken the other's bubble do? Record gestures, facial expressions, emotional responses, and words exchanged.

Experiment: See how close you can stand to someone in a crowd without touching him or her. Try breaking someone's bubble of space with a very light touch of your elbow or arm. What is the person's response? What happens? (Warning: This may provoke an angry response!)

Avoiding eye contact in an elevator.　**Elizabeth Coppolino**

Rule: When standing in elevators, Americans usually face the door, speak quietly, and try to avoid touching one another. If a stranger enters an elevator where there is only one other person, he or she will stand on the opposite side of the elevator. As more people get on the elevator, they occupy the corners first and then try to disperse themselves evenly throughout the available space.

Observation: Observe people in elevators. Which direction are they facing? If you are alone in an elevator and someone comes in, where does that person stand? As more people enter the elevator, where do they stand? Do the people talk to one another? How loudly do they speak? Do strangers touch? What happens in a crowded elevator when someone in the back has to get off?

Experiment: Get on an elevator where there is only one person and stand next to that individual. What is the person's reaction? In an elevator where there are a number of people, turn and face the group with your back to the door. How do the people react? Have a conversation with someone in a crowded elevator and don't lower your voice. How do you think people feel about this? Note their facial expressions.

 L. Suggestions for Further Reading

- Ralph Waldo Emerson, *Self-Reliance*
- Henry David Thoreau, *Walden*
- Sherwood Anderson, *Winesburg, Ohio*
- Thomas Paine, *The Age of Reason*
- Dee Brown, *Bury My Heart at Wounded Knee*
- O. E. Rölvaag, *Giants in the Earth*
- Michael J. Weiss, *Latitudes & Attitudes: An Atlas of American Tastes, Trends, Politics, and Passions*
- Sam Roberts, *Who We Are: A Portrait of America Based On the Latest U.S. Census*

 M. Recommended Movies

- *La Bamba*
- *The Immigrants*

Immigrants seeking a new life in the "Land of Opportunity"   **By Courtesy of the Statue of Liberty National Monument**

CHAPTER 2

Traditional American Values and Beliefs

We hold these truths to be self-evident, that all men are created equal, that they are endowed by their Creator with certain inalienable rights, that among these are Life, Liberty and the pursuit of Happiness.

The Declaration of Independence

Before You Read

1. Why do some people want to come and live in the United States?
2. What do you think Americans believe is the best thing about their country?
3. What is the "American Dream"?

The Context of Traditional American Values: Racial, Ethnic, Religious, and Cultural Diversity

As the 21st century begins, the United States probably has a greater diversity of racial, ethnic, cultural, and religious groups than any other nation on earth. From the beginning of the history of the United States, there has been diversity—Native Americans throughout the North American continent, Spanish settlers in the Southwest and in Florida, French missionaries and fur traders along the Mississippi River, black slaves brought from African countries, Dutch settlers in New York, Germans in Pennsylvania, and, of course, the British colonists, whose culture eventually provided the language and the foundation for the political and economic systems that developed in the United States.

Most early Americans recognized this diversity, or pluralism, as a fact of life. The large variety of ethnic, cultural, and religious groups meant that accepting diversity was the only practical choice, even if some people were not enthusiastic about it. However, in time, many Americans came to see strength in their country's diversity. Today, there is more recognition of the value of cultural pluralism than at any other time in the history of the United States.

New immigrants on Ellis Island at the turn of the century   **By Courtesy of the Statue of Liberty National Monument**

When we examine the system of basic values that emerged in the late 1700s and began to define the American character, we must remember this context of cultural pluralism. How could a nation of such enormous diversity produce a recognizable national identity?

Historically, the United States has been viewed as "the land of opportunity," attracting immigrants from all over the world. The opportunities they believed they would find in America and the experiences they actually had when they arrived nurtured this set of values. In this chapter, we will examine six basic values that have become "traditional" American values. Three represent traditional reasons why immigrants have been drawn to America: the chance for individual freedom, equality of opportunity, and material wealth. In order to achieve these benefits, however, there were prices to be paid: self-reliance, competition, and hard work. In time, these prices themselves became a part of the traditional value system.

Individual Freedom and Self-Reliance

The earliest settlers came to the North American continent to establish colonies that were free from the controls that existed in European societies. They wanted to escape the controls placed on their lives by kings and governments, priests and churches, noblemen and aristocrats. To a great extent, they succeeded. In 1776, the British colonial settlers declared their independence from England and established a new nation, the United States of America. In so doing, they **overthrew** the king of England and declared that the power to govern would lie in the hands of the people. They were now free from the power of the kings. In 1789, when they wrote the Constitution for their new nation, they separated church and state so that there would never be a government-supported church. This greatly limited the power of the church. Also, in writing the Constitution, they expressly forbade titles of nobility to ensure that an aristocratic society would not develop. There would be no ruling class of nobility in the new nation.

The historic decisions made by those first settlers have had a **profound** effect on the shaping of the American character. By limiting the power of the government and the churches and **eliminating** a formal aristocracy, they created a climate of freedom where the emphasis was on the individual. The United States came to be associated in their minds with the concept of *individual freedom*. This is probably the most basic of all the American values. Scholars and outside observers often call this value *individualism*, but many Americans use the word *freedom*. Perhaps the word *freedom* is one of the most respected popular words in the United States today.

By freedom, Americans mean the desire and the ability of all individuals to control their own destiny without outside interference from the government, a ruling noble class, the church, or any other organized authority. The desire to be free of controls was a basic value of the new nation in 1776, and it has continued to attract immigrants to this country.

There is, however, a price to be paid for this individual freedom: *self-reliance*. Individuals must learn to rely on themselves or risk losing freedom. This means achieving both financial and emotional independence from their parents as early as possible, usually by age 18 or 21. It means that Americans believe they should take care of themselves, solve their own problems, and "stand on their own two feet." De Tocqueville observed the Americans' belief in self-reliance nearly 200 years ago in the 1830s:

> *They owe nothing to any man, they expect nothing from any man; they **acquire** the habit of always considering themselves as standing alone, and they are **apt** to imagine that their whole destiny is in their own hands.*

This strong belief in self-reliance continues today as a traditional basic American value. It is perhaps one of the most difficult aspects of the American character to understand, but it is profoundly important. Most Americans believe that they must be self-reliant in order to keep their freedom. If they rely too much on the support of their families or the government or any organization, they may lose some of their freedom to do what they want.

Special parking helps the handicapped be self-reliant **JoAnn Crandall**

If people are dependent, they risk losing freedom as well as the respect of their **peers**. Even if they are not truly self-reliant, most Americans believe they must at least appear to be so. In order to be in the mainstream of American life—to have power and/or respect—individuals must be seen as self-reliant. Although receiving financial support from **charity**, family, or the government is allowed, it is never admired. Many people believe that such individuals are setting a bad example, which may weaken the American character as a whole.

The sight of beggars on city streets and the **plight** of the homeless may inspire sympathy but also concern. Although Americans provide a lot of financial support to people in need through charities or government programs, they expect that help to be short-lived. Eventually, people should take care of themselves.

Equality of Opportunity and Competition

The second important reason why immigrants have traditionally been drawn to the United States is the belief that everyone has a chance to succeed here. Generations of immigrants, from the earliest settlers to the present day, have come to the United States with this expectation. They have felt that because individuals are free from excessive political, religious, and social controls, they have a better chance for personal success. Of particular importance is the lack of a **hereditary** aristocracy.

Because titles of nobility were forbidden in the Constitution, no formal class system developed in the United States. In the early years of American history, many immigrants chose to leave the older European societies because they believed that they had a better chance to succeed in America. In "the old country," their place in life was determined largely by the social class into which they were born. They knew that in America they would not have to live among noble families who possessed great power and wealth inherited and accumulated over hundreds of years.

The hopes and dreams of many of these early immigrants were fulfilled in their new country. The lower social class into which many were born did not prevent them from trying to rise to a higher social position. Many found that they did indeed have a better chance to succeed in the United States than in the old country. Because millions of these immigrants succeeded, Americans came to believe in *equality of opportunity*. When de Tocqueville visited the United States in the 1830s, he was impressed by the great uniformity of conditions of life in the new nation. He wrote:

> The more I advanced in the study of American society, the more I perceived that... equality of condition is the fundamental fact from which all others seem to be derived.

It is important to understand what most Americans mean when they say they believe in equality of opportunity. They do not mean that everyone is—or should be—equal. However, they do mean that each individual should have an equal chance for success. Americans see much of life as a race for success. For them, equality means that everyone should have an equal chance to enter the race and win. In other words, equality of opportunity may be thought of as an ethical rule. It helps ensure that the race for success is a fair one and that a person does not win just because he or she was born into a wealthy family, or lose because of race or religion. This American concept of "fair play" is an important aspect of the belief in equality of opportunity. President Abraham Lincoln expressed this belief in the 1860s when he said:

> We... wish to allow the humblest man an equal chance to get rich with everybody else. When one starts poor, as most do in the race of life, free society is such that he knows he can better his condition; he knows that there is no fixed condition of labor for his whole life.

There is, however, a price to be paid for this equality of opportunity: *competition*. If much of life is seen as a race, then a person must run the race in order to succeed; a person must compete with others. If every person has an equal chance to succeed in the United States, then it is every person's duty to try. Americans match their energy and intelligence against that of others in a competitive contest for success. People who like to compete and are more successful than others are honored by being called *winners*. On the other hand, those who do not like to compete and are not successful when they try are often dishonored by being called *losers*. This is especially true for American men, and it is becoming more and more true for women.

The pressures of competition in the life of an American begin in childhood and continue until retirement from work. Learning to compete successfully is part of growing up in the United States, and competition is encouraged by strong programs of competitive sports provided by the public schools and community groups.

The pressure to compete causes Americans to be energetic, but it also places a constant emotional strain on them. When they retire (traditionally at age 65), they are at last free from the pressures of competition. But then a new problem arises. They may feel useless and unwanted in a society that gives so much **prestige** to those who compete well. This is one reason why older people in the United States do not have as much honor and respect as they have in other, less competitive societies. In fact, any group of people who do not compete successfully—for whatever reason—do not fit into the mainstream of American life as well as those who do compete.

Workers in an asparagus-processing plant   **Roxane Fridirici**

The American Ways

Material Wealth and Hard Work

The third reason why immigrants have traditionally come to the United States is to have a better life—that is, to raise their standard of living. For the vast majority of the immigrants who came here, it was probably the most compelling reason for leaving their homeland. Because of its incredibly **abundant** natural resources, the United States appeared to be a "land of plenty" where millions could come to seek their fortunes. Of course, most immigrants did not "get rich overnight," and many of them suffered terribly, but the majority of them were eventually able to improve upon their former standard of living. Even if they were not able to achieve the economic success they wanted, they could be fairly certain that their children would have the opportunity for a better life. The phrase "going from rags to riches" became a **slogan** for the great American Dream. Because of the vast riches of the North American continent, the dream came true for many of the immigrants. They achieved material success; they became very attached to material things. *Material wealth* became a value to the American people.

Placing a high value on material possessions is called *materialism*, but this is a word that most Americans find offensive. To say that a person is *materialistic* is an insult. To an American, this means that this person values material possessions above all else. Americans do not like to be called *materialistic* because they feel that this unfairly accuses them of loving only material things and of having no religious values. In fact, most Americans do have other values and ideals. Nevertheless, acquiring and maintaining a large number of material possessions is of great importance to most Americans. Why is this so?

Probably the main reason is that material wealth has traditionally been a widely accepted measure of social status in the United States. Because Americans rejected the European system of hereditary aristocracy and titles of nobility, they had to find a substitute for judging social status. The quality and quantity of an individual's material possessions became an accepted measure of success and social status. Moreover, as we shall see in later chapters, the Puritan work ethic associated material success with godliness.

Americans have paid a price, however, for their material wealth: *hard work*. The North American continent was rich in natural resources when the first settlers arrived, but all these resources were undeveloped. Only by hard work could these natural resources be converted into material possessions, allowing a more comfortable standard of living. Hard work has been both necessary and rewarding for most Americans throughout their history. Because of this, they came to see material possessions as the natural reward for their hard work. In some ways, material possessions were seen not only as **tangible** evidence of people's work but also of their abilities. In the late 1700s, James Madison, the father of the American Constitution, stated that the difference in material possessions reflected a difference in personal abilities.

As the United States has shifted from an industry-based economy to one that is service or information-based, there has been a decline in high-paying jobs

Having a nice home in the suburbs: part of the great "American Dream"   **Elizabeth Coppolino**

for factory workers. It is now much more difficult for the average worker to go "from rags to riches" in the United States, and many wonder what has happened to the traditional "American Dream." As the United States competes in a global economy, many workers are losing their old jobs and finding that they and their family members must now work longer hours for less money and fewer benefits. Faced with a decline in their standard of living, these people no longer believe that hard work necessarily brings great material rewards.

Most Americans, however, still believe in the value of hard work. They believe that people should hold jobs and not live off **welfare** payments from the government. In the 1990s, the welfare system came under attack. In a time when many people were working harder than ever "to make ends meet," there was enormous resentment against groups such as "welfare mothers," young women who do not marry or hold a job but have children and are supported by payments from the government.

In understanding the relationship between what Americans believe and how they live, it is important to distinguish between idealism and reality. American values such as equality of opportunity and self-reliance are ideals that may not necessarily describe the reality of American life. Equality of opportunity, for example, is an ideal that is not always put into practice. In reality, some people have a better chance for success than others. Those who are born into rich families have more opportunities than those who are born into poorer families. Inheriting money does give a person a decided advantage. Many black Americans have fewer opportunities than the average white American, and many women have fewer opportunities than men, in spite of laws designed to promote equality of opportunity for all individuals. And many immigrants today have fewer opportunities than those who came before them, when there were more high-paying factory jobs, and the economy was growing more rapidly.

The fact that American ideals are only partly carried out in real life does not **diminish** their importance. Many Americans still believe in them and are strongly affected by them in their everyday lives. It is easier to understand what Americans are thinking and feeling if we can understand what these basic traditional American values are and how they have influenced almost every facet of life in the United States.

The six basic values presented in this chapter—*individual freedom, self-reliance, equality of opportunity, competition, material wealth,* and *hard work*—do not tell the whole story of the American character. Rather, they should be thought of as **themes** that will be developed in our discussions on religion, family life, education, business, and politics. These themes will appear throughout the book as we continue to explore more facets of the American character and how it affects life in the United States.

■　■　■　■

New Words

overthrow　to take power away from a government by force; to defeat

profound　deep; very important

eliminate　to end; to exclude

apt　to be likely to do something (will probably do it)

peer　a person of the same age or status (as another person)

charity　an organization that gives money or other help to the poor

plight　a bad (or sad or serious) condition or state

hereditary　that which can be inherited (Note: *hereditary* and *heritage* refer to intangibles; *inheritance* refers to things such as property that can be inherited.)

prestige　honor and respect

abundant　plentiful

slogan　a popular or well-known saying

tangible　real; able to be seen and touched

welfare　money, food, medical assistance, and other social services provided by the government to "needy" or poor people

diminish　to lessen

theme　main idea

A. Vocabulary Check

Complete the crossword puzzle using words from the New Words list.

Across

1. likely to do something
4. deep, meaningful
7. something real that you can touch
9. an organization to help poor people
12. honor and respect
13. government payments to the poor
14. main idea

Down

2. someone who is your age and has a similar lifestyle
3. a popular saying
5. to take control over the government and force the leaders out
6. to make smaller
8. something that can be inherited
10. plentiful
11. to do away with or exclude
12. a serious condition

B. Comprehension Check

Write the letter of the best answer according to the information in the chapter.

_____ 1. The *main* reason the early settlers came to the North American continent and established colonies was because they wanted to be free from
   a. the power of kings, priests, and noblemen.
   b. the influence of their families.
   c. the problems of poverty and hunger.

_____ 2. There are no titles of nobility in the United States today because
   a. no one likes aristocrats.
   b. the church does not allow it.
   c. they are forbidden by the Constitution.

_____ 3. The price that Americans pay for their individual freedom is
   a. self-reliance.
   b. competition.
   c. hard work.

_____ 4. The American belief in self-reliance means that
   a. receiving money from charity, family, or the government is never allowed.
   b. if a person is very dependent on others, he or she will be respected by others.
   c. people must take care of themselves and be independent or risk losing their personal freedom.

_____ 5. The American belief in equality of opportunity means that
   a. all Americans are rich.
   b. Americans believe that everyone should be equal.
   c. everyone should have an equal chance to succeed.

_____ 6. In the United States, learning to compete successfully is
   a. part of growing up.
   b. not seen as healthy by most people.
   c. not necessary, because Americans believe in equality.

_____ 7. Traditionally, immigrants have been able to raise their standard of living by coming to the United States because
   a. Americans value money and nothing else.
   b. there have been such abundant natural resources.
   c. the rich have shared their wealth with the poor.

_____ 8. Americans see their material possessions as
   a. having nothing to do with social status.
   b. the natural reward for their hard work.
   c. no indication of a person's abilities.

_____ 9. A belief in the value of hard work
      a. developed because it was necessary to work hard to convert national resources into material goods.
      b. developed because the immigrants who came here had a natural love of hard work.
      c. has never been a part of the American value system because people have so much.

_____ 10. In reality, such American ideals as equality of opportunity and self-reliance
      a. are not real because there is no equality in the United States.
      b. are always put into practice in the United States and truly describe American life.
      c. are only partly carried out in real life but are still important because people believe in them.

C. Questions for Discussion

1. Americans believe strongly in self-reliance and the freedom and independence of the individual. At what age do young people become financially and emotionally independent from their parents in your country? At what age do they leave home?

2. Can most people stand alone and solve their own problems? Should they? How much should people depend on their families? Which is more important to you, pleasing your family or having the freedom to do what you want? What are the advantages and disadvantages of being very independent?

3. What gives people high status in your country? How important is the social class into which a person is born? Has there ever been a system that separated the social classes in a formal way—titles of nobility, for example? How can a person move into a higher social class? Were most of the people who have the wealth and power in your country born into a high social class?

4. Is it healthy for a young person to want to compete? Should everyone in a country have an equal chance to succeed, or are there other factors that are more important? Which is more important, competing or cooperating? Which does your culture value more? Why?

5. What is the "mainstream" of a society? Who is in the mainstream of life in your country? What are these people like? Who is excluded? What could cause someone to leave the mainstream? How would that person's life be different? What is life like for people in your country who are not in the mainstream?

D. Cloze Summary Paragraph

This paragraph summarizes the chapter. Fill in each blank with any ̶
makes sense.

The earliest settlers came _____*to*_____ North America because they

_____ to be free from _____ placed on their lives _____

European governments, churches, and _____ societies. They created a

_____ nation where the emphasis _____ on the freedom of

_____ individual. The price paid _____ individual freedom is

self-reliance; _____ are expected to take _____ of themselves

and not _____ on others. A second _____ why immigrants have

come _____ the United States is _____ equality of opportunity.

Americans _____ that everyone should have _____ equal chance

to succeed, _____ the price for this _____ is competition for

everyone. _____ third reason why immigrants _____ come is

to raise _____ standard of living. Material _____ has become

the measure _____ success and social status, _____ hard work

is the _____. Material possessions are seen _____ the natural

reward for _____ work. Although these six _____ values may

not always _____ put into practice in _____, they are ideals

which _____ every aspect of American _____.

E. Ask Yourself

Do you agree or disagree with each of the statements on the following page? Put
a check under the number that indicates how you feel.

+2 = Strongly agree
+1 = Agree
 0 = No opinion
-1 = Disagree
-2 = Strongly disagree

	+2	**+1**	**0**	**-1**	**-2**
1. The welfare of the individual is more important than the welfare of the group.	___	___	___	___	___
2. Our destiny is in our own hands.	___	___	___	___	___
3. People should take care of themselves, solve their own problems, and stand on their own two feet.	___	___	___	___	___
4. If I could have a better life in another country, I would go and live there.	___	___	___	___	___
5. Earning a lot of money is more important than having an interesting job.	___	___	___	___	___
6. The government should take care of the poor and homeless.	___	___	___	___	___
7. Life is basically a competitive race for success.	___	___	___	___	___
8. Money and material possessions are the best indicators of high social status.	___	___	___	___	___
9. People who work hard deserve to have a higher standard of living than others.	___	___	___	___	___
10. If I work hard, I am sure I can be a success and get what I want in life.	___	___	___	___	___

Now divide the room into plus and minus sections, with the zero in the middle. Hang up pieces of paper with 0, +1, +2, -1 and -2. As you face the front of the room, the left side should have +1 in the front left corner and +2 in the back left corner. The 0 should be in the middle of the front of the room. On the right side, the -1 should be in the right front corner, and the -2 should be in the back right corner. As the teacher reads the statements, walk to the part of the room that reflects whether you agree or disagree with the statement, and how strongly. Explain why you have made your choice.

 F. Ask Americans

Interview several Americans of different ages, and ask them about their basic beliefs. Ask each one the following questions and record their answers.

1. Do you agree or disagree with these statements:
    a. People should place more emphasis on working hard and doing a good job than on what gives them personal satisfaction and pleasure.
    b. Working hard and doing a good job give me personal satisfaction and pleasure.

2. Some people say that people get ahead by their own hard work; others say that lucky breaks and help from other people are more important. Which do you think is more important?

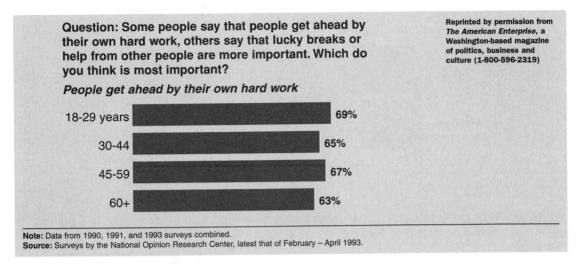

Question: Some people say that people get ahead by their own hard work, others say that lucky breaks or help from other people are more important. Which do you think is most important?

Reprinted by permission from *The American Enterprise*, a Washington-based magazine of politics, business and culture (1-800-596-2319)

People get ahead by their own hard work

18-29 years	69%
30-44	65%
45-59	67%
60+	63%

Note: Data from 1990, 1991, and 1993 surveys combined.
Source: Surveys by the National Opinion Research Center, latest that of February – April 1993.

3. Do you agree or disagree with this statement: In this country if you work hard, eventually you will get ahead.

4. How important is success? Is it *very important, somewhat important, somewhat unimportant,* or *very unimportant* to be successful in your work?

5. In recent years, many of the traditional values toward such things as work, sexual morality, and respect for authority have been questioned by those who think that these values no longer provide good guidelines on how to live and behave. How useful do you think traditional values are today?

The following polls contain questions about the American welfare system. Ask several Americans these questions, and compare the answers you get with the percentages in the polls.

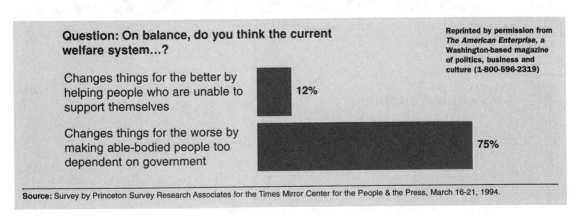

Question: On balance, do you think the current welfare system...?

Reprinted by permission from *The American Enterprise*, a Washington-based magazine of politics, business and culture (1-800-596-2319)

Changes things for the better by helping people who are unable to support themselves	12%
Changes things for the worse by making able-bodied people too dependent on government	75%

Source: Survey by Princeton Survey Research Associates for the Times Mirror Center for the People & the Press, March 16-21, 1994.

Question: In your view are most people who receive welfare payments genuinely in need of help or are they taking advantage of the system?

Most people who receive welfare are taking advantage of the system

White response ████████ 69%

Black response ██████ 61%

Reprinted by permission from *The American Enterprise*, a Washington-based magazine of politics, business and culture (1-800-596-2319)

Source: Survey by the Gallup Organization for CNN and *USA TODAY*, April 16-18, 1994.

Question: I am going to read a list of some things government could do as part of a plan to help welfare recipients get off welfare and become self-sufficient. Please tell me whether you would favor or oppose each one...

Reprinted by permission from *The American Enterprise*, a Washington-based magazine of politics, business and culture (1-800-596-2319)

██ **Black response**   ██ **White response**

Help provide childcare so a parent can work or look for work	Provide job training to teach welfare recipients new skills	Pay the costs of commuting to a job or job-training classes	Provide a gov't paid job to welfare recipients when there are not enough private sector jobs available	Cut off all benefits to people who have not found a job or become self sufficient after two years	Finance welfare benefits by reducing or eliminating some existing benefits
97% / 90%	95% / 94%	70% / 65%	79% / 57%	50% / 70%	67% / 80%

Source: Survey by the Gallup Organization for CNN and *USA TODAY*, April 16–18, 1994.
American Enterprise, Jan. – Feb. 1995.

 G. People Watching

Do this experiment, and record the results in your journal.

Rule: Americans usually stand about two and a half feet apart and at a slight angle (not facing each other directly) for ordinary conversation. They may touch when greeting each other by shaking hands (during a formal introduction), or by placing a hand briefly on the other's arm or shoulder (friends only). Some people kiss on the cheek or hug when greeting a friend. Note that the hug usually is not a full-body hug; only the shoulder and upper part of the bodies touch.

Bill Cosby shaking hands and "clowning around"
Courtesy: Mayor's Office, Chicago

Observation: Observe people who are standing and talking. How far apart are they? Do they touch as they speak? What do you think their relationship is? Observe people greeting each other. What do they do? What is their relationship? Observe formal introductions. Do the people shake hands? Do women usually shake hands? If a man and a woman are introduced, who extends a hand first?

Experiment: Ask someone on the street for directions. When you are standing two or three feet apart and the other person seems comfortable with the distance, take a step closer. What is the person's reaction? Try standing more than two to three feet from the other person. What does the other person do? Try facing the person directly as you talk instead of standing at an angle. What happens?

 H. Think, Pair, Share

In a recent advertisement for a popular car, the company offered a free copy of a *Life Magazine* issue, entitled "More Reflections on the Meaning of Life," to people who test-drove the car. The ad suggests that your life will be more meaningful if you own this car. People in different countries have different feelings about cars.

Think about what a car means to you personally. Write the answers to these questions, share your answers with a partner, and then you and your partner may share your answers with another pair of students.

1. Which cars have high status in your country, and which ones have low status?

2. If you could have any car in the world, which one would you choose? Why?

3. What does having a car mean to you personally?

4. What kinds of car ads do you think are most effective?

I. Observing the Media: Small Group Discussion

Look for advertisements in American magazines and newspapers that depict American people of high status. Bring in ads that imply if you buy a particular product you will have high status and gain admiration and respect. Discuss the products, how they are pictured, and the messages the ads are sending. Make a collage on a big piece of paper with your group.

J. Making Comparisons

In his book *Latitudes & Attitudes*, Michael J. Weiss has profiles that highlight lifestyle and demographic features (statistics about the population) for 211 American markets. The first part of the book shows these consumer markets on U.S. maps such as the ones on pages 14 and 216 (Chapter 10). The second part has profiles of the market areas such as the ones on pages 39 and 40. It is important to remember that these profiles make generalizations about how large numbers of consumers spend their money. Advertisers use this information to determine whether there are significant numbers of people who might buy their products in a particular geographical area. If the market is large enough for their product, they will try to sell it there. If there are not enough potential customers, however, they will spend their advertising money in another area.

Weiss says that these consumer maps change over time as potential buyers evaluate the 25,000 new products they see every year. For example, video games were first introduced in coastal cities, but they are now most popular in heartland communities. Baking "from scratch" (not using a prepared mix) used to be a "downscale" part of daily life, but it is now more of an "upscale" hobby. Weiss cautions that this detailed market information might be used to persuade Americans to spend more money than they should, particularly when they use credit cards. He notes that a consumer group, The Media Foundation, tries to warn Americans about the dangers of materialism. In one of their ads, they joked about a well-dressed young man with the slogan, "I buy. Therefore I am."

The three authors of this book live in two very different market areas—Washington, D.C., and Bowling Green, Kentucky. Jodi Crandall lives in a racially and ethnically mixed area of Washington; Maryanne Datesman lives in a Virginia suburb of Washington; and Ned Kearny lives in the small town of Bowling Green, Kentucky. All three teach in universities and have similar interests, but they live in different environments. The lifestyles of many people around them in the Washington and Bowling Green areas reflect some of the contrasts between coastal American cities and heartland small towns, as shown in the two market profiles. The lists of "What's hot" (popular) and "What's not" compare each market with the national average. They list in order: lifestyle highlights, sports/leisure, household products, television, music/radio, periodicals (magazines), food, drink, cars/trucks, financial, and politics/issues.

Washington, DC

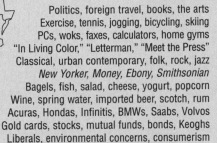

From Michael Weiss, *Latitudes and Attitudes: An Atlas of American Tastes, Trends, Politics, and Passions*. Boston: Little, Brown and Company, 1994.

What's Hot

Politics, foreign travel, books, the arts
Exercise, tennis, jogging, bicycling, skiing
PCs, woks, faxes, calculators, home gyms
"In Living Color," "Letterman," "Meet the Press"
Classical, urban contemporary, folk, rock, jazz
New Yorker, Money, Ebony, Smithsonian
Bagels, fish, salad, cheese, yogurt, popcorn
Wine, spring water, imported beer, scotch, rum
Acuras, Hondas, Infinitis, BMWs, Saabs, Volvos
Gold cards, stocks, mutual funds, bonds, Keoghs
Liberals, environmental concerns, consumerism

What's Not

Crafts, casinos, mobile homes, sweepstakes, cats
Bowling, hunting, camping, fishing, sewing
Tillers, 126/110 cameras, recliners, microwaves
"Love Connection," "Major Dad," "Current Affair"
Golden oldies, country, religious radio
Field & Stream, Soap Opera Digest, Star
Sausage, pork & beans, biscuits, doughnuts, Fritos
Powdered drinks, milk, lemon-lime soda, cocoa
Pontiacs, Chevrolets, Oldsmobiles, Chryslers
Life insurance, first mortgages, money orders
Moderates, death penalty, pro-lifers

THE NATION'S CAPITAL is the kind of company town where the workers are button-down bureaucrats and the boss is a free-spending Uncle Sam. Washington residents stand near the top when it comes to brains (nearly two out of three have gone to college), bucks (half of all households earn more than $50,000 a year), and workaholics (there are more two-career couples here than anywhere else). And it ranks among the nation's best markets for interest in politics, computers, the arts, and foreign travel. With young singles drawn to the dozen area colleges and high-glamour, low-pay Capitol Hill jobs, Washington is also a haven for the athletic-minded, with high rates for exercise, jogging, tennis, and downhill skiing. Despite problems typical of most urban cores— crime, drug abuse, and illiteracy—the market takes its character from its affluent suburbs, where residents splurge on half-million-dollar-plus homes (three times the U.S. average) and drive luxury cars by BMW, Ferrari, and Mercedes-Benz. Politically, the area is a liberal stronghold, where environmentalists and consumer advocates are considered heroes. Socially, this is a conservative town, where, according to interior designers, the most requested piece of bedroom furniture is a good reading lamp.

Family on the front porch JoAnn Crandall

Affluent metropolitan sprawl

Racially diverse singles

College educations

Jobs in business, education, and public administration

Key Demographics:

Total population: 4,911,402
Median household income: $50,424

Primary ages of adults: 25–44
Median home value: $165,118

From Michael Weiss,
*Latitudes and
Attitudes: An Atlas of
American Tastes,
Trends, Politics, and
Passions.* Boston:
Little, Brown and
Company, 1994.

Bowling Green, Kentucky

What's Hot	**What's Not**
Home furnishing, muscle cars, gardening, pets	The arts, foreign travel, dancing, unions
Horseback riding, target shooting, fishing	Bicycling, skiing, sailing, exercise
Microwaves, tires, washers, mobile homes	PCs, comedy records, 35mm cameras
Network news, "Blossom," "Family Matters"	"Wonder Years," "Simpsons," NBA basketball
Country, religious radio, college sports	Jazz, rhythm & blues, Broadway musicals
Sports Afield, Star, Country Living	*Discover, Shape, Bon Appetit, Ebony*
Bacon, frankfurters, white bread, gum	Beef, frozen yogurt, rice cakes, chocolates
Tea, cola, orange juice, powdered drinks	Imported wine, draft beer, Diet 7-Up
Lincolns, Buicks, Plymouths, Chevy Camaros	Nissans, Toyotas, VWs, Hondas, Infiniti M30s
Mail-order medical and life insurance, loans	Annuities, stocks, mutual funds
Conservatives, privacy rights, death penalty	Liberals, school sex ed, military cutbacks

Mini-Corvette race **Marshall Ray**

TOURISTS KNOW IT as the only place to buy a drink between Nashville and Louisville. But Bowling Green more closely resembles other Bible Belt cities with a lifestyle steeped in tradition. Folks place their trust in God—reading the Bible and listening to religious radio are popular pastimes—and in work accomplished by their own hand. They hunt, fish, garden, and sew at rates far above the national average. And residents are skeptical of the latest trends, caring little for fashion clothing and gourmet cooking, rarely cluttering their coffee tables with publications like *GQ,* the *New Yorker,* and *Omni.* Perhaps the one area where they care about cutting-edge development is cars: they tend to work on them, watch auto races, and take visitors to tour the local General Motors Corvette plant. Yet even with automobiles, there's a traditional streak: Bowling Green residents tend to buy American. In one 1992 survey, nine out of ten of the most popular models were made in the U.S. while 52 of the 53 least popular had foreign name plates.

Lower-middle-class agricultural center

Predominantly white singles and families

Less than high school educations

Farm, labor, and manufacturing jobs

Key Demographics:

Total population:	125,401	Primary ages of adults:	35–54
Median household income:	$22,937	Median home value:	$52,466

Read the two profiles on pages 39 and 40 and answer these questions:

1. In which location would you expect to find more political conservatives?
2. If you were selling Hondas, which market would you choose?
3. If you were selling microwaves, which market would you advertise in?
4. Which market has more young single people?
5. In which part of the country do people buy more American cars than foreign cars?
6. Who takes more trips to foreign countries?
7. Who has more PCs (personal computers)?
8. Where could you buy a nice house for $100,000?
9. Where do people drink more alcoholic beverages?
10. If you were selling exercise equipment, which market would you advertise in?

 ## K. Suggestions for Writing

1. Refugees from other countries are sometimes puzzled because Americans give them a great deal of help (both financial aid and personal support) when they first arrive, but then they are expected to be independent and self-supporting after a few months. What American values do you see operating here? Imagine that you are writing a letter to refugees who have been in the United States for one year. Explain to them why their American friends now expect them to "stand on their own two feet" and be self-supporting.

2. Write a brief summary comparing and contrasting the lifestyles of Washington and Bowling Green. Which place would you like to live in? Why?

3. "What's hot" and "what's not" in the community where you live? Write a brief report describing what you have observed about life in your area.

 ## L. Suggestions for Further Reading

- John F. Kennedy, *A Nation of Immigrants*
- Sandra Cisneros, *The House on Mango Street*
- Richard Rodriguez, *Hunger of Memory*
- Amy Tan, *The Kitchen God's Wife*

 ## M. Movies to Watch

- *The Joy Luck Club*
- *Thelma and Louise*

Religion in the United States: National Cathedral (Episcopal); Islamic mosque; Baha'i temple; Sikh temple; Hawaiian church (Protestant); Mormon temple; Buddhist temple; Jewish synagogue; Spanish chapel (Catholic) **Roxane Fridirici, JoAnn Crandall, Maryanne Kearny Datesman**

CHAPTER 3

The American Religious Heritage

The care of every man's soul belongs to himself.

Thomas Jefferson

Before You Read

1. What do you know about religion in the United States?
2. Do many Americans believe in God?
3. What religion is most popular in the United States?
4. Do Americans have a national religion?
5. How has religion shaped American values?

Freedom of Religion in the United States

The fundamental American belief in individual freedom and the right of individuals to practice their own religion is at the center of religious experience in the United States. The great diversity of ethnic backgrounds has produced religious pluralism; almost all of the religions of the world are now practiced in the United States. Ninety-three percent of all Americans say that they believe in God. Only 7 percent say they have no religious preferences or beliefs. About 87 percent of Americans are Christians, 2 percent are Jewish, and the other 4 percent belong to other religious faiths such as Moslem, Buddhist, or Hindu. Of the 87 percent who are Christian, 59 percent are Protestant, 27 percent Catholic, and 1 percent Eastern Orthodox. This is a pattern that has persisted for decades.

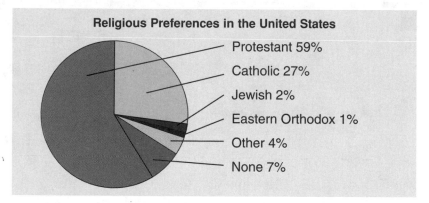

Religious Preferences in the United States

Protestant 59%

Catholic 27%

Jewish 2%

Eastern Orthodox 1%

Other 4%

None 7%

Although the overwhelming majority of Americans are Christians, all religions make important contributions to the American culture. There are now almost as many Moslems living in the United States as there are Jews. People of Hispanic origin now make up nearly one-half of the Catholic church. The Asian immigrants have brought with them the traditional religions of East Asia— Taoism, Confucianism, and Shintoism, as well as Buddhism. And the Native American religions are still practiced and studied today, particularly for their teachings about living in harmony with nature.

From the beginning of its history, religion has played an important role in the United States. The Catholic faith was first brought to the North American continent by the Spanish in the 1500s. For the next 300 years, Catholic missionaries and settlers from Spain and then Latin America came to what is now California and the Southwest. Many of the cities were named by these missionaries and settlers—San Francisco, Sante Fe, and San Antonio, for example. French Canadian Catholic missionaries also came with the explorers and traders from Quebec, down the Mississippi River to New Orleans.

In the 1600s, the European settlers began establishing colonies along the east coast of North America. Although there were some Catholics, the vast majority of these settlers were Protestants. As the new nation formed, it was the Protestant branch of the Christian faith that had the strongest effect on the development of the religious climate in the United States. Today, almost two-thirds of all Americans are Protestants.

The Development of Protestantism

The Protestant branch of the Christian faith broke away from the Roman Catholic church in Europe in the 16th century because of important differences in religious beliefs. (The Eastern Orthodox branch of the Christian faith had separated from the Roman Catholic Church in 1054.) At the time of the Protestant Reformation, the Roman Catholic church was the center of religious life in Western European countries; the Catholic **Pope** and the priests played the role of parent to the people in spiritual matters. They told people what was right and wrong, and they granted them forgiveness for **sins** against God and the Christian faith.

The Protestants, on the other hand, insisted that all individuals must stand alone before God. If people sinned, they should seek their forgiveness directly from God rather than from a priest speaking in God's name. In place of the power and authority of priests, Protestants substituted what they called the "priesthood of all believers." This meant that every individual was **solely** responsible for his or her own relationship with God.

Children's time during Sunday worship at Bruen Chapel United Methodist Church   **Maryanne Kearny Datesman**

After the Protestants broke away from the Catholic church, they found that they could not agree among themselves about many things. Therefore, the Protestants began to form separate churches, called **denominations**. (The largest Protestant denominations in the United States now are the Baptists, Methodists, Lutherans, Presbyterians, Episcopalians, and the United Church of Christ.) In the 1600s, the Catholic church did not recognize the rights of such Protestant churches to exist. There was much bitterness among some of the religious groups, and many Protestant denominations experienced religious **persecution**. The result of this persecution was that many Protestants were ready to leave their native countries in order to have freedom to practice their particular religious beliefs. Consequently, among the early settlers who came to America in the 1600s, there were many Protestants seeking religious freedom.

In the previous chapter, we noted that this desire for religious freedom was one of the strongest reasons why many colonial settlers came to America. Generally speaking, the lack of any established national religion in America appealed strongly to European Protestants, whether or not they were being persecuted. A large number of Protestant denominations were established in America. At first, some denominations hoped to force their views and beliefs on others, but the colonies were simply too large for any one denomination to gain control over the others. The idea of separation of church and state became accepted. When the Constitution was adopted in 1789, the government was forbidden to establish a national church; no denomination was to be favored over the others. The government and the church had to remain separate. Under these conditions, a variety of different Protestant denominations developed and grew, with each denomination having a "live and let live" attitude toward the others. Diversity was accepted and strengthened.

Protestantism in the United States

To someone not familiar with the Protestant faith, the religious scene in the United States may be confusing. The various Protestant denominations have completely separate church organizations, and although there are many similarities, there are also significant differences in their religious teachings and beliefs. Some Protestant denominations forbid dancing, playing cards, and drinking alcohol, for example, while others do not.

What causes this religious diversity? Perhaps the major cause is the Protestant belief that the individual, not the organized church, should be the center of religious life. This idea was brought to America and firmly established by European Protestants, and it is one reason why no single church has become the center of religious life in the nation. American religious tradition has encouraged not only the development of numerous denominations but also a tolerance and acceptance of all faiths that express the religious preferences of different individuals. This climate of religious freedom has, of course, strengthened the development of cultural pluralism in the United States.

The Protestant Heritage: Self-Improvement

Although many Protestant denominations exist in the United States today, all of them share a common heritage that has been a powerful force in shaping the values and beliefs of Americans. One of the most important values associated with American Protestantism is the value of self-improvement. Protestant Christianity, like Roman Catholic Christianity, often emphasizes the natural sinfulness of human nature. However, since Protestants do not go to priests for forgiveness of their sins, individuals are left alone before God to improve themselves or suffer **eternal** punishment by God for their sinful acts. In this way, Protestantism encourages a strong and restless desire for self-improvement.

The need for self-improvement, once established, reaches far beyond self-improvement in the purely moral or religious sense. It can be seen in countless books that explain how people can be happier and more successful in life by improving everything from their vocabulary to their tennis game, or even their whole personality. Books of this type are often referred to as *self-help* books. They are the natural products of a culture in which people believe that "God helps those who help themselves."

One of the most popular self-help books ever written in the United States was written by a Protestant minister, Norman Vincent Peale. As its title states, it stresses *The Power of Positive Thinking*. According to Peale, the key to self-improvement and success is self-confidence. Reading the Bible is like doing regular daily exercises; it can improve one's self-confidence and ensure personal success in life.

Americans buy hundreds of millions of self-help books a year, and typically, half of the *New York Times* best-seller list of nonfiction books are related to self-help. In addition to that, Americans attend thousands of self-help seminars and

Woman looking at self-help books in bookstore   **Maryanne Kearny Datesman**

support group meetings to help them stop smoking or drinking, lose weight, be better parents, have happier relationships, and, of course, develop self-confidence.

Material Success, Hard Work, and Self-Discipline

The achievement of material success is probably the most widely respected form of self-improvement in the United States. Many scholars believe that the nation's Protestant heritage is largely responsible for bringing this about. The idea of mixing materialism and religion may seem contradictory; religion is considered to be concerned with spiritual matters, not material possessions. How can the two mix?

Some of the early European Protestant leaders believed that people who were blessed by God might be recognized in the world by their material success. Other Protestant leaders, particularly in the United States, made an even stronger connection between gaining material wealth and being blessed by God. In 1900, for example, Bishop William Lawrence **proclaimed**, "Godliness is **in league with** riches…. Material prosperity is helping to make the national character sweeter, more joyous, more unselfish, more Christlike."

American Protestantism, however, has never encouraged the idea of gaining wealth without hard work and self-discipline. Many scholars believe that the emphasis of Protestantism on these two values made an important contribution to the industrial growth of the United States. The Protestant view of hard work and discipline differed from the older tradition of the Catholic church where the most highly valued work was that performed by priests and others whose lives were given completely to the organized church. The work and self-discipline of those whose occupations were outside the church might have been considered admirable but not holy. Protestant leaders brought about a different attitude toward work, first in Europe, and later in the New World, by viewing the work of all people—farmers, merchants, and laborers—as holy.

Protestants also believed that the capacity for self-discipline was a holy characteristic blessed by God. Self-discipline was often defined as the willingness to save and invest one's money rather than spend it on immediate pleasures. Protestant tradition, therefore, may have played an important part in creating a good climate for the industrial growth of the United States, which depended on hard work and willingness to save and invest money. The belief in hard work and self-discipline in pursuit of material gain and other goals is often referred to as "the Protestant work ethic," or "the **Puritan** work ethic."

It is important to understand that this work ethic has had an influence far beyond the Protestant Church. Many religious groups in the United States share belief in what is called the Protestant work ethic. Americans who have no attachment to a particular church, Protestant or Catholic, have still been influenced by the work ethic in their daily lives.

It is interesting to note that in the last few decades, there has been a shift both in the work ethic and in the meaning of work. Yankelovich and other researchers report that in the past, most Americans did not expect their work to be interesting or enjoyable. In the 1950s, for example, most people saw their jobs primarily as a source of income. Now, by a margin of four to one, they expect their work to give them a sense of personal satisfaction and fulfillment, in addition to their income. Some people are also beginning to question whether working long hours to have success and material wealth is really worth the sacrifice. Perhaps less might be better.

Volunteerism and Humanitarianism

The Protestant idea of self-improvement includes more than achieving material gain through hard work and self-discipline. It includes the idea of improving oneself by helping others. Individuals, in other words, make themselves into better persons by contributing some of their time or money to charitable, educational, or religious causes that are designed to help others. The philosophy is sometimes called **volunteerism**, or **humanitarianism**.

Historically, some of the extremely wealthy Americans have made generous contributions to help others. In the early 1900s, for example, Andrew Carnegie, a famous American businessman, gave away more than 300 million dollars to help support schools and universities and to build public libraries in thousands of communities in the United States. John D. Rockefeller, another famous businessman, in explaining why he gave a large sum from his private fortune to establish a university, said: "The good Lord gave me my money, so how could I withhold it from the University of Chicago?" The motive for humanitarianism and volunteerism is strong: Many Americans believe that they must devote part of their time and wealth to religious or humanitarian causes in order to be acceptable in the eyes of God and in the eyes of other Americans. Many businesses encourage their employees to do volunteer work, and individuals may get tax credits for money given to charity.

Peace Corps volunteer teacher with villagers of Nzere in Central African Republic **Peace Corps**

Born-Again Christians and the Religious Right

Perhaps the most dramatic example of the idea of self-improvement in American Protestantism is the experience of being "born again." Some individuals who have had this experience say that before it occurred they were hopelessly lost in their own sinfulness. Then they opened their hearts to God and to His Son, Jesus Christ, and their lives were completely changed. They say this experience is sometimes very emotional, and afterward, their lives are so completely changed that they describe the experience as being "born again." A number of the Christian radio and television shows have been led by born-again evangelists such as Billy Graham and Jerry Falwell.

Many of the born-again Christians belong to Protestant churches that are politically very conservative. About 16 percent of Americans now identify themselves as part of the religious conservative political movement. Although many conservative Christians from different Protestant denominations (and a number of Catholic churches) have traditionally had their differences, the issue of legalized abortion has brought them together to form political activist groups. In recent years, under names such as "The Moral Majority," the "Religious Right," the "Christian Right," or "Religious Conservatives," the Christian Conservatives have joined together to oppose legalized abortion and the **ban** on prayer in the public schools. They have been particularly successful in gaining power within the Republican political party, and they have actively campaigned for candidates who support their views.

A National Religion

In the countries from which the American colonists emigrated, the dominant values of the nation were often supported by an organized national church. American Protestants made certain that no organized national church would exist in their young country.

Americans, however, have developed a number of informal practices that combine national **patriotism** with religion. A number of scholars have referred to these practices as the "national religion" of the United States. The main function of this national religion is to provide support for the dominant values of the nation. Thus, it does in an informal and less organized way what nationally organized churches did for European nations in earlier times.

The informal national religion in the United States mixes patriotism with religious ideas in songs and in ceremonies that proclaim God's blessing on America, its basic values, and its actions as a nation. The national religion can be observed on many occasions when Americans gather together—on national holidays, at political conventions, and especially at sports events. Before a ballgame, the players and fans stand up for the national anthem, and sometimes a religious leader will offer a prayer. This practice is taken so seriously that in 1996, the National Basketball Association (NBA) actually suspended a professional basketball player who refused to stand during the national anthem.

Baseball players stand for the singing of the national anthem at Yankee Stadium. **Ken Karp**

The NBA stated that he could not play in games unless he agreed to follow their rule requiring players to stand in a respectful manner during the national anthem.

Patriotic songs such as "God Bless America," "America the Beautiful," and "My Country 'Tis of Thee" are as well known to most Americans as their national anthem. These songs are sung frequently on public occasions and may also be sung at Protestant worship services, expressing the idea that the United States has received God's special blessing. Expressions of the national religion can also be seen when the United States sends military forces overseas; the Gulf War provided good examples of the mixing of prayer and patriotism.

Some observers of American society believe that the various practices that are called the national religion can have harmful effects. Sometimes these practices can help to create a climate in which disagreement with current national practices is discouraged or not tolerated. In the 1960s, for example, some citizens considered the young people who protested against the war in Vietnam to be "un-American." They told the young protesters, "America—love it or leave it." This phrase became a slogan that illustrated their excessive patriotism.

When the national religion helps to create a climate that encourages excessive conformity with **prevailing** national practices, it can have a harmful effect. However, it usually serves a different function: to express the belief of most Americans that it is important to be a nation of people who believe in God and are loved and protected by God.

The earliest Protestant settlers believed that by coming to America, they were carrying out God's plan. This belief gave them confidence that they would succeed. Today, Americans still need to believe that their nation will continue to succeed, and the national religion helps to answer this need by reminding them

Family members gather for a church wedding   **Roxanne Fridirici**

of their religious heritage. It is a means of maintaining their national self-confidence in a rapidly changing world.

America's Protestant heritage seems to have encouraged certain basic values that members of many diverse non-Protestant faiths find easy to accept. This has helped to unite many different religious groups in the United States without requiring any to abandon their faiths. Cultural and religious pluralism has also created a context of tolerance that further strengthens the American reality of many different religions living peacefully within a single nation.

■ ■ ■ ■

 ## New Words

Pope the leader of the Roman Catholic Church

sin an act that breaks God's laws; something that is morally wrong

solely only; by oneself alone

denomination a particular religious body with special beliefs that are different from the beliefs of other groups with the same religious faith

persecution cruel treatment; causing one to suffer for religious beliefs

eternal everlasting; having no end

support group a group of people that share a common problem (such as having cancer or going through a divorce) and meet regularly to give each other encouragement and support

proclaim to make known, to declare officially

in league with working together

Puritan a Protestant group with very strict religious practices (This group had political power in some of the American colonies.)

volunteerism the practice of volunteering one's services to help others (without pay)

humanitarianism trying to improve life for human beings by giving them better living conditions; helping others

ban an order that prohibits or forbids something

patriotism love for and loyalty to one's country

prevailing most common or general

 ## A. Vocabulary Check

Write the letter of the correct phrase next to each word.

_____ 1.	sin	a.	people who meet to encourage each other
_____ 2.	denomination	b.	a religious leader
_____ 3.	ban	c.	cruelty; causing suffering
_____ 4.	eternal	d.	only
_____ 5.	humanitarianism	e.	most popular
_____ 6.	Puritan	f.	love of country
_____ 7.	in league with	g.	improving life for others
_____ 8.	patriotism	h.	giving time to serve others without pay
_____ 9.	persecution	i.	working with
_____ 10.	Pope	j.	make a strong statement
_____ 11.	prevailing	k.	a morally wrong act
_____ 12.	proclaim	l.	an early religious group
_____ 13.	solely	m.	Protestant church such as Methodist or Baptist
_____ 14.	volunteerism	n.	continuing forever
_____ 15.	support group	o.	no smoking laws

B. Comprehension Check

Write **T** *if the statement is true and* **F** *if it is false according to the information in the chapter.*

_____ 1. Although there is cultural pluralism in the United States, there is no religious pluralism.

_____ 2. The Protestant denominations (such as Methodist, Baptist, Presbyterian) are all part of the Roman Catholic church.

_____ 3. No single church has become the center of religious life in the United States because the emphasis is on the individual, not a particular church.

_____ 4. Many Catholics settled in colonial America to escape religious persecution by the Protestants in Europe.

_____ 5. The Constitution of the United States separates church and state and forbids the government from ever establishing a national church.

_____ 6. Protestantism encourages a strong desire for self-improvement.

_____ 7. Some American Protestant leaders have said that people who are rich have been blessed by God.

_____ 8. The Protestant work ethic is the belief that people should share their time and their wealth to help others.

_____ 9. A majority of Americans now consider themselves part of the religious, politically conservative movement.

_____ 10. The national religion of the United States is a mixture of religion and patriotism that expresses the belief that God has blessed America and its values.

C. Questions for Discussion

1. Which is the center of religious life in your country: the church or the individual? Explain. Do the majority of the people in your country belong to one particular church or religious faith? Is there a government-supported church or official religion? How much power do religious leaders have?

2. What is considered a sin in your religion? How are these sins forgiven in your religion? Do you think that human nature is basically sinful or good? What does your religion teach about self-improvement? Are there self-help books in your country? Do you agree with Norman Vincent Peale that the key to self-improvement and success is self-confidence?

3. What is the "Protestant work ethic"? How did it help the new Americ..
nation grow? Do you have a similar ethic in your country? Which is mo..
important: religious faith or doing the right thing?

4. What is humanitarianism? Is this philosophy part of your religion? In your
opinion, what responsibility do the wealthy have? Do people in your
country volunteer their time to help the poor? What do they do?

5. Is there any mixing of religion and patriotism in your country? Are there
prayers at non-religious public events? Where? Soccer games? At school?

 D. Cloze Summary Paragraph

This paragraph summarizes the chapter. Fill in each blank with any word that makes sense.

Although there are many _____different_____ Christian churches in the

_____ States, the majority of _____ are Protestant

denominations. European _____ separated from the Catholic

_____ in the 1500s because _____ differences in beliefs. In

_____ 1600s most of the _____ settlers who came to

_____ were Protestant, and Protestantism _____ the

dominant religious influence. _____ there are no priests

_____ the Protestant church, individuals _____ alone

before God, and _____ is a strong emphasis _____ the need

for self-improvement. _____ may improve themselves by

_____ material success through hard _____ and

self-discipline, and by helping _____. Some Americans have a

_____-again religious experience. The _____ Constitution

forbids government support _____ a national church, but

_____ do mix religion and _____ in a form of

_____ religion. Its main function _____ to provide support

for _____ dominant values and proclaim _____ blessing on

a and _____ values. Today, the United _____ has

‿us pluralism, and _____ of the religions of _____

‿d are practiced here.

 ## E. Ask Americans

About two-thirds of all Americans are members of a church and attend at least once a month. According to Gallup polls taken in the mid-1990s, 64 percent believe that religion is still relevant, but 69 percent feel that religion is losing influence in the society.

INFLUENCE, RELEVANCE OF RELIGION IN TODAY'S SOCIETY

Questions: At the present time, do you think religion as a whole is increasing its influence on American life or losing its influence? Do you believe that religion can answer all or most of today's problems, or that religion is largely old-fashioned and out-of-date?

	Influence?				Still relevant?				
	Increasing	Losing	Same (vol.)	No opinion	Yes	No	Other (vol.)	No opinion	No. of interviews
National	27%	69%	2%	2%	64%	20%	9%	7%	1014
SEX									
Male	25	70	2	3	55	24	12	9	517
Female	38	69	1	2	72	16	7	5	497
AGE									
18-29 years	32	59	5	4	59	28	8	5	185
30-49 years	16	83	1	*	61	23	11	5	439
50-64 years	25	72	2	1	77	9	9	5	188
65 & older	27	64	2	7	66	14	7	13	190
REGION									
East	25	72	*	33	59	24	11	6	252
Midwest	25	71	2	2	66	18	8	8	244
South	25	71	2	2	77	12	7	4	308
West	33	62	2	3	47	27	15	11	210
COMMUNITY									
Urban	27	69	2	2	56	25	10	9	403
Suburban	26	69	2	3	65	19	10	6	335
Rural	25	71	1	3	76	14	6	4	263

*Less than one percent.
Source: *The Gallup Poll Monthly*, April 1994.

The Gallup Poll

Interview several Americans of different ages and ask them about their religion. Ask each one the following questions and record their answers, then compare your findings with your classmates.

1. What is your religious preference—Protestant, Catholic, Jewish, or another faith? If Protestant, what denomination is that?

2. Have you happened to attend a church, synagogue, or temple in the last seven days?

3. How important would you say religion is in your own life—would you say very important, fairly important, or not very important?

4. How often do you attend religious services?

5. Do you believe in God or a universal spirit? If yes, how would you describe God?

6. Do you believe that there is life after death? What happens to a person's soul after death?

7. Do you believe in angels? Do you believe that you have a guardian angel? Have you ever seen an angel or felt one's presence?

8. Would you say that you have been born again or have had a born-again experience—that is, an identifiable turning point in your life?

9. Do you feel the need to experience spiritual growth? Have you ever had a mystical experience?

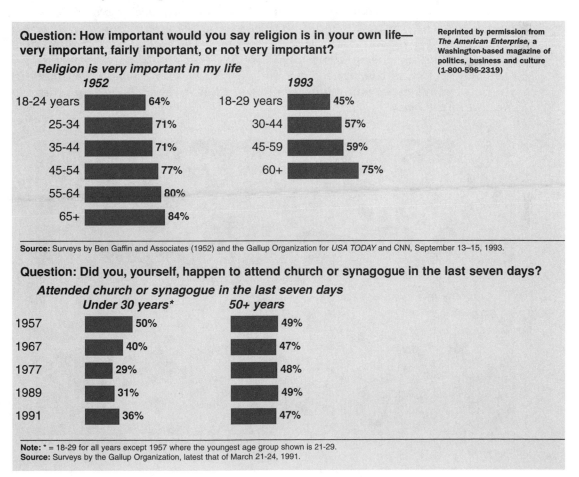

Question: How important would you say religion is in your own life—very important, fairly important, or not very important?

Reprinted by permission from *The American Enterprise*, a Washington-based magazine of politics, business and culture (1-800-596-2319)

Religion is very important in my life

1952

18-24 years	64%
25-34	71%
35-44	71%
45-54	77%
55-64	80%
65+	84%

1993

18-29 years	45%
30-44	57%
45-59	59%
60+	75%

Source: Surveys by Ben Gaffin and Associates (1952) and the Gallup Organization for *USA TODAY* and CNN, September 13–15, 1993.

Question: Did you, yourself, happen to attend church or synagogue in the last seven days?

Attended church or synagogue in the last seven days

	Under 30 years*	50+ years
1957	50%	49%
1967	40%	47%
1977	29%	48%
1989	31%	49%
1991	36%	47%

Note: * = 18-29 for all years except 1957 where the youngest age group shown is 21-29.
Source: Surveys by the Gallup Organization, latest that of March 21-24, 1991.

F.   Round Robin/Round Table

More than 50 percent of adult Americans and over 60 percent of American teenagers volunteer some of their time to help others. Adult volunteers spend an average of over four hours a week and teens more than three hours a week in various service projects. Some people are involved in preparing or distributing food to the homeless, the poor, and the elderly. Others work in animal shelters, collect clothing or household goods for the poor, volunteer time in hospitals and nursing homes, tutor children, help illiterate adults learn to read, drive people to the doctor, collect money for charities, pick up trash in a park, volunteer time in a political campaign, or do other community service. Some schools now require students to do a certain number of hours of community service before graduation.

Imagine that you are planning volunteer activities for your community. What needs does your community have? What activities could adults do? What activities could teenagers do? Working in groups of four to six, discuss what needs to be done by volunteers. Then pass around a piece of paper to record your ideas. The first time around, each person in the group should write down at least one activity that could be done by adults. The second time around, turn the paper over and write down the activities that would be appropriate for teenagers to do. As you write down your ideas, explain them to the others in your group. When the paper has been around twice, report the group's ideas to the rest of the class.

Volunteer organizations of Modesto, California. Note the town motto: "Water, Wealth, Contentment, and Health."
Roxane Fridirici

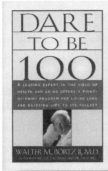
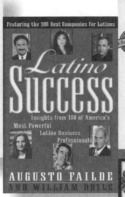
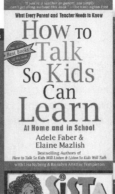

*Dare to be 100 by
Walter M. Bortz II, MD © 1996, Latino Success
by Augusto Failde © 1996, How to Talk So Kids
Can Learn At Home and in School by Adele Faber
& Elaine Mazlish (with Lisa Nyberg & Rosalyn
Anstine Templeton) © 1995, The Millionaire's Secrets: Life Lessons in Wisdom
and Wealth by Mark Fisher © 1996, Sista Girlfren' Breaks it Down... When
Mom's Not Around by Francheska Ahmed-Cawthrone, Illustrations by Barbara
Brandon © 1996, The 7 Habits of Highly Effective People: Powerful Lessons in
Personal Change by Stephen R. Covey © 1989. All copyrights held by authors.*

 G. Observing the Media

*Look at the illustrated titles of some popular American
self-help books. What aspects of life do they promise to improve? What
conclusions about American values can you draw from these titles? Collect other
titles by visiting an American bookstore, checking* Books in Print, *best-seller lists,
and by looking at ads for books in magazines and newspapers.*

H. Suggestions for Writing or Making an Oral Report

Some people say that they "live to work" while others "work to live." What
do they mean? Which phrase would best describe Americans who are heavily
influenced by the Protestant work ethic? Sometimes this belief in hard work for
material success or another goal can cause people to become workaholics, who
are unable to stop working, as alcoholics are unable to stop drinking alcohol.
They may work such long hours that they neglect their families and find it
difficult to relax.

Make a list of the pros and cons of working hard.

*Look for articles on workaholics, and write an essay or give an oral report on one
of the following topics:*

- It Is Possible to Work Too Hard
- How People View Work in My Country
- Two Different Views of Work: Living to Work and Working to Live

I. Proverbs and Sayings

There are a number of proverbs and sayings about right and wrong. For example, the golden rule, *Do to others as you would have them do to you*, means that you should treat people the way you want them to treat you.

Ask Americans to tell you proverbs and sayings about religion, hard work, and saving or spending money. Here are some examples to get you started. Ask Americans to explain these sayings to you.

1. God helps those who help themselves.
2. Early to bed and early to rise makes a man healthy, wealthy, and wise.
3. Save something for a rainy day.
4. Eat, drink, and be merry, for tomorrow you die.
5. Idle hands are the devil's workshop.

 J. Ask Yourself

Religion plays an important role in the lives of individuals and in a society. Think about your own beliefs.

1. Do you believe in God?
2. Do you believe in guardian angels?
3. Have you ever had an experience where you felt that you were being protected or guided by some spiritual power?
4. What do you think happens to our souls after we die?
5. What is the role of organized religion (if any) in your life? Do you belong to a religious faith?
6. Do you think it is important for children to be taught about religion? Will you raise your children in a religious faith?
7. Ideally, what role do you think religion should play in society?

If you feel comfortable discussing these questions, share your answers with a partner or with a small group of classmates.

All cultures have ceremonies to mark the important milestones and other important events in a person's life, and many of these ceremonies have a religious origin. How does your culture mark each of the following milestones and events? Which of these occasions may be celebrated with a religious ceremony? Discuss these with your classmates.
- The birth of a child
- Naming a child
- When a child becomes a member of a religious group
- When a child passes into adulthood (or puberty)

The García family celebrates a baptism   **Vivian García**

- Courtship and engagement
- Marriage
- Moving into a new home
- Starting a new job or career
- Divorce
- Death and burial
- Mourning the dead
- Remembering ancestors or others who have died

Are there any other milestones that your culture celebrates with special ceremonies?

 ## K. Suggestions for Further Reading

- Jonathan Edwards, *Sinners in the Hands of an Angry God*
- Nathaniel Hawthorne, *The Scarlet Letter*
- Nathaniel Hawthorne, *Young Goodman Brown*
- Herman Melville, *Billy Budd*
- Studs Terkel, *Working*
- Jacob Neuser, Editor, *World Religions in America: An Introduction*

 ## L. Recommended Movies

- *Elmer Gantry*
- *Witness*
- *The Scarlet Letter*
- *Leap of Faith*

Clint Eastwood as William Munny in Unforgiven   **AP/Wide World Photos**

CHAPTER 4

The Frontier Heritage

This ever retreating frontier of free land is the key to American development.

Frederick Jackson Turner

Before You Read

1. What is a "frontier"?
2. What American movies about the Old West have you seen?
3. What are the characteristics of American movie heroes?
4. Why do so many Americans own guns?

The Impact of the American Frontier

Although the American civilization took over and replaced the frontier over a century ago, the heritage of the frontier is still evident in the United States today. Many people are still **fascinated** by the frontier because it has been particularly important in shaping American values. When Ronald Reagan was President in the 1980s, he liked to recall the image of life on the frontier. He was often photographed on his western ranch—chopping wood or riding his horse, and wearing his cowboy hat. For many years, the frontier experience was **romanticized** in popular movies and television shows that featured cowboy heroes fighting Indian villains. Little attention was given to the tragic story of what really happened to the Native Americans. Today, most Americans are more aware of the darker side of the settling of the continent, when thousands of Native American Indians were killed, their lands were taken, and much of their culture was destroyed.

The frontier experience began when the first colonists settled on the east coast of the continent in the 1600s. It ended about 1890 when the last western lands were settled.

The American frontier consisted of the relatively unsettled regions of the United States, usually found in the western part of the country. Here, both land and life were more **rugged** and primitive than in the more settled eastern part. As one frontier area was settled, people began moving farther west into the next unsettled area, sweeping aside the Native Americans as they went. By settling one frontier area after another, Americans moved across an entire continent, 2,700 miles wide. They came to believe that it was their destiny to control all the land, and eventually they did. The Native Americans were given small portions of land called *reservations* to control, but the United States government broke many promises and created much misery for the Indian nations.

Recently, Americans have come to a more balanced view of the settling of the West. However, many Americans still see many aspects of the frontier, its people and their beliefs, as good, inspiring examples of traditional American values in their original and purest form. How did the frontier movement, which lasted more than two centuries, help to shape these basic American values?

To be sure, the frontier provided many inspiring examples of hard work as forests were turned into towns, and towns into large cities. The competitive race for success was rarely more colorful or adventurous than on the western frontier. The rush for gold in California, for silver in Montana, and for fertile land in all the western territories provided endless stories of high adventure. When it was announced that almost two million acres of good land in Oklahoma would be opened for settlement in April 1889, thousands of settlers gathered on the border waiting for the exact time to be announced. When it was, they **literally** raced into the territory in wagons and on horseback to claim the best land they could find for themselves.

The 1889 rush to claim land in Oklahoma **Library of Congress**

Although daily life on the frontier was usually less dramatic than the frontier adventure stories would lead one to believe, even the ordinary daily life of frontier men and women **exemplified** national values in a form that seemed purer to many Americans than the life of those living in the more settled, more cultivated eastern United States.

Individualism, self-reliance, and equality of opportunity have perhaps been the values most closely associated with the frontier heritage of America. Throughout their history, Americans have tended to view the frontier settler as the model of the free individual. This is probably because there was less control over the individual on the frontier than anywhere else in the United States. There were few laws and few established social or political institutions to confine people living on the frontier. In the United States, where freedom from outside social controls has traditionally been valued, the frontier has been idealized, and it still serves as a basis for a **nostalgic** view of the early United States, a simpler time that was lost when the country became urbanized and more complex.

Self-Reliance and the Rugged Individualist

Closely associated with the frontier ideal of the free individual is the ideal of self-reliance. If the people living on the frontier were free of many of society's rules, they were also denied many of society's comforts and conveniences. They had to be self-reliant. They often constructed their own houses, hunted, tended their own gardens, and made their own clothing and household items.

The self-reliant frontiersman has been idealized by Americans, who have made him the model of the classic American male hero with "rugged individualism." This hero is a man who has been made physically tough and rugged by the conditions of frontier life. He is skilled with guns and other weapons. He needs no help from others. He usually has no strong ties or obligations to women and children. He is

An 1859 gold mining camp in Colorado **Library of Congress**

kind and polite to them, but he prefers "to go his own way" and not be tied down by them. Standing alone, he can meet all the dangers that life on the frontier brings. He is strong enough to extend his protection beyond himself to others.

There are two types of "heroic rugged individualists." Each is drawn from a different stage of life on the frontier. In the early frontier, which existed before the Civil War of the 1860s, the main struggle was man against the wilderness. Daniel Boone is probably the best-known hero of this era. Boone explored the wilderness country of Kentucky in the 1760s and 1770s. On one trip, he stayed in the wilderness for two years, successfully matching his strength and skills against the dangers of untamed nature and hostile Native American Indians. In 1778, Boone was captured by Native Americans, who were so impressed with his physical strength and skills that they made him a member of their tribe. Later he succeeded in making a daring escape. Boone's heroic strength is seen primarily in his ability to master the **harsh** challenges of the wilderness. Although he had to fight against Indians from time to time, he is admired mainly as a survivor and conqueror of the wilderness, not as a fighter.

The second type of heroic rugged individualist is drawn from the last phase of the western frontier, which lasted from the 1860s until the 1890s. By this time, the wilderness was largely conquered. The struggle now was no longer man against nature but man against man. Cattleman and cowboys* fought against farmers, outlaws, Native Americans, and each other for control of the remaining western lands. The traditions of law and order were not yet well established, and physical violence was frequent. The frontier became known as the *Wild West*.

---

* Cattlemen were men who raised large herds of cattle as a business and needed large areas of land on which their cattle could graze before being sent to market. Cowboys usually worked for the cattlemen. They would spend most of the day on horseback rounding up the cattle or taking them on long drives to market.

It is not surprising, then, that the hero drawn from this period is primarily a fighter. He is admired for his ability to beat other men in **fist** fights, or to win in a gunfight. The principal source of his heroism is his physical **prowess**, and he is strong enough to defeat two or three ordinary men at one time. This rugged individualist is typically a defender of good against evil.

The hero of the Wild West is based on memories of a number of gunfighters and lawmen of the time, men such as Jesse James and Wyatt Earp. Although none of these men achieved the fame of Daniel Boone, the Wild West hero has had more impact on the American idea of heroism than the hero of the earlier wilderness frontier. It is the Wild West hero who has inspired countless western movies; until the 1960s, 25 percent of all American movies made were westerns.

American Macho

Through movies and television programs, this Wild West hero has helped shape the American idea of *macho* or male strength. For the most part, almost all American male heroes on radio, television, and in movies have traditionally had the common ability to demonstrate their strength through physical violence. Once the western macho hero had been created, the model for this hero was used in other settings—for soldiers in battle and tough detectives and policemen fighting crime. From John Wayne to Rambo and the Terminator, these heroes can fight with their fists or with their guns, or both. Although there are movie and TV heroes who are respected more for their intelligence and sensitivity than their physical prowess, the classic macho male heroes still dominate much of American entertainment and are popular in video games. Now there are even female heroes who have to be tough and fight or kill their enemies.

The image of the rugged individualist has been criticized for overlooking many factors that played a central part in the development of the frontier. The

On a western ranch, cowboys prepare to round up the cattle **Standard Oil Co.**

rugged individualist image overstates the importance of complete self-reliance and understates the importance of cooperation in building a new nation out of the wilderness. Second, because the image is entirely masculine, it overlooks the importance of pioneer women: their strength, hard work, and resourcefulness, and their civilizing influence on the untamed frontier.

Finally, the rugged individualist image is criticized because of its emphasis on violence and the use of guns to solve problems. On the frontier, men did use guns to hunt and protect themselves and their families, but Western movies romanticized and glorified gunfights in the old West. The good guys and the bad guys shot it out in classic westerns such as *High Noon*. Gradually, however, the western hero was largely replaced in the movies by the soldier or the crime fighter, guns still blazing, and the violence in movies, and later on TV, increased. Incidentally, the classic old western movies always featured the "good guys" wearing white hats, while the "bad guys" wore black hats.

As Americans watch the level of violence rise in their society, many are questioning the impact of these entertainment heroes on the lives and imaginations of young people. At the very least, many young people have become **de-sensitized** to the sight of violence and killings. By the mid-1990s, guns had become a severe problem in the lives of many children. It is all too easy for teenagers to get guns, and they are much more at risk of being killed by them than adults are. These problems are particularly bad in the inner cities, where many young gang members carry guns.

Arnold Schwarzenegger as The Terminator with Edward Furlong in the movie T2: Judgment Day   **AP/Wide World Photos**

Americans have a long history of owning guns, and many people strongly believe having a gun in their house is an important right. In fact, the right to bear arms is even guaranteed in the Constitution, although there is debate about what the founding fathers meant by that. Today there are over 200 million guns in the United States, and there is at least one gun in more than half of U.S. households. Worried about rising crime rates, many people continue to believe that owning a gun is the best way to protect their homes and families from being robbed or attacked. After the Los Angeles riots of the early 1990s, the sale of guns rose sharply in that area. Statistically, however, families with guns in their homes are 13 times more likely to be shot by another family member than they are by someone trying to break into their house.

It should be pointed out that most Americans favor stricter government controls on the sale of guns, but there are already so many guns on the streets that the problem is enormous. The millions who oppose gun controls feel strongly enough about the issue that they have created powerful political pressure groups, such as the National Rifle Association (NRA), which has worked to prevent most gun control legislation from passing. They argue that limiting gun sales will keep law-abiding citizens from owning guns, not criminals. In 1994, the Brady Bill banned the sale of many automatic assault weapons, and a new crime bill was passed in an effort to stop the violence. However, an effort to repeal the ban on assault weapons was launched almost immediately.

Inventiveness and the Can-Do Spirit

While the frontier idealized the rugged individual as the great American hero, it also respected the inventive individual. The need for self-reliance on the frontier encouraged a spirit of inventiveness. Frontier men and women not only had to provide most of their daily life essentials, but they were also constantly facing new problems and situations that demanded new solutions. Under these circumstances, they soon learned to experiment with new ways of doing things.

Observers from other countries were very impressed by the frontiersman's ability to invent useful new farm tools. They were equally impressed by the pioneer woman's ability to make clothing, candles, soap, and many other items needed for the daily life of her family. Lord Bryce, a famous English observer of American life, believed that the inventive skills of American pioneers enabled them to succeed at tasks beyond the abilities of most ordinary men and women in other countries. Although Americans in the more settled eastern regions of the United States created many of the most important inventions in the new nation, the western frontier had the effect of spreading the spirit of inventiveness throughout the population and helping it to become a national character trait.

The willingness to experiment and invent led to another American trait, a *can-do* spirit, a sense of optimism that every problem has a solution. Americans like to believe that a difficult problem can be solved immediately—an impossible one may take a little longer. They take pride in meeting challenges and overcoming difficult **obstacles**. This can-do spirit has traditionally given Americans a sense of optimism about themselves and their country. Many like to say that if the United States can land a man on the moon, no problem on earth is impossible. In the 1830s, de Tocqueville said that no other country in the world "more confidently seizes the future" than the United States. Traditionally, when times are hard, political leaders remind Americans of their frontier heritage and the tough determination of their pioneer ancestors; the can-do spirit has become a source of pride and inspiration.

Equality of Opportunity

The frontier is an expression of individual freedom and self-reliance in its purest (and most extreme) form, and it is also a pure expression of the ideal of equality of opportunity. On the western frontier, there was more of a tendency for people to treat each other as social equals than in the more settled eastern regions of the country. On the frontier, the highest importance was placed on what people could do in their own lifetime. Hardly any notice was taken of their ancestors. Frontier people were fond of saying, "What's above the ground is more important than what's beneath the ground."

Because so little attention was paid to a person's family background, the frontier offered a new beginning for many Americans who were seeking opportunities to advance themselves. One English visitor to the United States in the early 1800s observed that if Americans experienced disappointment or failure in business, in politics, or even in love, they moved west to make a new beginning. The frontier offered millions of Americans a source of hope for a fresh start in the competitive race for success and for a better life. On the frontier, there was a continuing need for new farmers, skilled laborers, merchants, lawyers, and political leaders.

There were fewer differences in wealth between rich and poor on the frontier than in the more settled regions of the nation. People lived, dressed, and acted more alike on the frontier than in other parts of the United States. The feeling of equality was shared by hired helpers who refused to be called "servants" or to be treated as such. One European visitor observed: "The **clumsy gait** and bent body of our peasant is hardly ever seen here… Everyone walks **erect** and easy." Wealthy travelers to the frontier were warned not to show off their wealth or to act superior to others if they wished to be treated politely.

The American frontier may not be "the key" to American development, as Frederick Jackson Turner said, but it is certainly one major factor. The frontier provided the space and conditions that helped to strengthen the American ideals

A 19th-century frontier family in front of their sod house   **Library of Congress**

Cowboys ride bucking broncos in a modern-day Western rodeo   **Roxane Fridirici**

of individual freedom, self-reliance, and equality of opportunity. On the frontier, these ideals were enlarged and made workable. Frontier ideas and customs were continuously passed along to the more settled parts of the United States as newer frontier regions took the place of older ones during a westward march of settlers that lasted more than two centuries. In this way, many of the frontier values became national values.

■ ■ ■ ■

 ## New Words

fascinate to interest greatly

romanticize to make something sound better than it really is

rugged rough; tough

literally exactly

exemplify to be an example of

nostalgic fond of something in the past

harsh difficult; severe

fist the hand with the fingers closed in tightly

prowess unusual ability or skill; great bravery

de-sensitized lacking sensitivity; unable to feel any emotion

obstacle something that stands in the way and prevents action, movement, or success

clumsy gait awkward way of walking

erect standing up straight

 ## A. Vocabulary Check

Complete the sentences using words or phrases from the New Words list.

1. In many "action" movies, the heroes are expected to be able to fight with their _____.

2. Many heroes are known for their physical _____.

3. Soldiers guarding the Tomb of the Unknown Soldier are expected to stand _____.

4. Some people prefer to _____ life on the frontier; they do not want to look at its negative aspects.

5. Someone who drops things, trips, and bumps into furniture probably has a _____ _____.

6. I saw a lady laugh so hard she _____ fell off her chair.

7. The pioneers who lived on the frontier had a hard life, so they had to be _____.

8. If you are reading a book that is so interesting that you can't put it down, you are _____ by the book.

9. Frontier people displayed examples of the American national values; these people _____ these values.

10. People living on the frontier had to overcome many difficulties and _____, such as clearing the land, in order to succeed.

11. Americans like to remember the days on the frontier; they feel _____ about the old West.

12. Conditions on the frontier were often _____, and the people had to work hard just to survive.

13. Some Americans worry that their children are becoming _____ to the violence and killing on television. It doesn't seem to bother them to see someone get hurt or even killed.

B. Comprehension Check

Write **T** *if the statement is true and* **F** *if it is false according to the information in the chapter.*

_____ 1. The frontier experience began about 1890 and is still continuing in the American West today.

_____ 2. One reason why many Americans are still fascinated by the frontier is that, for many, this period represents a time when the traditional basic American values were expressed in their purest form.

_____ 3. The settling of the frontier did little to affect the lives of the Native American Indians.

_____ 4. There are two types of the "rugged individual" hero: The first is a man who fights against the wilderness, and the second is a man who fights against man.

_____ 5. The primary qualities of the American macho hero are intelligence, sensitivity, and caring for others.

_____ 6. It is difficult for the average American to buy a gun, so very few people own them.

_____ 7. Members of the NRA (and many gun owners) believe that the right to own a gun is guaranteed in the United States Constitution.

_____ 8. The can-do spirit came from the willingness of the pioneers to work together on a cooperative project for the good of all.

_____ 9. On the frontier, family name and ancestry were more important than what a person could do.

_____ 10. There was a great distance between the rich and the poor on the frontier, and social class was more important than in the more settled regions.

C. Questions for Discussion

1. Do children in your country play with toy guns or swords? What effect does seeing violence on TV or in movies have on children? What happens when children become de-sensitized to violence?

2. Why is there nostalgia for the American frontier days? What evidence of this trend do you see today? Is there anything similar to the frontier experience in the history of your country? Is there a historical period that has been romanticized?

3. What is the American concept of macho? How does this compare with your own concept of manliness? What qualities does a "man's man" have? What

experiences help a boy become a man in your country? How do women in your country respond to a macho man? Is there such a thing as a macho woman?

4. What qualities should a true hero have? What qualities do heroes in movies and TV shows in your country have? Who are some of your own personal heroes? Why do you admire and respect these people?

5. Do many people in your country own guns? What kinds of gun control laws are there? How does one buy a gun? What kinds of guns are most popular: handguns or rifles? Would you have a gun in your own home? Why? How do you feel about guns?

6. Do you agree or disagree with this saying: "What's above the ground is more important than what's beneath the ground"? In your country, how much emphasis is placed on what a person can do? Which do you think is more important: a person's family background or what that person can do?

 D. Cloze Summary Paragraph

This paragraph summarizes the chapter. Fill in each blank with any word that makes sense.

The American frontier has ____*had*____ a strong influence on _____ values, particularly individualism, self-reliance, _____ equality of opportunity. Individuals _____ great freedom on the _____, but they had to _____ very self-reliant. These qualities _____ idealized in the concept _____ rugged individualism. There are _____ types of American heroes _____ are rugged individualists. The _____ comes out of the _____ before 1860 when the _____ was man against nature. _____ second comes from the _____ West era, 1860 to _____, when the struggle was _____ against man. The Wild _____ hero is the basis _____ the American macho hero _____ western movies and TV _____. He is a fighter _____ solves his problems by _____ his fists or his _____. Guns are still popular _____ America today, and many _____ own them. The frontier _____ encouraged inventiveness and a _____ spirit. There was great _____ of opportunity on the _____, and there were few _____ in wealth or social _____. People moved west to _____ frontier to get a _____ start in life. Although _____ frontier disappeared more than _____ hundred years ago, it _____ fascinates and influences Americans _____.

E. Observing the Media

1. The American cowboy has long been a symbol of the American belief in rugged individualism and the frontier spirit. What is there about cowboys that exemplifies the values discussed in this chapter: individualism, self-reliance, inventiveness, the can-do spirit, and equality of opportunity? Describe cowboys as you have seen them in American movies and on TV shows.

2. Cowboys and the Old West are frequently used in advertisements for cigarettes, blue jeans, trucks, cars, and other American products. What image do they have? Why does this image help sell this or that product? Collect examples of ads in magazines and newspapers that use cowboys or western themes. (If possible, observe and report on TV ads also.) For each, explain what the message is to the people who may buy this product.

3. Watch American TV shows that have male heroes. How do they compare with the description of American macho presented in this chapter? What personality traits do they have? Compare the heroes of several shows. Would you describe them as…

   - having sex appeal?
   - being admired by beautiful women?
   - having no involvement in long-term relationships with a woman (not married; no children; no family)?
   - being a loner (few friends, mysterious)?
   - having an ideal or a goal in life?
   - fighting against injustice?
   - being a man's man?
   - moving from place to place?
   - being good with his fists?
   - being good with a gun?

F. Proverbs and Sayings

Ask Americans to explain these proverbs and sayings. Then ask them for other examples of sayings about succeeding on your own *or* being tough.

1. Pull yourself up by the bootstraps.
2. If at first you don't succeed, try, try again.
3. Actions speak louder than words.
4. Life is what you make it.
5. Every problem has a solution.

 G. Ask Yourself

Do you agree or disagree with each of the statements below? Put a check under the number that indicates how you feel.

+2 = Strongly agree
+1 = Agree
 0 = No opinion
-1 = Disagree
-2 = Strongly disagree

	+2	+1	0	-1	-2
1. I really love action movies that have a lot of gunfights.	___	___	___	___	___
2. A real man should be able to defend himself well and even win in a fist fight.	___	___	___	___	___
3. Intelligence and sensitivity in a man are more important than physical strength.	___	___	___	___	___
4. Watching fights in movies and on TV shows probably doesn't hurt children.	___	___	___	___	___
5. Using physical violence is not the best way to solve a problem.	___	___	___	___	___
6. Women really like macho men.	___	___	___	___	___
7. Having a gun in your home is a good way to protect yourself against robbers.	___	___	___	___	___
8. I believe people should not own guns and there should be strict laws controlling the sale of them.	___	___	___	___	___
9. Every problem has a solution.	___	___	___	___	___
10. What you do is more important than who you are.	___	___	___	___	___

Now divide the room into plus and minus sections, with the zero in the middle (see Exercise E in Chapter 2). Hang up pieces of paper with 0, +1, +2, -1, and -2. As the teacher reads the statements, walk to the part of the room that reflects whether you agree or disagree with the statement, and how strongly. Explain your choice.

H. Ask Americans

Read the statements from Exercise G to several Americans, and ask them if they agree or disagree with each statement.

I.   Think, Pair, Share

Some Americans are nostalgic for the Old West. What period of your country's history is romanticized? If you could travel back in time to anywhere in the world, what place and what period in history would you like to visit?

Write your answer on a piece of paper, then share you answer with a partner and then with another pair.

Shiprock—an Indian sacred place in New Mexico   **Roxane Fridirici**

American astronaut David R. Scott salutes the U.S. flag on the moon, 1971 **NASA**

 ## J. Suggestions for Writing or Making an Oral Report

1. American rugged individualism, the can-do spirit, and an optimistic belief in the future were exemplified on July 20, 1969, when man first walked on the moon. That was the day when the Apollo XI Mission landed. As Neil Armstrong climbed down the ladder from the spacecraft to the surface of the moon, he declared, "One small step for man. One giant leap for mankind." What did he mean? In what way was it a "giant leap" for mankind? The plaque on the lunar lander left on the moon reads, "We came in peace for all mankind." (Would Armstrong use the word *mankind* today?) Why did the astronauts plant a flag on the moon? How does this relate to staking a claim for land on the frontier? What values do you see reflected in the pride Americans feel about the moon landing? Write an essay discussing these values and how they relate to the frontier experience. Or write an essay (or have a debate) about who should "own" or "control" space, the moon and planets.

2. Americans have strong opinions about the gun control issue. What do *you* think? Write an essay (or have a debate) summarizing the arguments for and against gun control laws. Or imagine that you are living in a city where guns are a problem. Write a letter to a hunter who lives out in the country urging him to support gun control laws. Explain how his right to own an automatic weapon is interfering with your right to live in peace and safety in the city.

3. Americans believe in the importance of teaching their children to be independent and self-reliant, and in preparing them to leave home and live on their own, usually at age 18, when most young people go off to college or get a full-time job. Perhaps this philosophy has something to do with Americans' ancestors and how the frontier was settled. Ellen Goodman, a popular columnist, observes:

The whole country was settled by one generation of leavers after the next—people who moved to a new frontier or a new neighborhood or a new job, who continually left relationships for opportunities. It was considered unreasonable, almost unpatriotic, for parents to "cling." And it still is.

The result of this is an emphasis on raising children to be independent and separate from their parents. The goal of parenting in America is to make children competent and confident enough to leave "the nest." What do you think of this philosophy? Is this the goal of parenting in your country? Compare and contrast this philosophy of child raising with that of your country.

Mother and daughter   **Maryanne Kearny Datesman**

K. People Watching

Americans are very conscious of space and have a strong sense of territory—that is, the idea that a particular space belongs to them. Children usually have their own room; the kitchen may belong to Mom; Dad may have a special chair in the living room or den, or he may have a workshop. Observe Americans at home, in a public place, or in a social situation to see how they use space. (Watch TV shows, if you are not in the United States.) If someone has been sitting in a particular chair and gets up, does the person tend to come back to the same chair? When someone asks, "Is that seat taken?" what does that person mean?

Conduct the following experiment and record the results in your journal.

Rule: When an American sits down at a table where a stranger is sitting alone, the American will choose a seat across from the other person or at least one chair away. The space is divided in half between them, and personal belongings must be kept on each person's respective side of an imaginary boundary line.

Observation: Observe people sitting in a public place where there are tables, such as a cafeteria or library. What happens when a stranger sits down at a table where a person is sitting alone? If someone sits down next to a stranger, what happens? How do the people acknowledge each other's presence? Does the person who was sitting there first move his or her belongings?

Experiment: Choose a table where a stranger is sitting alone and sit down in the next chair. What happens? Sit across from someone at a table and put some personal belongings (such as books) on the table in front of you. Push them toward the other person so that they are more than halfway across the table. What is the person's reaction?

As you read the morning newspaper, you quickly come to an undeniable conclusion. Our world is in rough shape. Our environment. Our families. Our values.

A SANE, RATIONAL ARGUMENT FOR GIVING THE ENTIRE COUNTRY BACK TO THE INDIANS.

Now, the only way we can change the world we live in, is to change the way we think. And a good place to start is by becoming better acquainted with the traditional American Indian beliefs. For reasons of economy, we'll briefly mention how traditional American Indian thinking applies to just four timely issues: The destruction of the wilderness. The breakdown of the family. Greed. And international turmoil.

The destruction of the wilderness. You can't watch television for fifteen minutes without hearing about another toxic dump or another endangered species. To the American Indian, nature is more than a collection of water and landforms, it's their religion and thus it's treated with the appropriate respect. There is the belief that everything must be kept in balance and to disrupt this balance (pollution, over-hunting, over-developing, etc.) will only result in tragedy.

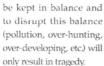

The breakdown of the American family. It's a sad and widely accepted fact. In traditional American Indian culture, though, the family is not only strong, it spans many generations. The children are also raised by the aunts and uncles and elders for Indians believe it's best for a child to learn from as many people as possible to give them a more well-rounded education. Also, child abuse was unheard-of in the traditional American Indian world. In their journals, Lewis and Clark often commented with amazement how the Indians never struck their children.

Greed. So many modern problems can be directly traced to that emotion. The American Indians, though, believe wealth and success only means that you're able to give more to others, and materialism only removes one further from God.

The international problems. Most often they occur because one culture becomes intolerant of another. The American Indians, on the other hand, believe all cultures are equally important. The Indians often used the analogy of the wagon wheel to explain this belief. The spokes represent all the various cultures, each one unique unto itself. None of the spokes could ever be removed or shortened or lengthened, because they are all absolutely necessary for the wheel (the earth) to turn.

As stated earlier, these are only four examples demonstrating how relevant traditional American Indian beliefs are. But the greater problem is that the American Indian culture is in danger of becoming extinct. 200 years of forced assimilation has done everything possible to dilute and destroy their world. And the greatest hope for survival is through the 26 tribal colleges. The tribal colleges were formed to keep the tribal ways alive and to reintroduce them to a generation of Indians who may know nothing about their heritage. The results have been remarkable. More Indians are becoming educated, tribal pride is increasing, and the old ways are being restored and preserved.

The tribal colleges, though, are struggling financially and to survive this decade, they are going to need your help.

So please call 1-800-776-FUND. And help save a culture that could save ours.

AMERICAN INDIAN COLLEGE FUND

American Indian College Fund, 217 East 85th St., Suite 201 PA, New York, NY 10028. We would like to give a special thanks to US West for all their concern and support.

American Indian College Fund

L. What's Your Opinion? Small Group Discussion

Read the ad for the American Indian College Fund on page 80. What is the purpose of the ad? What are the four traditional American Indian values explained in the ad? What do you think of these values? Why would Americans have trouble following their advice?

M. Suggestions for Further Reading

- John Steinbeck, *The Grapes of Wrath*
- Jack London, *The Call of the Wild*
- Stephen Crane, *The Red Badge of Courage*
- James Fenimore Cooper, *The Leatherstocking Tales*
- Willa Cather, *O Pioneers!*
- Dee Brown, *Bury My Heart at Wounded Knee*
- Vine Deloria, *Custer Died for Your Sins: An Indian Manifesto*

N. Recommended Movies

- *High Noon*
- *Shane*
- *Rio Bravo*
- *Far and Away*
- *The Virginian*
- *Dances with Wolves*
- *Lakota Woman*
- *Unforgiven*

A Native American woman talks about contemporary Indian life
Laimute E. Druskis

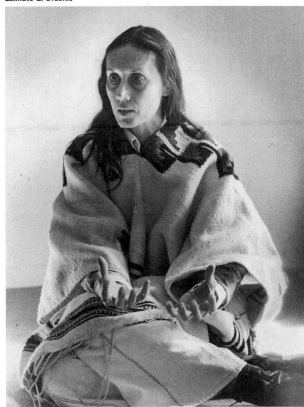

A playstructure made from recycled plastic containers, aluminum cans and soup cans   **Maryanne Kearny Datesman**

CHAPTER 5

The Heritage of Abundance

For millions of people throughout this world, during the past three centuries, America has symbolized plenty, wealth and abundance of goods.

David Potter

Before You Read

1. What do you think is abundant in American society? What effect does abundance have on people?

2. What products do you see advertised on television in your country? Do TV ads influence you to buy the products?

3. What do you think American consumers like? Why?

A History of Abundance

Although the population of the United States accounts for only 5 percent of the total population of the world, Americans use up about 25 percent of the world's energy per year, generating more than four pounds of **trash** and **garbage** per person each day. Only a country that has great abundance could afford to throw so much away. America has sometimes been criticized as a "throw-away" country, a land where there is so much abundance that people are sometimes viewed as wasteful. Scholars like David Potter, an American historian, believe that the abundant material wealth of the United States has been a major factor in the development of the American character.

This abundance is the gift of nature. In what is now the continental United States, there are more than three million square miles of land. When the European settlers first arrived in the 17th and 18th centuries, most of this land was rich, fertile farmland, with an abundance of trees and animals. Only about one million Native Americans lived on this land, and they had neither the weapons nor the organization necessary to keep the European settlers out. One writer has said that never again can human beings discover such a large area of rich, unfarmed land, with such a small population and such great undeveloped natural resources.

But it would be a mistake to say that the abundant natural resources of North America were the only reason why the United States became a wealthy nation. The beliefs, determination, and hard work of the early settlers were equally important.

In aristocratic European nations, the American settlers left behind the material wealth and comforts of the ruling classes that were guaranteed by their birth. Therefore, as de Tocqueville said, the wealthy took these things for granted and placed little importance on material things. The poor people in those aristocratic nations also did not concern themselves with wealth, since they knew that they had so little hope of becoming wealthy or changing their status.

In the early years of the United States, however, wealth and social position were not permanently determined at birth. The idea of equality of opportunity in America made the level of material wealth of both the rich and the poor much less certain. At any time, the rich might lose some of their wealth, and the poor might increase theirs. Therefore, all classes in American society thought about protecting their material possessions and looked for ways to acquire more. De Tocqueville believed that this was not so much a matter of greed; rather, it was a matter of their insecurity. People might be naturally insecure if their material wealth, and that of their children, could change so rapidly either upward or downward during a lifetime, or even during a single generation.

De Tocqueville concluded that it was extremely important both to rich Americans and poor Americans to increase their personal wealth and material comforts. Therefore, the entire population joined in the great task of increasing the nation's material abundance as quickly as possible.

De Tocqueville visited the United States 50 years after the nation had won its independence from England. He was impressed with the great progress made in such a short time. Although the country was still in an early stage of development, and there was not much money available for investment, the United States had already made great progress in both trading and manufacturing. It had already become the world's second leading sea power and had constructed the longest railroads in the world. De Tocqueville worried, however, about the effect of all this material success. In such a society, materialism could be made into a moral value in itself rather than a means to an end.

De Tocqueville's concern, to a large extent, became a reality. In the process of creating a land of abundance, Americans began to judge themselves by materialistic standards. Unlike many countries, where the love of material things was seen as a **vice**, a mark of weak moral character, in the United States it was seen as a virtue: a positive **incentive** to work hard and a reward for successful efforts.

Traditionally, the people of the United States have been proud of their nation's ability to produce material wealth so that they could maintain a high standard of living. This helps to explain why Americans use materialistic standards not only to judge themselves as individuals but also to judge themselves as a nation. And the opportunity to share in the good life has attracted immigrants to the United States for generations.

Inside Pentagon City shopping mall, Arlington, Virginia **Maryanne Kearny Datesman**

The Heritage of Abundance

From Producers to Consumers

The emphasis on producing wealth and maintaining a high standard of living has not always been the same. In the 1700s and 1800s, most Americans thought of themselves more as producers than consumers. As farmers, they produced food and many of their own household goods. Later, as factory workers, they produced manufactured goods. The real change came with the invention of the radio and the arrival of mass advertising in the 1920s. Along with the radio programs came short advertisements, or **commercials**, asking the listener to buy a certain product. Business companies paid for radio programs that agreed to run commercials advertising their products.

When television began in the 1950s, it used the same technique that radio had developed: entertainment programs accompanied by short commercials. However, television soon passed radio as a source of both family entertainment and mass advertising. By the 1990s, 98 percent of all homes in the United States had at least one television set (the average number was 2.1), and the family TV was in use about six hours a day. Today, the average American sees about 50,000 commercials a year. When popular events such as the Super Bowl are on, mass advertising may reach 50 million or more viewers during a single program.

What impact has all this mass advertising had? It has created the age of the consumer. Big producers came to believe that the best way to increase both their production and their profits was to convince millions of Americans, through mass advertising, to consume more products. The older picture of the American as producer gave way to a newer picture of the American as a consumer.

Television sets on sale in a department store   **Maryanne Kearny Datesman**

Historian David Potter believes that mass advertising in the United States is now so important in size and influence that it should be viewed as an institution, such as the school or the church. However, unlike schools and churches, mass advertising does not seek to improve the individual. Its only purpose is to convince people to consume more and more products.

Commercial Television Versus Public Television and the Internet

Because some businesses **sponsor** certain television shows, they may work with the creators of the programs and have some say over the content. If they do not like what is happening on the show, the sponsors can withdraw their support. Some critics believe that the control of television by mass advertising has affected the quality of the programs. Others argue that commercial television gives the American public what it wants. Only popular programs stay on the air; others are quickly canceled. Moreover, television offers a wide variety of entertainment, sports, and news programs in the average family's living room at a very low cost.

There is, of course, an alternative to commercial television where programs are paid for by sponsors. Public television is not paid for by mass advertising; therefore, it has no commercials. It is paid for by contributions from individual viewers (the public) who want higher-quality television, **donations** by private companies, and government grants. The programs on public television are generally superior in educational and cultural content to the programs on commercial television. Even though public television is watched by a large number of Americans, commercial television still attracts much larger audiences. (This would seem to support the argument of those who claim that commercial television gives the general public what it wants to see.)

Both commercial and public television programs are also available on cable TV or satellite TV for a monthly fee. In addition, a subscriber can pay extra for movie channels and other entertainment services. Cable television, now in more than 60 percent of American homes, may offer viewers more than 100 channels. Satellite TV, gaining in popularity, may offer more than 500 channels.

As the information superhighway develops, and all means of communication begin to merge, more and more options become available to the home user. More than one-third of the American households now have personal computers, and communication over the Internet and the World Wide Web is rising rapidly.*

Americans face a constant **dilemma**—how to balance the right to free speech with the need to protect children and maintain standards of **decency**.

---

* The Internet and World Wide Web are communication systems that connect computers around the world. Individuals can send each other "E-mail" (electronic-mail) messages from their home or office computers, and they can get information from the "home page" of businesses, libraries, government agencies, museums, schools, newspapers, TV stations, and countless other private and public organizations.

American schools and universities now require students to use computers   **Elizabeth Coppolino**

Because Americans place such a high value on individual freedom, particularly freedom of speech, they have traditionally been very hesitant to **censor**, or even restrict, the flow of information by any means of communication. True censorship occurs when the government sets the standards; most Americans would prefer that the entertainment industry regulate itself. The movie industry currently rates movies (G for General, PG for Parental Guidance, PG-13 for movies not appropriate for children under 13, R for movies Restricted to age 17 and older). Many people believe that it is important for the industry also to rate TV programs. And now that many American children have access to the Internet, there is a debate over whether and how to regulate it.

What American Consumers Like

People in the mass advertising business and others who study American society have been very interested in the question: What does the American consumer like? Max Lerner, a well-known scholar who has studied American society, has said that American consumers are particularly fond of three things: comfort, cleanliness, and novelty.

Lerner believes that the American love of comfort perhaps goes back to the frontier experience, where life was tough and there were very few comforts. This experience may have created a strong desire in the pioneers and their children for goods that would make life more comfortable. Today, the Americans' love of comfort is seen in the way they furnish their homes, design their cars, and travel. How Americans choose a new mattress for their bed is an example of the American love of comfort. Many Americans will go to a store where beds are set up, and they will lie down on several mattresses to see which one is the most comfortable.

Cleanliness is also highly valued by Americans. There is a strong emphasis on keeping all parts of the body clean, and Americans see lots of TV commercials for soap, shampoo, **deodorants**, and mouthwash. Perhaps the Puritan heritage has played some role in the desire for cleanliness. The Puritans, a strict Protestant church group who were among the first settlers of America, stressed the need to **cleanse** the body of dirt and of all evil tendencies, such as sexual desire. The saying "Cleanliness is next to Godliness" reflects the belief of most Americans that it is important to keep not only their bodies but also their clothes, their houses, their cars, and even their pets clean and smelling good. Indeed, many Americans are offended by anyone who does not follow their accepted standards of cleanliness.

Along with cleanliness and comfort, Americans love having things that are new and different. Perhaps this love of novelty comes from their pride in their inventiveness. Americans have always been interested in inventing new products and improving old ones. They like to see changes in cars, clothing, and products for the home. Advertisements encourage people to get rid of old products and try new ones, whether the old ones still work or not. And if they cannot afford to buy something now, advertisers encourage consumers to charge it on a credit card. "Buy now—pay later."

In addition to the three qualities that Lerner mentions, there is a fourth quality that American consumers like very much—convenience. During the last 40 years, there has been a dramatic increase in such labor-saving devices as automatic washing machines, clothes dryers, dishwashers, food processors, microwave ovens, garbage disposals, and power lawn mowers. Today, all of these, and many more, are found in a typical suburban home. These labor-saving devices are designed to reduce the time spent on housework. However, the time that Americans save is quickly spent on other activities.

A drugstore offers a wide selection of deodorants **Maryanne Kearny Datesman**

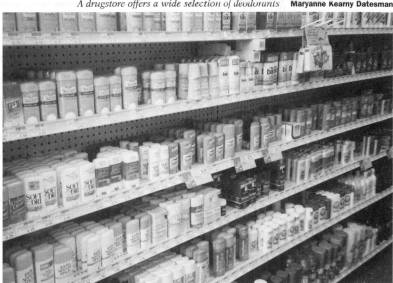

The American desire for convenience also created the concept of fast-food restaurants, found in every city and almost every small town in the United States, and now exported all over the world. These fast-food restaurants, such as McDonald's and KFC (Kentucky Fried Chicken), serve sandwiches, salads, fried chicken, seafood, and other food to hurried customers in five minutes or less, often at a drive-up window. There are also a wide variety of restaurants that will deliver Chinese food, pizza, and other dishes to people's homes in about a half-hour. In many areas there are "take-out taxis" that will deliver food from the menus of 20 or 30 different restaurants for a small charge. For those who prefer to prepare their food at home, American grocery stores are full of convenience foods that are packaged and ready to cook or even precooked.

Like microwaves and dishwashers, fast-food and take-out restaurants are convenient because they save the American consumer time that would otherwise be spent fixing meals or cleaning up. These conveniences, however, do not mean that Americans are less busy. More than half of all the women in the United States are currently employed. This includes mothers with children under the age of 18. More than half the women with little children under the age of six hold jobs. Sixty-eight percent of the women who have school-age children (age six and over) are employed. Families with working mothers need all the time-savers they can get.

American fast-food restaurants are spreading around the world   **Eugene Gordon, Anita Duncan, and Maryanne Kearny Datesman**

The American Ways

Thus, the conveniences that Americans desire reflect not so much a **leisurely** lifestyle as a busy lifestyle in which even minutes of time are too valuable to be wasted. Alexis de Tocqueville was one of the first to see in this a curious **paradox** in the American character. He observed that Americans were so busy working to acquire comforts and conveniences that they were unable to relax and to enjoy leisure time when they had it. Today, as in de Tocqueville's time, many Americans have what one medical doctor has called "the hurry sickness."

The Ever-Expanding Pie

During the first 200 years of their nation's existence (1776–1976), Americans were never forced to change their great optimism about wealth and abundance. They viewed the material wealth of the United States as an ever-expanding pie. In other countries, people believe that the rich take a larger piece of the pie and the poor get a smaller piece. Americans, however, have believed that their economic pie would just continue to grow so that all people could get a bigger piece of a bigger pie. This expectation was based on the early experience that as the new nation grew, the pie of wealth and abundance grew at an even faster rate. In the 1800s, the nation grew in size, as new western lands were settled and became states. In the 1900s, when the continent had been settled, Americans invented new products and techniques of production, such as Henry Ford's mass production of cars on the assembly line. The expanding economy created new jobs, and the pie continued to grow larger and larger. Under these circumstances, Americans came to believe that their heritage of abundance would last as far as they could see into the future.

The belief in an everlasting heritage of abundance had many good effects. It made Americans an optimistic people with confidence that human problems could be solved. It greatly reduced the conflict between the rich and poor that has torn many older nations apart. Perhaps most important, the belief in an always growing abundance gave strong support to such basic national values as freedom, self-reliance, equality of opportunity, competition, and hard work. It seemed to Americans that their high standard of living was a reward for practicing these values.

The Decline of American Abundance

Perhaps the most important change in American life in the last two decades has been a slow but steady decline in the standard of living of many Americans, particularly the young. In the late 1970s, the energy crisis and the economic recession warned Americans that there might be a limit to their abundant natural resources and the lifestyle that these natural resources had supported. The 1980s brought a general turnaround in the economy, but it was the rich who got richer; the poor got poorer, and the number of people in the middle class decreased.

A high standard of living has been at the heart of the American Dream—a house in the suburbs, one or two cars, a secure job, and enough money to go on vacations and to send the children to college. But the cost of all these things has been rising, while the number of high-paying jobs—particularly in factories—has been declining.

The new jobs are often in the service economy (not in manufacturing), with relatively low pay and poor benefits. As a result, younger Americans must work harder than their parents did to have the same standard of living. Young parents are finding that it is necessary for both of them to work outside the home in order to maintain their lifestyle. The average number of hours per week that Americans work rose from 41 hours in the 1970s to 47 hours in the 1990s, with many professionals (doctors, lawyers, business people) working 50 or 60 hours per week.

Although Americans are working harder and have less and less leisure time, many still cannot keep up with rising costs. During the 1980s, housing costs rose twice as fast as incomes did. The result is that in the 1990s, people have to spend a larger percent of their income on owning a home or renting an apartment. Today, more than half of American families cannot afford to buy a median-priced house in the area in which they are living. This breaks down to 43 percent of white, 77 percent of black, and 74 percent of Hispanic households that cannot afford to buy a nice home. Even a modest house is beyond the economic reach of a total of 48 percent of the households.

What of the future?

On the positive side, the decline in American abundance has caused people to become less wasteful and more protective of their environment. Many Americans now recycle aluminum and tin cans, plastic and paper bags, plastic and glass containers, office paper, and newspapers. Children study about environmental issues in school—about care of the local environment, and the problems of planet earth, such as air and water pollution, global warming, and the threat to endangered species. Businesses sometimes "adopt" sections of roads, and the company's employees volunteer their time to keep the trash picked up. Communities conduct environmental impact studies before developing empty land. Sometimes a local community chooses to keep its rural lifestyle and protect its historical lands. The people reject development even if it means losing potential new jobs. For example, the citizens of a rural community near Washington, D.C., were able to stop the Disney company from building a new theme park in their area, even though Virginia state officials were in favor of the development.

On the negative side, old habits are hard to change, and it is difficult to predict what the future holds. Most Americans are pessimistic about the economic future of their country and its ability to expand forever. As Daniel Yankelovich, a public opinion expert, observed:

Ad Council Symbol, EPA symbol and EDF symbol

©1994 EDF

Buy recycled. It would mean the world to them.

Thanks to you, all sorts of everyday products are being made from materials you've recycled. But to keep recycling working for the future, you need to look for these products and buy them. For a free brochure, call 1-800-CALL-EDF.

Ad Council A Public Service of This Publication

♻EPA

ENVIRONMENTAL DEFENSE FUND EDF

Americans in all walks of life are now adjusting their expectations downward and adapting to what they see as a more difficult, less open, less fair, more demanding, and more stressful economic environment.

Because of the profound effect abundance has had on the American belief system, this widespread perception of its decline could have important consequences. Whether the traditional American values will remain strong in the coming decades or **undergo** basic changes is impossible to predict with certainty. Only time will tell.

 # New Words

trash; garbage waste material to be thrown away

vice a serious fault of character

incentive something that encourages a person to work hard to accomplish a goal

commercial an advertisement on television or radio

sponsor to pay money in return for advertising; the person or organization that pays the money

donation a gift

dilemma a difficult choice between doing two things

decency social acceptability

censor to examine information and exclude anything that is unacceptable

deodorant a man-made chemical substance that destroys or hides unpleasant smells, especially those of the human body

cleanse to make clean or pure

leisurely without hurrying; "leisure time" is time when one is free from employment and duties of any kind

paradox a surprising or unlikely combination of opposing qualities, ideas, etc.; a seeming contradiction

undergo to experience something

A. Vocabulary Check

Write the letter of the correct definition next to each word.

_____ 1. cleanse
_____ 2. commercial
_____ 3. censor
_____ 4. deodorant
_____ 5. donation
_____ 6. decency
_____ 7. incentive
_____ 8. leisurely
_____ 9. trash and garbage
_____ 10. paradox
_____ 11. sponsor
_____ 12. undergo
_____ 13. dilemma
_____ 14. vice

a. telling lies
b. a problem that requires a hard choice to solve
c. used paper, cans, uneaten food
d. not rushing; taking your time
e. a company paying for a TV show
f. to get rid of dirt or impurities
g. money given to a charity
h. to have something happen to you
i. a product used to reduce body odor
j. a scholarship to go to college
k. to remove inappropriate materials from a movie or book
l. homeless people in a rich country
m. standards society accepts
n. something that tries to persuade you to buy a product

B. Comprehension Check

Write the letter of the best answer according to the information in the chapter.

_____ 1. The most important reason why the United States became a wealthy nation is that
    a. the North American continent was rich in undeveloped resources.
    b. the values of the American people inspired them to develop a wilderness continent into a wealthy nation.
    c. the American government encouraged them to develop the resources.

_____ 2. De Tocqueville believed that in a nation such as the United States, where wealth and social position are not determined by birth,
    a. the rich are not worried about keeping their wealth.
    b. everyone is worried about either acquiring wealth or holding on to it if they have it.
    c. people worry about money so much because they are basically very greedy.

_____ 3. Americans think of themselves more as consumers than producers because
- a. few people are still farmers.
- b. mass advertising has had such a great impact.
- c. they are concerned about competing on the international market.

_____ 4. Programs on public television
- a. are sponsored by businesses who have some control over the content of the program.
- b. are not available on cable TV.
- c. are usually of higher educational quality than programs on commercial television.

_____ 5. Americans believe that censorship of material on television
- a. should be extremely strict because children must be protected.
- b. is a difficult issue because they believe in the right of free speech.
- c. is the responsibility of the government, not the people who create the programs.

_____ 6. Based on information in the _What American Consumers Like_ section, which one of these statements _is_ true?
- a. The Puritans thought that there was something evil about sexual desire.
- b. When buying a chair, most Americans would be more concerned about its beauty than its comfort.
- c. Most Americans don't wear deodorants because they like the natural odors of the body.

_____ 7. Which of these is _implied_ but not stated directly in that section of the chapter?
- a. Fast food is not as nutritious as home-cooked food.
- b. Most of the cooking is done by women.
- c. Men use credit cards more than women.

_____ 8. The view that a country's economy is an ever-expanding pie
- a. is held by most nations in the world today.
- b. was held by Americans and reinforced by their experiences until recently.
- c. is still held by the majority of the American people today.

_____ 9. Based on information in _The Decline of American Abundance_ section, which one of these statements is _not_ true?
- a. The cost of a college education is rising.
- b. There are not many new factory jobs being created.
- c. The cost of housing has risen about as much as the average income has increased.

_____ 10. The decline in abundance in the United States
- a. is temporary, and most people are not worried about it.
- b. has caused people to recycle and use resources more wisely.
- c. has encouraged people to develop land as quickly as possible to get more money.

C. Questions for Discussion

1. Which is more important for economic growth: a good supply of natural resources or the values of the people in the society? Give examples. How has the presence or absence of natural resources affected various countries' economic growth? What about your country?

2. What are the commercials like on TV in your country? Are they all grouped together at a certain time of day, or do they appear during and between programs? What kind of ads are there? What should the role of mass advertising on radio and TV be? Should the advertising industry be regulated? Why?

3. Does your country have public TV programs in addition to those paid for by sponsors? What should be the role of television in a society? What is its role in your country? What effect does TV have on the morals of the people? What are the standards of decency for television programs in your country? What words cannot be said? What cannot be shown? How do you feel about censorship?

4. How do people in your country feel about deodorants? Are they used by most people? Are they advertised on TV? What do you think about the American view of cleanliness? In your country what things must be kept clean?

5. Why are fast-food restaurants so popular? Which ones do you have in your country? How about convenience foods—canned goods, frozen foods, TV dinners, "instant" foods? Are they popular in your country? Have you tried them?

 D. Cloze Summary Paragraph

This paragraph summarizes the chapter. Fill in each blank with any word that makes sense.

The United States became ___*a*___ wealthy nation because of _____ abundant undeveloped natural resources _____ the values of the _____ people, which inspired them _____ build a land of _____ material wealth. Their belief _____ equality of opportunity meant _____ everyone had the chance _____ succeed, or to fail. _____, everyone became concerned about _____ money and keeping it. _____ started using materialistic standards

_____ judge themselves both as _____ and as a nation. _____ advertising on radio and _____ has caused Americans _____ think of themselves more _____ consumers than producers. (Public _____, by contrast, does not _____ any commercials.) Advertisements appeal _____ Americans' love of comfort, _____, novelty, and convenience. Americans _____ to believe that abundance _____ last forever; now economic _____ are worse, and people _____ becoming more pessimistic about _____ future. If abundance declines, _____ will be the effect _____ American values in the _____?

 ## E. People Watching

Observe what Americans throw away. Visit a fast-food restaurant, and count the containers that are thrown away from one person's meal. Visit a supermarket, and note the kinds of "convenience" or packaged foods available. Be sure to check all the departments. Some examples you will find are: salad in a bag, fruit already cut up and ready to eat, many rice and pasta boxed dinners, ready-to-cook meat and poultry dishes, and lots of frozen dinners. Notice what Americans are buying at the grocery store. How does this compare with grocery shoppers in your country?

 ## F. Proverbs and Sayings

Americans have a strong _sense of time_ as a resource—something to be used, saved, spent, shared, and so forth. How they talk about time is an indication of how they feel about it. Add to the list of time expressions below by asking Americans for suggestions, by listening to conversations, and by watching TV. What value does time have for Americans?

1. A stitch in time saves nine.
2. Time is money.
3. Time and the tide wait for no man.
4. I don't have time for that today.
5. Can you give me a few minutes of your time?
6. We lost a lot of time on that.

G. Think, Pair, Share

If you won or inherited one million dollars, which of these things, if any, do you think you would do? Check as many as you like.

———— 1.	Put in a savings account	———— 10. Buy a boat
———— 2.	Buy a new home	———— 11. Buy a vacation house
———— 3.	Invest for your old age	———— 12. Buy a plane
———— 4.	Start/buy your own business	———— 13. Share with your family
———— 5.	Invest in stocks	———— 14. Contribute to your church
———— 6.	Take a vacation	———— 15. Contribute to charities
———— 7.	Buy a new car	———— 16. Other (your choice)
———— 8.	Refurnish your house	_____
———— 9.	Quit your job	_____

Now arrange the 15 items in order of their importance to you. Which is the first thing you would spend your money on? Which is the last? Compare your answers with those of your partner, and then share your answers with another pair of students.

H. Ask Americans

What do you think "the good life" is? Americans were asked to choose from the list that follows. Which things do you think most people chose? Predict the answers of the Americans and mark them with the letter "A." Then check the things that you would want to have for "the good life." How many of these things do you (or your family) now have? After you have finished, share your answers with your classmates, and then make a chart showing the responses of everyone in the class. Be sure to indicate the predictions you made about the responses of Americans and also your own choices of what things you think are part of "the good life."

———— ————	4-day work week		———— ————	job that is interesting
———— ————	5-day work week		———— ————	job that pays much more than average
———— ————	car		———— ————	lot of money
———— ————	college education for my children		———— ————	one or more children
———— ————	college education for myself		———— ————	really nice clothes
———— ————	color TV		———— ————	second car
———— ————	happy marriage		———— ————	second color TV set
———— ————	a home you own		———— ————	swimming pool
———— ————	job that contributes to the welfare of society		———— ————	travel abroad
			———— ————	vacation home
			———— ————	yard and a lawn

Discovery Bay, CA   **Roxane Fridirici**

Now you can check your predictions and compare your own responses to those of Americans. Remember that part of the "American Dream" has been that each generation will have a better life than the previous one. Look at the following polls about what Americans think "the good life" is and whether they have it now or think they will eventually have it.

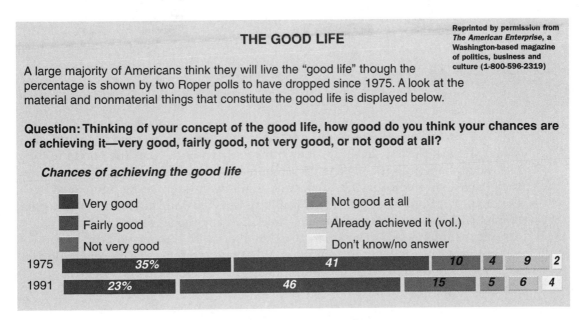

THE GOOD LIFE

Reprinted by permission from *The American Enterprise*, a Washington-based magazine of politics, business and culture (1-800-596-2319)

A large majority of Americans think they will live the "good life" though the percentage is shown by two Roper polls to have dropped since 1975. A look at the material and nonmaterial things that constitute the good life is displayed below.

Question: Thinking of your concept of the good life, how good do you think your chances are of achieving it—very good, fairly good, not very good, or not good at all?

Chances of achieving the good life

- Very good
- Fairly good
- Not very good
- Not good at all
- Already achieved it (vol.)
- Don't know/no answer

Year	Very good	Fairly good	Not very good	Not good at all	Already achieved it	Don't know
1975	35%	41	10	4	9	2
1991	23%	46	15	5	6	4

Question: We often hear people talk about what they want out of life. Here are a number of different things. When you think of the good life—the life you'd like to have, which of the things on this list, if any, are part of that good life as far as you are personally concerned?

Question: Now would you go down that list and call off all the things you now have?

■1975 ■1991

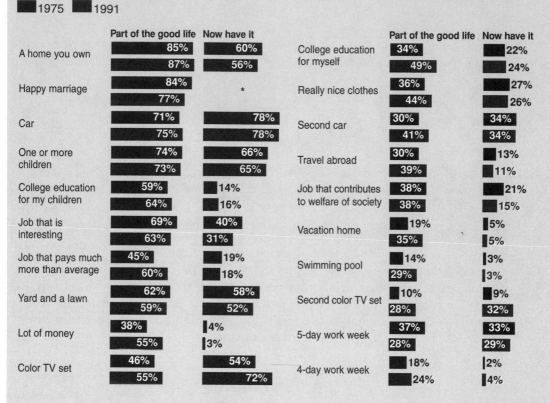

	Part of the good life	Now have it		Part of the good life	Now have it
A home you own	85% / 87%	60% / 56%	College education for myself	34% / 49%	22% / 24%
Happy marriage	84% / 77%	*	Really nice clothes	36% / 44%	27% / 26%
Car	71% / 75%	78% / 78%	Second car	30% / 41%	34% / 34%
One or more children	74% / 73%	66% / 65%	Travel abroad	30% / 39%	13% / 11%
College education for my children	59% / 64%	14% / 16%	Job that contributes to welfare of society	38% / 38%	21% / 15%
Job that is interesting	69% / 63%	40% / 31%	Vacation home	19% / 35%	5% / 5%
Job that pays much more than average	45% / 60%	19% / 18%	Swimming pool	14% / 29%	3% / 3%
Yard and a lawn	62% / 59%	58% / 52%	Second color TV set	10% / 28%	9% / 32%
Lot of money	38% / 55%	4% / 3%	5-day work week	37% / 28%	33% / 29%
Color TV set	46% / 55%	54% / 72%	4-day work week	18% / 24%	2% / 4%

Note: * Change in the composition of the sample made results for this category incomparable.
Source: Surveys by the Roper Organization (*Roper Reports* [92–1]), latest that of December 1–8, 1991.

Ask several Americans of different ages the questions in each of the polls. When you ask them what things they think are part of having "the good life," use the alphabetical list on page 98. Do not show them the poll results until after they have answered your questions. You do not want them to be influenced by the answers of other people. When you have finished your interviews, share your results with your classmates. Make a chart showing the answers of all the Americans interviewed. Then compare that chart with the one you did to show the answers of the people in your class. What similarities and differences do you see? You may want to write up your conclusions and make a class poster showing your charts.

I. Observing the Media

This chapter lists four things that Americans like: comfort, cleanliness, novelty, and convenience. Examine advertising on American TV, on radio, or in magazines and newspapers to see how businesses appeal to these four qualities in advertising their goods and services. Write a brief summary of each commercial appearing on radio or TV, and cut ads out of newspapers and magazines. Collect or describe ads for each of the four categories.

Look for these key words and phrases:

1. *Comfort:* luxury, luxurious, elegant, gracious, comfortable, classic, spacious, relax, enjoy, experience

2. *Cleanliness:* clean, deep cleaning, spotless, kills germs, fights odors, germ- or odor-free

3. *Novelty:* new, different, improved, better than before, brand new or all new, far removed from the real world, exotic, unusual; see, taste, or feel the difference

4. *Convenience:* convenient, fast, saves time, efficient, automatic, ready in a minute or in no time at all, instant, precooked, frozen, heat-and-serve

Questions to answer when analyzing the advertisement or commercial:

1. What is being sold?

2. What is the main reason given for buying this product or using this service?

3. Are there any hidden messages in this ad? How are these messages communicated?
    * Does buying this product lead to "success"?
    * Will it make you more attractive to the opposite sex?
    * Will it lead to "happiness"?
    * Will it give you more leisure time?

4. Who are the people in the ad, and what do they represent? (Example: A typical housewife struggling to keep her kitchen floor clean.)

5. Who is likely to use this product or service?

6. How would you rate this ad? What grade would you give it:
    A – excellent
    B – good
    C – fair
    D – poor
    F – terrible

7. After studying this ad, would you buy this product or service? Do you consider this product or service a luxury, or a necessity?

8. Do you have similar ads in your country? What do people in your country like?

J. **Small Group Discussion/Round Robin**

A motto of the environmental movement in the United States is to "think globally" but "act locally." Why do you think they chose this as a motto? How do these two relate? What can people do on a day-to-day basis to decrease water, air, or soil pollution? What can they do to protect the world's endangered species?

Look at the following poll. Who do you think should be responsible for cleaning up the environment? What is the role of the government? What should industry do? What can we do as individuals?

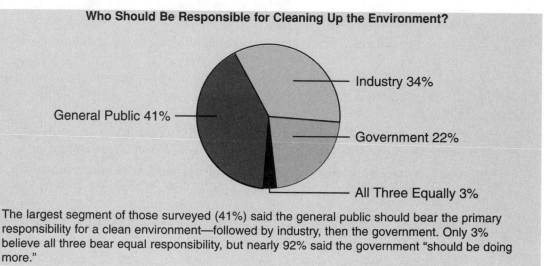

Who Should Be Responsible for Cleaning Up the Environment?

General Public 41%

Industry 34%

Government 22%

All Three Equally 3%

The largest segment of those surveyed (41%) said the general public should bear the primary responsibility for a clean environment—followed by industry, then the government. Only 3% believe all three bear equal responsibility, but nearly 92% said the government "should be doing more."

Reprinted with permission from Parade, © 1992

Round Robin: Draw a line down the center of a piece of paper. Label one side "What individuals can do to protect the environment" and the other side "What industries and governments can do to protect the environment." Pass the paper around the group several times. Each time the paper comes to you, add a suggestion to each list. Discuss your group's recommendations, and report to the rest of the class.

 K. **Suggestions for Research and Oral Reports**

Choose one of the following topics as the subject of a report; then go to the library and look for information in magazines, journals, books, and reference texts.

1. The "green" movement may have come to your town and your campus. By the mid-1990s, there were more than 2,000 of these environmental groups working on campus and government environmental issues in the United

States. What about your country? What are the environmental issues? If you are in the United States, find out about the environmental concerns on your campus and in your town. Are there recycling bins available? Are there local environmental groups? Are there local problems with pollution? For information about campus groups in the United States, you may wish to write Campus Green Vote, 1400 16th St., N.W., Washington, D.C. 20036.

2. From the mid-1970s to the mid-1990s, more than one million species vanished from the world's tropical rain forests, and the size of these forests shrank from 4.7 to 4.2 billion acres. Why are these rain forests important to everyone on the earth? Why are they being cut down? What can be done to protect them? Research both sides of the issue: the environmental value of the rain forests and the needs of the people who are cutting them down. Also look for what experts are recommending should be done.

 L. Suggestions for Further Reading

- Walt Whitman, *Leaves of Grass* (especially the poem "I Hear America Singing")
- Rachel Carson, *Silent Spring*
- Aldo Leopold, *A Sand County Almanac*

 M. Recommended Movies

- *Quiz Show*
- *The Paper*
- *A River Runs Through It*

The New York Stock Exchange **AP Photo/L.M. Otero**

CHAPTER 6

The World of American Business

The business of America is business.

President Calvin Coolidge

Before You Read

1. Why do you think *business* has high prestige in the United States?
2. Why do people want to go into business for themselves? Would you want to be your own boss?
3. What does it mean to "go from rags to riches"?
4. How is the workforce of the United States changing?

The Characteristics of American Business

It is essential to become familiar with two words in order to understand the meaning of *business* to Americans; they are *private* and *profit*. Businesses are directly or indirectly owned and operated by private individuals (or groups of individuals) in order to make a profit. In contrast to these privately owned, for-profit businesses, there are public government-owned and operated institutions as well as nonprofit institutions such as churches and nonprofit charitable organizations. These organizations and institutions are not to be confused with businesses. ·

The Prestige of Business and the Ideal of Competition

The statement by President Coolidge in the 1920s—"The business of America is business"—still points to an important truth today: Business institutions have more prestige in American society than any other kind of organization, including the government. Most Americans believe, for example, that businesses are more efficient and better-run than the federal government. Why do business institutions possess this great prestige?

One reason is that Americans view business as being more firmly based on the ideal of competition than other institutions in society. Since competition is seen as the major source of progress and prosperity by most Americans, competitive business institutions are respected. Competition is not only good in itself; it is the means by which other basic American values such as individual freedom, equality of opportunity, and hard work are protected.

Competition protects the freedom of the individual by ensuring that there is no monopoly of power. In contrast to one, all-powerful government, many businesses compete against each other for profits. Theoretically, if one business tries to take unfair advantage of its customers, it will lose to a competing business that treats its customers more fairly. Where many businesses compete for the customers' dollar, they cannot afford to give them inferior products or poor service.

A contrast is often made between business, which is competitive, and government, which is a monopoly. Because business is competitive, many Americans believe that it is more supportive of freedom than government, even though government leaders are elected by the people and business leaders are not. Many Americans, believe, then, that competition is as important, or even more important, than democracy in preserving freedom. So closely is competitive business associated with freedom in the minds of most Americans that the term *free enterprise* rather than the term *capitalism* is most often used to describe the American business system.

Competition in business is also believed to strengthen the ideal of equality of opportunity. Americans compare business competition to a race open to all, where success and status go to the **swiftest** person, regardless of social class background. Gaining success and status through competition is often seen as the American alternative to systems where social rank is based on family background. Business is therefore viewed as an expression of the idea of equality of opportunity rather than the aristocratic idea of inherited privilege.

Business competition is also seen by most Americans as encouraging hard work. If two business people are competing against each other, the one who works harder is likely to win. The one who spends less time and effort is likely to lose. Because business people must continually compete against each other, they must develop the habit of hard work in order not to fail.

Americans are aware that business institutions often do not live up to the ideals of competition and the support of freedom, equality of opportunity, and hard work. Americans sometimes distrust the motives of business people, believing that they are capable of putting profit before product safety, or a cleaner environment. Therefore, most Americans believe businesses need some government regulation, although they may disagree on how much. Even with these **flaws**, however, most Americans believe that business comes closer than other institutions to carrying out competition and other basic values in daily practice.

The Prestige of Business and the Dream of Getting Rich

There is a second reason why business institutions receive respect in the United States. One aspect of the great American Dream is to rise from poverty or modest wealth to great wealth. In the United States, this has usually been accomplished through successful business careers. All of the great private fortunes in the nation were built by people who were successful in business, many of whom started life with very little. Careers in business still offer the best opportunity for the ambitious individual to become wealthy.

Alexis de Tocqueville observed the great attractiveness of business careers for Americans as early as the 1830s. He wrote that Americans strongly preferred business to farming because business offered the opportunity to get rich more quickly. Even those who were farmers were possessed with a strong business spirit. They often ran small businesses to add to the money they made from farming. De Tocqueville also noticed that American farmers were often more interested in buying and selling land for a profit than in farming it. Thus, even in de Tocqueville's day, when most Americans were still farmers, the seeds of a business civilization had already been planted.

Not only is business seen as the best way for individuals to become rich, it is also seen as benefiting the entire nation. Through competition, more people gain wealth. By contrast, a socialistic system of production and distribution of goods (one that is owned and operated by the government) is seen as greatly inferior. A socialistic system is distrusted because of the monopoly of power held by the government that eliminates competition. There are few countries, if any, in the world where business institutions are so strongly preferred over government institutions as agencies for producing and distributing goods and for providing services. For example, the United States is one of the few industrialized countries in the world that does not have universal health care guaranteed and managed in some way by the government. Americans have traditionally preferred to have a system where health care providers compete with each other in a free market and individuals are free to choose their own doctors and hospitals, even if that means that some people go without health insurance.

Two Kinds of American Business Heroes

Because of the many beliefs that connect business to the wealth and the traditional values of the United States, people who are successful in business have sometimes become heroes to the American people. Two kinds of business heroes have gained widespread respect: "the **entrepreneur**" and the "organization man or woman." Entrepreneurs provide examples of traditional American values in their purest form, and these people are most likely to be idealized by the American public. The second kind of hero, "the organization man/woman," is seen as a less perfect example of basic American values, but he or she still commands great respect.

The Entrepreneur as Hero

Entrepreneurs are the purest kind of business heroes for a number of reasons. The first reason is that they succeed in building something great out of nothing. The people who, more than 100 years ago, built up the nation's great industries, such as steel, railroads, and oil refining, were usually entrepreneurs. They started with very little money or power and ended up as the heads of huge companies that earned enormous fortunes.

The fact that these early entrepreneurs built great industries out of very little made them seem to millions of Americans like the heroes of the early frontier days, who went into the vast wilderness of the United States and turned forests into farms, villages, and small cities. The entrepreneur, like the earlier hero of the frontier, was seen as a rugged individualist.

Entrepreneurs made so much out of so little that they became heroes to the common people in America. Entrepreneurs often began as common people themselves; without the aid of inherited social title or inherited money, they became "self-made" millionaires. They were thus perfect examples of the American idea of equality of opportunity in action.

The strong influence of the success stories of the early entrepreneurs can be found in the great popularity of the novels of Horatio Alger, which were published in late 19th- and early 20th-century America. About 17 million copies of these books were sold to the American public. The central theme of Alger's novels is that in the United States a poor city boy or a poor farm boy can become a wealthy and successful businessman if he works hard and relies on himself rather than depending on others. This is because the United States is a land of equality of opportunity where everyone has a chance to succeed.

By diligence, a quick-witted young fellow can rise from rags to riches.

A lot of people think the age of rags to riches died with Horatio Alger.

Are they wrong! The opportunities are out there as never before—if you have the drive and determination and guts to go after them.

Only *now* you don't have to hide your ambition.

Society has decided that it's OK to be frank about the drive for success.

If you're one of the fast-track people, you've probably been reading FORTUNE for years.

After all, when you're running with the best and the brightest, you need all the help you can get.

That's FORTUNE. It's the authority. It's the business magazine you rely on when you've *got* to be right.

It helps the movers and shakers decide how to move and what to shake. It's their early-warning system, alerting them to opportunities and dangers around the next corner.

In marketing, management, technology, everything—FORTUNE's where you get a vital couple of steps on your competition.

It's the business magazine that can help you make it—and keep it.

It's the business magazine to advertise in when you've got news for the fast-track people.

FORTUNE
How to succeed.

In Alger's first published novel, *Ragged Dick*, a poor city boy who shines shoes for a living becomes Richard Hunter, a successful and wealthy businessman. The hero rises "from rags to riches" and fulfills the American Dream. Dick succeeds only partly because he lives in a land of equality of opportunity. His success is also due to the fact that he practices the American virtues of self-reliance and hard work. According to Alger, Dick "knew that he had only himself to depend upon, and he determined to make the most of himself… which is the secret of success in nine cases out of ten." Dick was also a hard-working shoe shine boy, "energetic and **on the alert** for business." This quality marked him for success, explained Alger, because in all professions, "energy and industry are rewarded."

Although few Americans today read Horatio Alger's stories, they continue to be inspired by the idea of earning wealth and success as entrepreneurs who "make it on their own." A final characteristic of entrepreneurs that appeals to most Americans is their strong dislike of **submitting** to higher authority. Throughout their history, Americans have admired entrepreneurs who conduct their business and their lives without taking orders from anyone above them. Americans have great respect for those who can say, "I am my own boss."

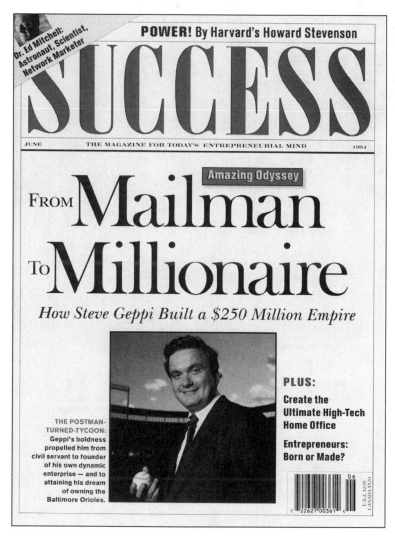

First appeared in SUCCESS, June 1994. Reprinted with permission of SUCCESS Holdings Company, LLC.

Today, many Americans are willing to take the big financial risk that is necessary to start their own small business. Although one out of every four new businesses fail within the first two years (and half of them within the first four years), small businesses account for three out of four of the new jobs created in the 1990s. The overwhelming majority of these jobs employ one to four people. Inspired by entrepreneur heroes like Steven Jobs, who started Apple Computer in his garage, Bill Gates, who developed Microsoft into a global giant, and Ross Perot, a self-made billionaire who ran for President, risk-taking entrepreneurs still **launch** their businesses with high hopes of "making it big."

Ross Perot's popularity provides an interesting illustration of the fact that Americans tend to have more respect for individuals who build a business from the beginning than they do for those who inherit a family business and manage it well. In the 1996 presidential campaign, another billionaire, Steve Forbes, tried unsuccessfully to get the Republican nomination. In contrast to the wealthy entrepreneur Ross Perot, Forbes inherited his fortune from his father, Malcolm Forbes. Although both men were extremely wealthy, Americans seemed to respect the self-made Perot more than the privileged Forbes. Indeed, many presidential candidates proudly state that they have come from poor or "working-class" families. They do not want to be known as "rich" or wealthy.

The Organization Man/Woman as Hero

The great entrepreneurs of the late 19th century built huge business organizations that needed a new generation of business leaders to run them. These leaders have often been called *organization men/women*. They are also heroes to Americans in the sense that they are role models of success in American society. They acquire power and wealth, but they do not have as strong a hero image as entrepreneurs because they are managing businesses that someone else started.

Lee Iacocca is an example of an "organization man" admired by Americans. Iacocca took over Chrysler Corporation when it was **on the verge of bankruptcy** in 1979. With the help of a government loan, he turned the company around and made it profitable, restoring American faith in the ability of the United States to compete in the global market. Some Americans urged Iacocca to run for president, although he, like Ross Perot, had never run for elected office.

It is interesting to note that as the United States came out of the 1980s—a decade of greed, **excess**, and in many cases dishonest business practices—Americans took a second look at their view of the business world. Although most Americans admire the earning power of entrepreneurs and would probably not want to put a limit on their income, they are less generous in their view of the "organization man/woman." In the early 1990s, highly paid corporate executives started to come under severe attack for their multi-million-dollar-a-year salaries. On the other hand, most Americans would probably say that self-made millionaires have the right to as much money as they can get.

American Business in the Global Marketplace

Fifty years ago, the operation of American business took place almost entirely in the United States. In the 1990s, this is no longer true. American business has become a part of a much larger global economy. In the 1950s, someone who bought a car from General Motors Corporation knew that the entire car was built in the United States. In the 1990s, however, if a person spent $20,000 for a General Motors car, $6,000 might go to South Korea for labor, $3,500 to Japan for advanced parts, $1,500 to Germany for design and styling, $800 to Taiwan, Singapore, and Japan for small parts, $500 to Britain for advertising, and $100 to Ireland and Barbados for data processing.

The United States is the single largest market in the world: a consumer society looking for goods from all over the world. It is also a country with products to sell, and much attention is being given to competing successfully in the global market of the 21st century. The United States cannot compete with the abundant supply of cheap labor that exists in the countries of the Pacific Rim and Latin America; therefore, many U.S. companies are moving their manufacturing operations to Asia or Latin America. In the 1990s, the NAFTA (North American Free Trade Agreement) treaty joined Canada, the United States, and Mexico as trading partners and created new opportunities and new markets. Old giant corporations such as IBM and AT&T laid off thousands of workers, **downsizing** to become more efficient and competitive. The auto industry that many were ready to pronounce dead has **revived** and is **flourishing**. American business now understands that it must be highly efficient if it is to compete successfully in the global marketplace.

The Changing American Workforce

Traditionally, white males have dominated American business—earning the highest salaries, achieving the greatest successes, and certainly **wielding** most of the **power**. They have been the "bosses," setting the standards and the working conditions for the rest of the working population.

The percentage of women entering the workforce rose steadily from the 1960s through the 1980s, leveling off in the 1990s. Some women have reached middle-management positions, but very few (only about 5 percent) are the chief executives of large corporations. Women are prevented from moving all the way to the top by what some call *the glass ceiling*, a **subtle** form of **discrimination**. The men above them often do not offer women the opportunities they need to advance in the company. Sometimes this happens because of a belief that a woman is not capable, but her boss may assume that she would not want the job because it might interfere with her family. In order to advance her career, for example, she might have to transfer to another city or take a job that has more responsibility and requires longer working hours. Interestingly, currently twice

ON THE JOB
Women and minorities in major job categories in 1994:

	Female	Black	Hispanic
Managerial, professional	48%	7%	5%
Technical, sales, admin. support	64%	10%	7%
Service	64%	17%	13%
Precision production, craft, repair	9%	8%	10%
Operators, fabricators, laborers	24%	15%	14%
Farming, forestry, fishing	19%	5%	17%

Note: Hispanics can be of any race.
Source: Bureau of Labor Statistics

Maryanne Kearny Datesman

as many new businesses in the United States are started by women as by men. Some women believe that it is easier for them to be successful as entrepreneurs than as "organization women" in male-dominated corporations.

Many jobs in corporate America are **fast track**, requiring that both women and men put their job first and their family second. Studies show that an employee perceived to be on the "mommy track" or the "daddy track" will not earn as much money or be given as much responsibility as the one willing to **sacrifice** time at home for time at the office. Some families are now beginning to question whether success is really worth the price. Some businesses provide **flexible working hours** and day-care centers in the building, but most do not. A number of women are choosing to drop out of the workforce and stay home with their children, or to find work they can do at home—working on a computer linked to their office, for example. About three million women a year now try their hands at starting their own small businesses, following the dream of the entrepreneur.

Dr. Wang, a National Cancer Institute Research scientist, examines a slide
National Institute of Health

One of the worst problems facing American women is that overall they earn about 75 cents for every dollar earned by American men. In spite of the ideal of equality of opportunity, women generally earn less money than men for doing the same work. Minorities often face similar discrimination in the workplace, earning less money than white workers with similar jobs.

In the future, the white American male may no longer have advantages over other workers. The recent arrival of millions of new immigrants is changing the makeup of the American workforce. A study done in 1987 called *Workforce 2000* provided the first predictions that more women and members of minority groups would be entering the workforce than white males. The study predicted that five-sixths of the net additions to the workforce by the year 2000 would be nonwhites, women, and immigrants; only 15 percent would be white males.

Studies show that within 10 or 20 years of their arrival, immigrants (or their children) will earn as much or more money than people born in the United States who have similar characteristics such as age, skills, and education. Some businesses now provide English as a Second Language courses at the workplace, and others conduct "diversity training" to promote understanding among the different racial and ethnic groups that now work together. Many believe that this multi-cultural workforce will ultimately help the United States compete in the global marketplace, since American workers will represent a **microcosm** of the world.

Although the institution of American business has undergone enormous changes in recent decades, it has remained the most prestigious institution in the United States. The business of America is still business.

■　■　■　■

New Words

swiftest fastest

flaw imperfection; a small sign of damage that makes something or someone not perfect

entrepreneur a person who makes the plans for a business and gets it going

on the alert quick to see and act

submit to agree to obey

launch to begin something new

on the verge of bankruptcy almost out of money

excess more than enough; too much

downsize to reduce the size of a business by eliminating workers

revive to bring back to life

flourish to be successful in business; to do well

wield power to exercise or use one's power

subtle not obvious; not easily seen

discrimination not treating all people the same; treating some people better than others

fast track allowing quick movement (the track that the fast train moves on); a job path allowing one to advance rapidly

sacrifice to give up something for a good purpose

flexible working hours a plan where employees must work a certain number of hours, but they can decide when to come to work and when to leave (Some may work from 9 to 5, while others may work from 7 to 3, for example.)

microcosm a small system representing the whole world; having the characteristics of the whole world

A. Vocabulary Check

Complete the crossword puzzle using words from the New Words list.

Across

4. not fixed; can be changed
7. fastest
8. to bring back to life
12. unequal treatment
16. aware of what is going on; ready to take action
17. to give up something

Down

1. too much
2. to make a company smaller
3. to agree to obey

4. a career path that lets you move up quickly
5. having no money
6. someone who starts his or her own business
9. to do well; to be prosperous
10. to use your power
11. to start something new
13. something that is not obvious
14. a small system that has characteristics of the whole world
15. imperfection

B. Comprehension Check

Write T *if the statement is true and* F *if it is false according to the information in the chapter.*

_____ 1. Most American businesses are directly or indirectly owned by the government.

_____ 2. In the United States, business has great prestige because Americans believe that it supports ideals and values that are important to the country.

_____ 3. Americans believe that competition among businesses is good for the economy but it does little to protect the freedom of the individual.

_____ 4. To succeed in American business, people believe that family background and social position are more important than anything, including hard work.

_____ 5. Most Americans believe that success in business offers the best chance to fulfill the dream of being wealthy.

_____ 6. The "organization man/woman" is the most admired business hero since he or she started a successful business from practically nothing.

_____ 7. Horatio Alger's books were very popular because they told stories of people who went from rags to riches by starting successful businesses from practically nothing.

_____ 8. Recently, American businesses have become more competitive by hiring many new workers and enlarging their companies.

_____ 9. Women who put their husbands and children first may have difficulty getting top managerial jobs in the United States.

_____ 10. In the 21st century, white males will probably continue to wield most of the power in the American business world.

 C. Questions for Discussion

1. What qualities should a good business person have in order to be successful? Are these the same personal qualities that you would like your own boss to have? How would you feel about having a woman as your boss? Are there many women managers and executives in your country? Are there certain jobs that women traditionally do or do not do? Are many women with small children employed?

2. If you are looking for a job in your country, what do you have to do? How do you find out about job openings? How important are family reputation and connections? How is the job market in your country now? What jobs are easy/hard to get?

3. What is the best way to get rich in your country? Is it through a business or a professional career? What kinds of business career opportunities promise the most money? Are there high-paying factory jobs in your country?

4. Who do you admire more: a person who inherits wealth or a self-made millionaire? an entrepreneur or an "organization man/woman"? Which would you rather be? Why? If you started your own small business, what would it be? Is there some virtue to having to struggle to succeed in life?

5. What benefits do companies in your country provide for employees? Do they provide child care? Who provides health insurance? How many hours a week do people work? Do companies allow flexible work schedules? Do employees feel great loyalty to their companies? Why?

6. What are the fast-track jobs in your country? What price does a person pay to be on the fast track? What sacrifices do they make? Do you want a fast-track job? Are there any sacrifices that you would be unwilling to make to have a successful career?

 D. Cloze Summary Paragraph

This paragraph summarizes the chapter. Fill in each blank with any word that makes sense.

American businesses are privately ___owned___ and are operated for _____ profit. Americans have great _____ for business because they _____ business competition protects the _____ American values of individual _____, equality of opportunity, and _____ work. Business is also _____ because Americans believe it _____ the best opportunity for _____ individuals and the nation _____ a whole to become _____. Entrepreneurs are respected heroes _____ they create a successful _____ out of nothing. They _____ self-made individuals who are _____ own bosses. Horatio Alger _____ stories about such people _____ went from rags to _____. Nowadays successful business people _____ more likely to be "_____ men/women" who take over _____ run large organizations started _____ others. American businesses _____ compete in a global _____; many companies have downsized _____ become more productive. As _____ 21st century begins, there _____ be many changes in _____ American workforce. Although white _____ dominated the workplace in _____ past, in the future _____ will be fewer of _____ and there will be _____ minorities and women. Having _____ multicultural workforce could be _____ advantage for competing in _____ global marketplace.

 E. People Watching

Who works in the United States? What ages? Men, women, teenagers, the elderly? What kind of jobs do they do? To answer these questions, if you are in the United States, look around you in various businesses open to the public: restaurants, banks, stores, drugstores, supermarkets, clubs, dry cleaners, doctors' offices, theaters, and so on. If you are near a university, check to see who is working in the library and the cafeteria. (If you are not in the United States, you may gather information from Americans in your country or by watching American TV commercials, reading newspapers or magazines, and doing research in the library.)

Observation: Observe people working in at least ten different places and record your results in the following chart:

	Kind of Job	Sex of Worker	Age of Worker	Other Observations
1.				
2.				
3.				
4.				
5.				
6.				
7.				
8.				
9.				
10.				

Interview two Americans of different ages, and ask them about their work. Ask each one the following questions, and record their answers.

1. What is your current work status?

   a   b   **a   b**
   ___ ___ Self-employed   ___ ___ Unemployed
   ___ ___ Work full time   ___ ___ Student
   ___ ___ Work part time   ___ ___ Homemaker
   ___ ___ Retired

2. If you are currently employed, where do you work and what is your job? How long have you worked there?

3. What other jobs have you had? Did you work to earn money as a child, teenager, or college student?

4. Would you consider the job you now have to be a permanent job?

5. Do you have a college degree or vocational training for the job you hold now? How useful is a college degree in your line of work?

6. Have you ever changed careers? Would you ever consider doing so? Why, or why not?

7. If you had enough money to live comfortably, would you prefer to:

   a   b   **a   b**
   ___ ___ Work full time   ___ ___ Do volunteer work
   ___ ___ Work part time   ___ ___ Work at home caring for
                                            the family

8. Given a choice, would you prefer to have more time, or more money?

9. How much do you think others value you for fulfilling your responsibilities?

   a   b   **a   b**
   ___ ___ Very valued   ___ ___ Not too valued
   ___ ___ Somewhat valued   ___ ___ Not at all valued

10. Which of these workplace issues is your greatest worry?

    a   b
    ___ ___ Employers providing fewer benefits
    ___ ___ Balancing work and family life
    ___ ___ Pressure from work affecting family
    ___ ___ Not being valued by employer
    ___ ___ Lack of opportunities to advance
    ___ ___ Possibility of job loss
    ___ ___ Lack of opportunities to grow and learn
    ___ ___ Sexual harassment

Compare their answers to questions 1, 7, 8, 9, and 10 with the poll results on the following page. Report your findings to the class.

WORKING WOMEN: FINDINGS FROM A SWEEPING NEW STUDY

Working women may sense real obstacles to professional advancement today, but lack of education or training isn't viewed as a big barrier. That's one of the findings in a sweeping new survey by the Families and Work Institute, the Whirlpool Foundation and Louis Harris and Associates. Additional results from the study follow.

What's your current work status?

Self-employed	8%
Work full time	45%
Work part time	15%
Retired	1%
Unemployed	4%
Student	7%
Homemaker	17%

If you had enough money to live comfortably, would you prefer to:

	Women	Men
Work full time	15%	33%
Work part time	33%	28%
Do volunteer work	20%	17%
Work at home caring for the family	31%	21%

Share of family income earned by working women:

	Total	White	Black
All	18%	17%	32%
More than half	11%	11%	9%
About half	26%	27%	26%
Less than half	44%	46%	33%

Given a choice, would you prefer to have more time or more money?

	Total	White	Black
More time	44%	46%	31%
More money	50%	47%	63%

How much do you think others value you for fulfilling your responsibilities:

	At home	At work
Very valued	59%	59%
Somewhat valued	35%	37%
Not too valued	4%	3%
Not at all valued	1%	1%

Which of these workplace issues is your greatest worry?

Employers providing fewer benefits	19%
Balancing work and family life	13%
Pressure from work affecting family	13%
Not being valued by employer	10%
Lack of opportunities for women to advance	10%
Possibility of job loss for men	9%
Lack of opportunities to grow and learn	5%
Sexual harassment	5%
Possibility of job loss for women	5%

Of the 80 percent of women who expect the next generation of women to have *more* opportunities, the top reasons:

More opportunities in the workplace	51%
More education	37%
Less discrimination against women	22%

Of the 15 percent of women who expect the next generation of women to have *fewer* opportunities, the top reasons:

Scarce market, slower economy	33%
Younger generation lazy, fun-loving	17%
Education not as good or accessible	12%

COMPILED BY DORIAN FRIEDMAN

USN&WR – Basic data: Louis Harris and Associates/ Families and Work Institute/ Whirlpool Foundation survey of 1,502 American women and 460 men where noted. Totals may not add up to 100 percent.

Families and Work Institute and the Whirlpool Foundation, May 22, 1995

G.   What's Your Opinion? Think, Pair, Share

Most businesses in America require those applying for a job to submit a résumé, that is, a summary of their work experience, education, and qualifications. Jerrold G. Simon, Ed. D., psychologist and career development specialist at Harvard Business School, who has counseled over a thousand people in their search for jobs, has written an article to tell people how to go after the job they really want. The article, "How to Write a Résumé," was printed as an advertisement in a news magazine. Throughout the article is the implied message, "You must sell yourself." That is, you must assert yourself and convince a prospective employer that you are the best person for the job:

'Who am I? What do I want to do?' Writing your résumé forces you to think about yourself.

The most qualified people don't always get the job. It goes to the person who presents himself more persuasively in person and on paper. So don't

*just list where you were and what you did. This is your chance to tell how
well you did. Were you the best salesman? Did you cut operating costs?
Give numbers, statistics, percentages, increases in sales or profits.*

Think about this advice, and then write answers to the following questions:

1. Would following this advice get you a good job in your country?
2. What American values do you recognize here?
3. If you were trying to "sell yourself" in a résumé, what points would you make?

Share your answers with a partner and then with another pair of students.

 H. Suggestions for Writing or Making an Oral Report

Choose one of the following topics for your report.

1. Look at the graph on page 123 that shows the growing occupations in the
   United States. What kinds of education and skills are needed for these new
   jobs? What is the outlook in your country? Are jobs that require advanced
   education on the increase or decrease? Imagine that you are a parent of a
   young person getting ready to make important decisions about what
   education or training to get in order to eventually have a good job. What
   advice would you give? Or, imagine that you are advising the policy
   planners of your country. What recommendations would you make about
   preparing a workforce for the 21st century?

2. Compare the way American businesses operate with the way businesses
   operate in your country. For example, compare a typical transaction at a
   shop. How do the activities differ? Consider these points:
   a. When the employees work
   b. Who the employees are
   c. The pace of the business transaction
   d. Whether the shopkeeper waits on one person or several people at a time
   e. The atmosphere of the shop
   f. Whether the employees know the customers or not
   g. How long the employees have worked there
   h. The relationship between the employees and their employer

3. During the 1980s, salaries for leaders of American companies rose to
   unbelievable highs. The average CEO (Chief Executive Officer) now earns one
   to four million dollars a year. For example, many of the workers at a large toy
   company make less than five dollars an hour, while the CEO makes over $3,000
   an hour (over six million dollars a year). In other countries, such as Germany
   and Japan, CEOs generally do not have such extremely high salaries. What
   about your country? Recently, many American stockholders have begun to
   challenge these high salaries. Imagine you are a stockholder in a company
   where the CEO is paid more than a million dollars a year. Write a letter to the
   CEO complaining about that person's salary. What benefits would there be to
   the company if less money were spent on the CEO's salary? Imagine that you
   are the CEO. Answer the letter, giving reasons why your salary is justified.

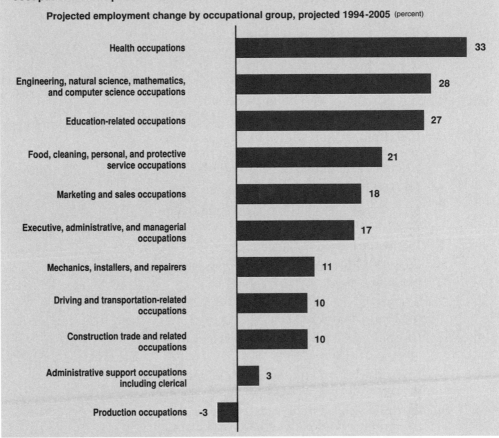

Occupational Employment

The fastest growing cluster is health occupations, followed closely by engineering, natural science, mathematics, and computer-related occupations. The largest occupation, administrative support including clerical, is projected to increase 3 percent and production occupations are expected to decline.

Projected employment change by occupational group, projected 1994-2005 (percent)

Occupational group	Percent
Health occupations	33
Engineering, natural science, mathematics, and computer science occupations	28
Education-related occupations	27
Food, cleaning, personal, and protective service occupations	21
Marketing and sales occupations	18
Executive, administrative, and managerial occupations	17
Mechanics, installers, and repairers	11
Driving and transportation-related occupations	10
Construction trade and related occupations	10
Administrative support occupations including clerical	3
Production occupations	-3

Source: Occupational Outlook Quarterly, Fall 1995

 ## I. Proverbs and Sayings

Ask Americans to explain these proverbs and sayings to you. Then ask them for other examples of sayings about competition, winning, or success.

1. When the going gets tough, the tough get going.
2. Every man for himself.
3. May the best man win.
4. To the winner belong the spoils.
5. It's a dog-eat-dog world.
6. Take care of number 1.

J. Ask Yourself

Do you agree or disagree with each of the statements below? Put a check under the number that indicates how you feel.

+2 = Strongly agree
+1 = Agree
 0 = No opinion or don't know
-1 = Disagree
-2 = Strongly disagree

	+2	+1	0	-1	-2
1. Entrepreneurs who build successful businesses are heroes.	___	___	___	___	___
2. I admire a person who is his or her own boss more than an "organization man/ woman" who must answer to others.	___	___	___	___	___
3. I would like to own my own business.	___	___	___	___	___
4. A medical doctor has more prestige than a business person.	___	___	___	___	___
5. Women and men make equally good bosses.	___	___	___	___	___
6. I would rather have a man for a boss than a woman.	___	___	___	___	___
7. The place where I live is more important to me than where I work.	___	___	___	___	___
8. I would take a job I liked for less pay over a job I didn't like for more pay.	___	___	___	___	___
9. I would work on an assembly line in a factory if the pay were good.	___	___	___	___	___
10. All things considered, socialism is better for a country and its people than capitalism.	___	___	___	___	___

K. Watch for This: Small Group Discussion

Read the explanation about how different cultures structure time, and then discuss the following questions with members of your small group. When you have finished, report your group's findings to the rest of the class.

Edward T. Hall has described two basic types of cultures, with regard to the ways those cultures deal with time. He calls these *monochronic* and *polychronic* cultures. In monochronic cultures, people do "one thing at a time." In polychronic cultures, people do "many things at a time." For example, in a monochronic culture, when someone has a business appointment, that person expects to have the complete attention of the other party until the appointment has ended. On the other hand, in a polychronic culture, a person who has a business appointment expects there to be many others waiting and being dealt with at one time.

How are activities scheduled in your country? Is your culture monochronic *or* polychronic? *Which best describes the United States? Which would best describe the following situations? What other examples can you think of?*

1. You arrive at the airport an hour before your flight to find that there are large crowds pushing their way to the counter. Whoever pushes hardest gets to the front and gets waited on. The ticket agent behind the counter serves several people at once, focusing attention on the one who has made himself or herself most noticed.

Waiting in line at Dulles International Airport, near Washington, DC   **Maryanne Kearny Datesman**

2. The doctor has told you that he will meet you at the hospital at 10:00 A.M. to take care of a minor problem. You have difficulty finding transportation but finally arrive at 10:45. The doctor is seeing another patient and sends word that he will not be able to see you now. He will "squeeze you in" around his other appointments. You will probably have to wait until late afternoon.

L. Suggestions for Further Reading

- Theodore Dreiser, *An American Tragedy*
- Horatio Alger, *Ragged Dick* and *Mark, the Match Boy*
- Arthur Miller, *Death of a Salesman*
- F. Scott Fitzgerald, "The Diamond as Big as the Ritz"
- Sloan Wilson, *The Man in the Gray Flannel Suit*

- Ralph Nader, *Unsafe at Any Speed*
- Sinclair Lewis, *Babbitt*
- William H. Whyte, Jr., *The Organization Man*
- Ross Perot, *Not for Sale at Any Price*
- Kenneth Blanchard, *The One Minute Manager*

M. Recommended Movies

- *Death of a Salesman*
- *Trading Places*
- *The Secret of My Success*

- *Mr. Mom*
- *Working Girl*

Americans gather on the mall to celebrate Earth Day   **National Park Services, National Capital Area**

CHAPTER 7

Government and Politics in the United States

A wise and frugal Government shall restrain men from injuring one another, shall leave them otherwise free to regulate their own pursuits of industry and improvements.

Thomas Jefferson

Before You Read

1. What do you think is the most important role of a government?

2. In the United States, what is the relationship between the president and Congress? Who has more power?

3. What are the two major political parties in the United States? What is the main difference in their beliefs?

A Suspicion of Strong Government

The ideal of the free individual has had a profound effect on the way Americans view their government. Traditionally, there has been a deep suspicion that government is the natural enemy of freedom, even if it is elected by the people. The bigger and stronger the government becomes, the more dangerous most Americans believe it is to their individual freedom.

This suspicion of strong government goes back to the men who led the American Revolution in 1776. These men believed that the government of Great Britain was determined to discourage the freedom and economic opportunities of the American colonists by excessive taxes and other measures that would ultimately benefit the British aristocracy and monarchy. Thomas Paine, the famous revolutionary writer, expressed the view of other American revolutionists when he said, "Government even in its best state is but a necessary evil; in its worst state, an **intolerable** one."

The Organization of the American Government

The way in which the national government is organized in the United States Constitution provides an excellent illustration of the American suspicion of governmental power. The provisions of the Constitution are more concerned with keeping the government from doing evil than with enabling it to do good. The national government, for example, is divided into three separate branches. This division of governmental power is based on the belief that if any one part or branch of government has all, or even most of the power, it will become a threat to the freedom of individual citizens.

The legislative or lawmaking branch of the government is called the *Congress*. Congress has two houses—the *Senate*, with two Senators from each state regardless of its size, and the *House of Representatives*, consisting of a total of 435 Representatives divided among the 50 states by population. (In the House, states with large populations have more representatives than states with small populations, while in the Senate, each state has equal representation.) The *president*, or chief executive, heads the executive branch, which has responsibility to carry out the laws. The *Supreme Court* and lower national courts make up the **judicial** branch. The judicial branch settles disputes about the exact meaning of the law through court cases.

If any one of the three branches starts to **abuse** its power, the other two may join together to stop it, through a system of *checks and balances*. The Constitution is most careful in balancing the powers of the legislative and executive branches of the government because these two (Congress and the

The signing of the Declaration of Independence, a painting by John Trumbull **Library of Congress**

president) are the most powerful of the three branches. In almost every important area of governmental activity, such as the power to make laws, to declare war, or to conclude treaties with foreign countries, the Constitution gives each of these two branches enough power to prevent the other from acting on its own.

The president and both houses of Congress have almost complete political independence from each other because they are all chosen in separate elections. For example, the election of the Congress does not determine who will be elected president, and the presidential election does not determine who will be elected to either house of Congress. It is quite possible in the American system to have the leader of one political party win the presidency while the other major political party wins most of the seats in Congress. In fact, during the 1970s and 1980s, four of the five presidents were Republicans, while the Democrats typically controlled one or both houses of Congress. In the Congressional elections of 1994, however, the reverse situation occurred. While Bill Clinton, a Democrat, was president, the Republicans won control of both the House of Representatives and the Senate. It is important to note that the elections of the members of the two houses of Congress are separate from each other.* Thus, the Republicans may control one

---

* Members of the House of Representatives are elected for two-year terms, while Senators serve six-year terms. The terms are staggered so that only one-third of the Senators run for re-election each time the House elections are held.

house, while the Democrats may control the other. Both the House of Representatives and the Senate must agree on all legislation, however, before it becomes law.

Observers from other countries are often confused by the American system. The national government often seems to speak with two conflicting voices, that of the president and that of Congress. It is necessary for the president to sign bills passed by Congress in order for them to become law. If the president **vetoes** a legislative bill passed by Congress—that is, if he refuses to sign it—the bill dies unless two-thirds of both the House and Senate vote to override the veto. This rarely happens. On the other hand, a treaty with a foreign government signed by the president dies if the Senate refuses to **ratify** it—that is, votes to accept it.

Although the American system of divided governmental power strikes many observers as inefficient and even disorganized, most Americans still strongly believe in it for two reasons. It has been able to meet the challenges of the past, and it gives strong protection to individual freedoms.

In addition to dividing government powers into three branches, the Constitution includes a *Bill of Rights*, which is designed to protect specific individual rights and freedoms from government interference. Some of the guarantees in the Bill of Rights concern the freedom of expression. The government may not interfere with an individual's freedom of speech or freedom of religious worship. The Bill of Rights also guarantees the right of a fair criminal procedure for those accused of breaking laws. Thus, the Bill of Rights is another statement of the American belief in the importance of individual freedom.

The Ideal of the Free Individual

In the late 1700s, most Americans expected the new national government created by the Constitution to leave them alone to pursue their individual goals. They believed that the central purpose of government was to create the conditions most favorable to the development of the free individual.

Before the Civil War of the 1860s, the American ideal of the free individual was the frontier settler and the small farmer. President Thomas Jefferson expressed this ideal when he said: "Those who labor in the earth are the chosen people of God, if ever he had a chosen people…." Jefferson glorified farmers for being free individuals who relied on no one but themselves for their daily needs. He believed that farmers, being dependent on none but themselves, were the most honest of citizens. Throughout his life, Jefferson favored a small, weak form of government, which he believed would encourage the development of a nation of free, self-reliant farmer citizens.

From the end of the Civil War until the Great Depression of the 1930s, the successful business person replaced the farmer and the frontier settler as the ideal expression of the free individual. The prevailing view of Americans during this time was that government should not interfere in the activities of business. If it were to do so, it would threaten the development of free individuals whose

Thomas Jefferson and Declaration of Independence, Jefferson Memorial, Washington, DC **Maryanne Kearny Datesman**

competitive spirit, self-reliance, and hard work were developing the United States into a land of greater and greater material prosperity.

Government, therefore, remained small and inactive in relation to the great size of the nation and the amount of power of business corporations. There were some government regulations over business during this period, but these had only a small impact on business practices. From the 1870s until the 1930s, business organizations and ideas dominated American government and politics. The Republican party, one of the nation's two major political parties, provided the means for maintaining this dominance. The Republicans were more successful than their rivals, the Democrats, in electing presidents and congressmen during this period, and the Republicans strongly supported government policies favorable to business.

The Development of Big Government: The Welfare State

Traditionally, Republicans have favored letting businesses compete with little or no government regulation: Let the free enterprise system regulate itself in the marketplace. On the other hand, Democrats have traditionally favored using government to regulate businesses and protect consumers and also to solve social problems. Not surprisingly, it was a Democratic president who presided over the creation of "big government."

The Great Depression of the 1930s greatly weakened the businessperson's position as the American ideal of the free individual, and "big business" lost respect. The Depression also created the need for emergency government action to help the needy on a scale never before seen in peacetime. As a result, the idea that government should be small and inactive was largely abandoned. Moreover, the ideal of the free individual underwent some very important changes.

The widespread unemployment and other economic hardships of the Depression gave rise to the new **assumption** that individuals could not be expected to rely solely on themselves in providing for their economic security. This new assumption, in turn, led to a large and active role for the national government in helping individuals meet their daily needs. The Democratic party,

President Lyndon B. Johnson signs the legislation creating "The Great Society," a collection of welfare programs **Stoughton**

led by President Franklin Roosevelt, brought about a number of changes in the 1930s, which he referred to as a *New Deal* for Americans.

Even with the return of prosperity after the Depression and World War II (1941–1945), the growth of government's role in helping to provide economic security for individuals did not end. It continued in the prosperous postwar years, and it was greatly expanded during the presidency of another Democrat, Lyndon Johnson, in the 1960s. Roosevelt's New Deal grew into what became a permanent "welfare state" that provided payments for retired persons, government checks for the unemployed, support for families with dependent children and no father to provide income, health care for the poor and the elderly, and other benefits for needy persons.

Although the welfare state has continued to grow, it has never been fully accepted by many Americans. They fear that economic security provided by the government will weaken self-reliance, an ideal that is closely associated in the minds of Americans with individual freedom.

Many Americans believe that although the welfare state began with good intentions, it is now at best a necessary evil. At worst, it presents a danger to individual freedom by making an increasing number of Americans dependent on the government instead of on themselves. In this way, the strong traditions of individualism and self-reliance have made Americans less accepting of welfare programs than the citizens of other democracies such as those in Western Europe, which have more extensive welfare programs than those of the United States.

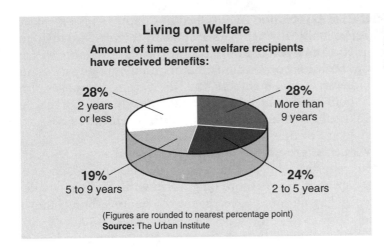

Living on Welfare

Amount of time current welfare recipients have received benefits:

28%
2 years
or less

28%
More than
9 years

19%
5 to 9 years

24%
2 to 5 years

(Figures are rounded to nearest percentage point)
Source: The Urban Institute

The welfare reform bill passed in 1996 was designed to prevent people from remaining on welfare for more than 2 to 5 years © **1993, USA TODAY**

Because welfare programs go against the basic value of self-reliance, many Americans believe that having to "go on welfare" to meet daily needs is a personal embarrassment and a mark of failure. Even people who have been supported by welfare payments for much of their lives complain that the system is **degrading** and causes them to lose self-respect. Reforming the welfare system has become an important political issue for both the Republicans and the Democrats. In 1996, a welfare reform bill was passed. It placed limits on the number of years people can receive welfare payments and gave states much more responsibility for deciding who is eligible for support.

The welfare system in the United States has also been troubled by racial problems that began with black slavery before the Civil War of the 1860s and continued with racial **segregation** in the South until the 1960s. Although American blacks have made significant gains in the last thirty years, many are still unable to escape from poverty and unemployment. For this reason, a large number of people who receive welfare benefits are black Americans. Sadly, some of the old racial prejudices against black Americans have been transferred to welfare programs. In reality, there are four or five times as many white people on welfare as there are African-Americans or members of other minorities.

The Role of Special Interest Groups

The great expansion of government programs since the 1930s is only partly due to the growth of welfare programs that help the poor and the needy. Practically all social and economic classes of Americans have seen the need to take advantage of, or to protect themselves from, the actions of government, especially the national government. To accomplish this, Americans with similar interests have formed special interest groups to more effectively influence the actions of government. These special interest groups are often called **lobbying** groups or *pressure* groups. Although lobbying groups have existed throughout the nation's history, they have grown significantly in both numbers and power in recent years.

The National Rifle Association (mentioned in Chapter 4) is an example of a powerful and effective lobby. Its members are mostly people who own guns for hunting, target practice, and personal protection. Yet the NRA receives a great deal of money from business corporations that manufacture guns. Because of the attitudes and interests of its members, the NRA strongly opposes almost all government restrictions on the sale of both handguns and rifles. Even though most of the general public favors gun controls, until recently, the NRA has been able to block the passage of most gun control legislation.

Although few interest groups have been as successful as the NRA, most well-organized interest groups have achieved a large measure of success. By organizing into groups that put pressure on government officials, people can gain more rewards and avoid more government restrictions than if they tried to do it as individuals.

With this principle in mind, business interest groups have multiplied in recent decades so that almost every major trade or business has its lobbyists in Washington. Labor unions, which were made strong during the New Deal years, have their influential lobbyists. So do farm groups. Interest groups representing ethnic groups such as African-Americans, Native Americans, Mexican-Americans, and Jewish Americans have also expanded. There are interest groups representing a variety of ideals or causes which want government support. These include equal rights for women, a clean environment, and greater protection for consumers. Even the people who receive welfare payments have a lobbying group called the Welfare Rights Organization. As one Congressman exclaimed, "Everybody in America has a lobby!"

The political tendency of recent decades is for the size of the government to bring about an increase in the number and size of interest groups, and for the greater demands made on the government by interest groups to increase the size of the government. Groups such as the AARP (American Association of Retired Persons) not only demand new government programs, regulations, and benefits for their members, they also strongly resist any attempts to reduce existing programs that they believe protect their interests. The result of this continuing cycle can be referred to as "interest group government." No single interest dominates government and politics as business groups did before the Great Depression. Instead, government and politics are based on reaching compromises with a large number of groups and pleasing as many as possible.

The New Individualism Versus the Old Individualism

Interest group government can be seen as expressing a new form of American individualism. Unlike frontier individualism or business individualism, individuals do not claim to succeed on their own but rather by forming groups to influence the government. Still, it is individuals, their rights, their interests, and their ambitions, not those of the group, that are the focus of attention. The interest group is no more than a tool to achieve the goals of the individual by influencing the government.

Although most Americans have benefited in some way from government-sponsored programs, many experts believe that interest group government is harmful to the United States. They believe it places emphasis on peoples' ability to influence the government rather than their ability to produce goods and services that enrich the society. Moreover, powerful interest groups pressure government leaders to give more benefits to Americans than the government can really afford. In this way, these groups have contributed greatly to the national debt, which has been a very serious problem since the 1980s.

The Democratic party emerged from the New Deal as the supporter of the idea that government should do more for all classes and all kinds of Americans. For this reason, poorer and less-privileged Americans tended to support the Democratic party. Blacks and other nonwhite minorities (such as Hispanics) are often underprivileged and have tended to vote for Democrats. Therefore, the Democratic party has traditionally been more racially and ethnically diverse than its political rival, the Republicans. The diversity of the Democratic party has been further broadened by the support it has received from most women's rights groups.

This diversity was reflected when Democrat Bill Clinton was elected president in 1992 after twelve years of Republican presidents. In naming his Cabinet, the top leaders of the government bureaucracy, President Clinton said that he wanted it to reflect the diversity of America. He then appointed six women, four blacks, and two Hispanics to his Cabinet.

President Bill Clinton gives his first "State of the Union" address to both houses of Congress, 1993. Vice President Al Gore and Speaker of the House Newt Gingrich are pictured on the left **AP Photo/J. Scott Applewhite.**

The Republican party was not changed by the New Deal as much as the Democrats were. The Republicans continued to stress anti-government and pro-business ideas much as they had before the Great Depression. While Democrats tended to see government action as part of the solution to many problems, Republicans tended to see government action as adding to America's problems. The best hope for America, Republicans argued, was to reduce the number of things government does, and to give American business more freedom from government taxes, rules, and requirements. Republicans gained most of their political strength from business groups and from the strong anti-government attitudes of millions of Americans. Moreover, Republicans argued that Democrats gave too much attention to the complaints of women's rights groups and racial and ethnic minority groups. Because of this, they said, Democrats had forgotten about the average citizens who see themselves as Americans first rather than as members of a particular group.

Many observers have questioned whether the traditional **stances** of either party truly serve the needs of the country. It may be that neither the Republican idea of national prosperity through the dominance of business groups, nor the Democratic idea of prosperity through government action to help the many diverse groups of Americans, is adequate to meet the common problems facing Americans at the dawn of the 21st century.

■ ■ ■ ■

 ## New Words

intolerable that which cannot be allowed; unbearable

judicial having to do with a court of law

abuse to use in a wrong way; to hurt or harm someone

veto to refuse to allow; to forbid; to refuse to sign a bill into law

ratify to approve an agreement and make it official

assumption something that is believed to be true

degrade to lower in the opinion of others

segregation the separation of one social or racial group from another

lobby a group of people who unite for or against an action so that those in power will support what they want; to try to influence the legislative process (to persuade Congress to vote the way the group wants)

stance way of thinking; viewpoint; attitude

A. Vocabulary Check

Match each word with its definition.

———— 1. lobby

———— 2. assumption

———— 3. intolerable

———— 4. judicial

———— 5. stance

———— 6. ratify

———— 7. degrade

———— 8. segregation

———— 9. veto

———— 10. abuse

a. unacceptable

b. what the Senate does to make a treaty official

c. mistreat; misuse

d. something you think is true

e. what the president does to a bill to prevent it from becoming law; a "no" vote

f. a pressure group that tries to influence government

g. the separation of people by race

h. make others think badly of someone

i. the viewpoint taken by a political party

j. the Supreme Court is part of this branch of the government

 ## B. Comprehension Check

Write the letter of the best answer according to the information in the chapter.

———— 1. Americans do not want to have a strong national government because
   a. they are afraid of their political leaders.
   b. they are afraid it will put limits on their individual freedom.
   c. they are much more concerned with national glory.

———— 2. The Constitution of the United States
   a. gives by far the most power to Congress.
   b. gives by far the most power to the president.
   c. tries to give each branch enough power to balance the others.

———— 3. The president of the United States
   a. has the power to make official treaties with foreign governments without the approval of Congress.
   b. can veto a law that has been passed by Congress.
   c. is elected if his political party wins most of the seats in Congress.

_____ 4. The Bill of Rights
   a. explains the rights of Congress and the rights of the president.
   b. guarantees citizens of the United States specific individual rights and freedoms.
   c. is part of the Declaration of Independence.

_____ 5. The American ideal of the free individual
   a. was exemplified by the farmers and the frontier settlers in the late 1700s and early 1800s.
   b. was exemplified by the businessman before the Civil War of the 1860s.
   c. caused the national government to grow in size and strength during the late 1800s.

_____ 6. The size and power of the United States government
   a. have remained the same since the nation began in the late 1700s.
   b. have decreased greatly since the Great Depression of the 1930s.
   c. have increased greatly since the Great Depression of the 1930s.

_____ 7. The welfare state
   a. was created during a time of great economic prosperity.
   b. started with President Roosevelt's New Deal.
   c. is based on the idea that all individuals should be self-reliant and responsible for their own welfare.

_____ 8. Stronger gun control laws are favored by
   a. the National Rifle Association.
   b. most of the American people.
   c. very few Americans.

_____ 9. Which statement about lobby groups is _not_ true?
   a. They have become less powerful in recent years.
   b. They try to influence the government and public opinion.
   c. They have caused the government to get larger.

_____ 10. Which statement about the traditional stances of the political parties is _false_?
   a. The Democrats believe that government should play a major role in solving society's problems.
   b. The Republicans believe that business and the free market can solve society's problems.
   c. The Republicans and the Democrats basically agree about the role of government, but they have different political beliefs.

C. Questions for Discussion

1. How is the government of your country organized? Is there a monarchy? Do you have a president? A prime minister? How are the leaders of your country chosen? Does the party that wins the most seats in the legislature choose the president (or prime minister)?

2. What are the qualifications for someone running for leadership in your country (president or prime minister)? Who are some of your most popular leaders? What personal qualities do they have?

3. What is a lobby group? What kind of special interest groups are there in the United States? Are there similar lobbies in your country? If so, how do they influence government officials? Who do you think is more trustworthy—business or government leaders?

4. How many political parties are there in your country? What are the major differences in their beliefs? Which party is in power now?

5. What are the main political issues in your country? When will the next election be? Who holds the real power in your country? What is the best/worst thing about your political system?

D. Cloze Summary Paragraph

This paragraph summarizes the chapter. Fill in each blank with any word that makes sense.

Americans believe that the _____*role*_____ of their government is

_____ protect their individual freedom. _____ Constitution divides

the powers _____ the government among the _____ branches: the

executive, the _____, and the judicial. This _____ any branch

from gaining _____ much power and threatening _____. Because

the ideal of _____ free individual was so _____, for many

years the _____ remained small and weak, _____ individuals to

pursue their _____ goals. In the 1930s, _____ was a severe

economic _____ and the role of _____ changed. Welfare

programs were _____ to help the needy, _____ the government grew much _____ and stronger. Also, many _____ groups were established to _____ the government. Today, almost _____ groups have a lobby _____ protect their interests and _____ for benefits from the _____. Traditionally, the Democratic party _____ favored having a big government _____ tries to solve society's _____ and regulates business activities. _____ Republican party has favored having _____ small government with few _____ over business activities. Although most Americans have _____ in some way from _____ programs, the majority of _____ are still suspicious of _____ power of big _____. They are more concerned about _____ own individual freedom than _____ common good of the _____ .

E. Ask Americans

Find out how Americans feel about their government. Compare their responses with the poll that follows.

I'm going to read you a list of institutions in American society. Please tell me how much confidence you have in each one—*a great deal, quite a lot, some, or very little?*

1. Banks
2. Big business
3. The police
4. Newspapers
5. The military
6. Public schools
7. The presidency
8. The criminal justice system
9. The U.S. Supreme Court
10. Television news
11. The medical system
12. Congress
13. Organized labor
14. The church or organized religion

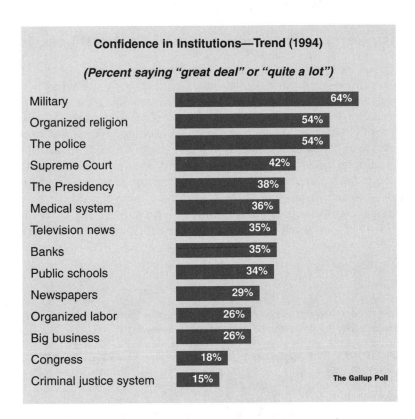

Confidence in Institutions—Trend (1994)

(Percent saying "great deal" or "quite a lot")

Institution	Percent
Military	64%
Organized religion	54%
The police	54%
Supreme Court	42%
The Presidency	38%
Medical system	36%
Television news	35%
Banks	35%
Public schools	34%
Newspapers	29%
Organized labor	26%
Big business	26%
Congress	18%
Criminal justice system	15%

The Gallup Poll

F. Think, Pair, Share

Which of the following things do you think your government should pay for? Put a check next to your choices, and indicate if you think the government should pay **all** *or just* **some** *of each of the following. Share your answers with a partner and then with another pair of students.*

		all	some
1.	Free medical care for all citizens	☐	☐
2.	Free education for all citizens	☐	☐
3.	Basic food and housing for all citizens	☐	☐
4.	Highways, roads, water systems, and other public works	☐	☐
5.	Complete care for the elderly	☐	☐
6.	Complete care for needy children	☐	☐
7.	Public transportation (trains, buses)	☐	☐

Which of these does your government now pay for?

G. Understanding Graphs: Small Group Discussion

Look at the following graph showing what percent of the U.S. budget goes for *mandatory* programs (those that must be paid) and what percent goes for *discretionary* items (those that the government has a choice about). What percent of the U.S. budget goes for interest on the national debt? What percent goes for "entitlement" programs such as Medicare (medical benefits for the elderly) and Medicaid (medical benefits for the poor)? An *entitlement* program means that if you fit a set of requirements, you are automatically entitled to receive government money from that program. Congress is changing the requirements for many of these programs, however, and the funding for entitlement programs is often debated. Who should be eligible for these programs? How much money should they receive, and for how long?

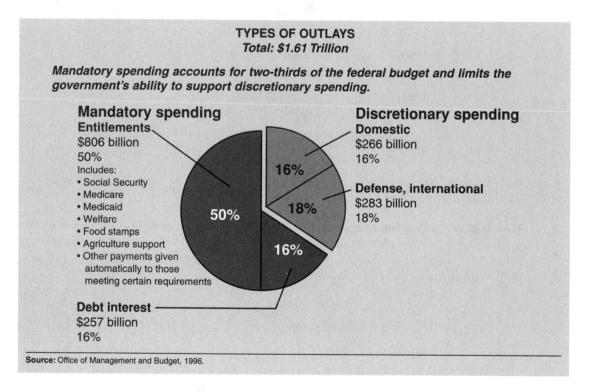

TYPES OF OUTLAYS
Total: $1.61 Trillion

Mandatory spending accounts for two-thirds of the federal budget and limits the government's ability to support discretionary spending.

Mandatory spending
Entitlements
$806 billion
50%
Includes:
• Social Security
• Medicare
• Medicaid
• Welfare
• Food stamps
• Agriculture support
• Other payments given automatically to those meeting certain requirements

Debt interest
$257 billion
16%

Discretionary spending
Domestic
$266 billion
16%

Defense, international
$283 billion
18%

50% 16% 18% 16%

Source: Office of Management and Budget, 1996.

 ## H. Suggestions for Research and Oral Reports

1. You may be surprised to learn that the president of the United States is not elected directly by the people but by the Electoral College. In presidential elections, people are actually voting for the "electors," and it is these electors who officially choose the President.

   With the Electoral College system, the winner of the majority of each state's popular votes gets all of that state's electoral votes. Though the number of electoral votes varies according to population, it is possible for a person to be elected president without carrying a majority of the popular (individual) votes. That happened in 1888, when Benjamin Harrison won the presidency even though Grover Cleveland had the majority of popular votes.

Look in an encyclopedia for an explanation of the Electoral College and its role in elections. At the time of a presidential election, you will see many articles about the Electoral College in newspapers and news magazines. How do Americans feel about this system?

2. Review the Bill of Rights and then decide if each of the following laws would be *unconstitutional* or not. What article of the Bill of Rights deals with each?
    a. You cannot hold a meeting to discuss corruption in government.
    b. A major city newspaper is prevented from reporting about the political activities of a member of the president's Cabinet.
    c. Your family is prevented from worshipping at a church that is new and is believed to be "strange."
    d. If you disagree with the president, you cannot legally say so in public.

3. In 1960, President John F. Kennedy appointed his brother Robert Kennedy to be Attorney General of the United States. In 1992, President Bill Clinton announced that he wanted to appoint his wife Hillary to an important government position, perhaps a Cabinet level post. Polls showed, however, that two-thirds of the American public disapproved of Hillary's having a major post, and Clinton was forced to reconsider. Why do you think Americans accepted the appointment of a president's brother but not a president's wife? What do you think about any president appointing a spouse or family member to government office? Write a "Letter to the Editor" (of a newspaper) expressing your opinion.

Al Gore and Bill Clinton campaigning in the presidential election, 1992   **AP Photo**

I.   Ask Americans about Political Labels

Being Republican or Democratic is becoming less important in American politics. Instead, a number of voters look to see which candidate is *liberal* and which is *conservative*. The Republican party has traditionally been conservative or *right wing*, while the Democratic party is considered more liberal or *left wing*. Many Americans consider themselves neither conservative nor liberal: they call themselves *middle of the road* or *moderate*.

What do you think the positions of liberals and conservatives would be on the following issues?

1. Control of handguns

2. Environmental protection

3. Guaranteed jobs and housing for everyone

4. Sex education courses

5. Legalization of marijuana

6. Government support (financial) for abortions

Ask several Americans whether they are opposed to or in favor of each of the six above issues. Then ask them whether they are liberals or conservatives. Compare their responses with your predictions.

 J.   People Watching

Americans sometimes say that it is dangerous to talk about two topics: religion and politics. It's often difficult to know what you should say to people when you first meet them. The questions you might ask others from your country may not be appropriate or acceptable in another society or culture.

Ask a number of Americans of different ages, of both sexes, and of different ethnic or racial backgrounds, if possible, the following questions. Record each person's reaction to each question. Write down not only what someone said but also how that person behaved. Did the person look surprised? Shocked? Embarrassed? What did the person do? Did the person look away? Did the person look down?

After you have finished asking the questions, ask each person whether there were any questions which that person felt should not be asked and why. Write your findings. Which questions are acceptable? Which are unacceptable? Which are acceptable in your country?

1. What is your name?

2. What do you do for a living?

3. Where are you from? (or: Where do you live?)

Answering interview questions   **Ken Karp**

4. Do you like your job?

5. How much do you make?

6. Are you a Republican or Democrat? Why?

7. Are you married? Why, or why not?

8. Do you have children? Why, or why not?

9. How old are you?

10. What is your religion?

 K. Suggestions for Further Reading

- Frank Norris, *The Octopus*
- Robert Penn Warren, *All the King's Men*
- James Agee, *Let Us Now Praise Famous Men*

 L. Recommended Movies

- *Dave*
- *The Silence of the Lambs*
- *Mr. Smith Goes to Washington*
- *The Candidate*
- *The American President*

Abraham Lincoln and the Gettysburg Address, Lincoln Memorial, Washington, DC   A. Devaney, Inc., N.Y.

CHAPTER 8

Ethnic and Racial Assimilation in the United States

So in this continent, the energy of Irish, Germans, Swedes, Poles and all the European tribes, of the Africans, and of the Polynesians—will construct a new race, a new religion, a new state.

Ralph Waldo Emerson

Before You Read

1. How did people from so many different countries create the "American culture" in the United States?

2. What group had the strongest influence on shaping the dominant American culture?

3. Why do you think some groups might assimilate to the American culture more than others?

4. What do you know about the history of African-Americans in the United States?

Melting Pot or Salad Bowl

The population of the United States includes a large variety of ethnic groups coming from many races, nationalities, and religions. The process by which these many groups have been made a part of a common cultural life with commonly shared values is called *assimilation*. Scholars disagree as to the extent to which assimilation has occurred in the United States. As we mentioned in Chapter 1, some have described the United States as a "melting pot" where various racial and ethnic groups have been combined into one culture. Others are inclined to see the United States as a "salad bowl" where the various groups have remained somewhat distinct and different from one another, creating a richly diverse country.

The truth probably lies somewhere between these two views. Since 1776, an enormous amount of racial and ethnic assimilation has taken place in the United States, yet some groups continue to feel a strong sense of separateness from the culture as a whole. Many of these groups are really *bicultural*. That is, they consider themselves Americans, but they also wish to retain the language and the cultural traditions of their original culture.

People of Hispanic origin were on the North American continent before settlers arrived from Europe in the early 1600s. In Florida and the Southwest, there were Spanish and Latin American settlements established centuries before the thirteen colonies joined together to form the United States in the late 1700s. Because of their long history and the continued influx of newcomers into the established communities, many Hispanics, or Latinos, have taken a special pride in maintaining their cultural traditions and the use of the Spanish language.

Generally speaking, over the years whites from different national and religious backgrounds have been gradually assimilated into the larger American culture, with some exceptions. For example, American Jews are one group of whites who have traditionally retained a strong sense of separateness from the larger culture. This may be a result of the long history of persecution in the Christian countries in Europe, the weaker forms of discrimination and anti-Jewish feeling that exist in the United States, and their own strong feeling of ethnic pride. Yet along with their sense of separateness, American Jews have a strong sense of being a part of the larger American culture in which they have achieved competitive success in almost every field.

The Establishment of the Dominant Culture

The first census of the new nation, conducted in 1790, counted about four million people, most of whom were white. Of the white citizens, more than 8 out of 10 traced their ancestry back to England. African-Americans made up a

Mulberry Street in the heart of the immigrant area of New York City in the early 1900s
Library of Congress

surprising 20 percent of the population, an all-time high. There were close to 700,000 slaves and about 60,000 "free Negroes." Only a few Native American Indians who paid taxes were included in the census count, but the total Native American population was probably about one million.

It was the white population that had the greater numbers, the money, and the political power in the new nation, and therefore this majority soon defined what the dominant culture would be. At the time of the American Revolution, the white population was largely English in origin, Protestant, and middle class. Such Americans are sometimes referred to as *WASPs* (White Anglo-Saxon Protestants). Their characteristics became the standard for judging other groups. Those having a different religion (such as the Irish Catholics), or those speaking a different language (such as the Germans, Dutch, and Swedes), were in the minority and would be disadvantaged unless they became assimilated. In the late 1700s, this assimilation occurred without great difficulty. According to historians Allan Nevins and Henry Steele Commager, "English, Irish, German,… Dutch, Swedish—**mingled** and intermarried with little thought of any difference."

The dominant American culture that grew out of the nation's early history, then, was English-speaking, Western European, Protestant, and middle class in character. It was this dominant culture that established what became the traditional values, described by de Tocqueville in the early 1830s. Immigrants with these characteristics were welcome, in part because Americans believed that these newcomers would probably give strong support to the basic values of the dominant culture such as freedom, equality of opportunity, and the desire to work hard for a higher material standard of living.

The Assimilation of Non-Protestant and Non-Western Europeans

As is the case in many cultures, the degree to which a minority group was seen as different from the characteristics of the dominant majority determined the extent of that group's acceptance. Although immigrants who were like the earlier settlers were accepted, those with significantly different characteristics tended to be viewed as a threat to traditional American values and way of life.

This was particularly true of the immigrants who arrived by the millions during the late 19th and early 20th centuries. Most of them came from poverty-stricken nations of southern and eastern Europe. They spoke languages other than English, and large numbers of them were Catholics or Jews.

Americans at the time were very fearful of this new flood of immigrants. They were afraid that these people were so accustomed to lives of poverty and dependence that they would not understand such traditional American values as freedom, self-reliance, and competition. There were so many new immigrants that they might even change the basic values of the nation in undesirable ways.

Americans tried to meet what they saw as a threat to their values by offering English instruction for the new immigrants and citizenship classes to teach them basic American beliefs. The immigrants, however, often felt that their American teachers disapproved of the traditions of their homeland. Moreover, learning about American values gave them little help in meeting their most important needs such as employment, food, and a place to live.

Far more helpful to the new immigrants were the "political bosses" of the larger cities of the northeastern United States, where most of the immigrants

Learning skills to make a living: A class for immigrants early in the 20th century **Library of Congress**

first arrived. Those bosses saw to many of the practical needs of the immigrants and were more accepting of the different homeland traditions. In exchange for their help, the political bosses expected the immigrants to keep them in power by voting for them in elections.

Many Americans strongly disapproved of the political bosses. This was partly because the bosses were frequently **corrupt**; that is, they often stole money from the city governments they controlled and engaged in other illegal practices. Perhaps more important to disapproving Americans, however, was the fact that the bosses seemed to be destroying such basic American values as self-reliance and competition.

The bosses, it seemed, were teaching the immigrants to be dependent on them rather than to rely on themselves. Moreover, the bosses were "buying" the votes of the immigrants in order to give themselves a monopoly of political power in many larger cities. This practice destroyed competition for political office, which Americans viewed as an important tradition in politics just as it was in other facets of American life.

Despite these criticisms, many scholars believe that the political bosses performed an important function in the late 19th and early 20th centuries. They helped to assimilate large numbers of new immigrants into the larger American culture by finding them jobs and housing, in return for their political support. Later the bosses also helped the sons and daughters of these immigrants to find employment, but the second generation usually had the advantage of growing up speaking English.

The fact that the United States had a rapidly expanding economy at the turn of the century made it possible for these new immigrants, often with the help of the bosses, to better their standard of living in the United States. As a result of these new opportunities and new rewards, immigrants came to accept most of the values of the larger American culture and were in turn accepted by the great majority of Americans. For white ethnic groups, therefore, it is generally true that their feeling of being a part of the larger culture—that is, American—is usually stronger than their feeling of belonging to a separate ethnic group—Irish, Italian, and Polish, among many others.

The African-American Experience

The process of assimilation in the United States has been much more successful for white ethnic groups than for nonwhite ethnic groups. Of the nonwhite ethnic groups, Americans of African descent have had the greatest difficulty in becoming assimilated into the larger culture. African-Americans were brought to the United States against their will to be sold as slaves. Except for the Native American Indian tribes who inhabited the United States before the first white settlers arrived, other ethnic groups came to America voluntarily—most as immigrants who wanted to better their living conditions.

The enslavement of African-Americans in the United States was a complete contradiction of such traditional basic American values as freedom and equality

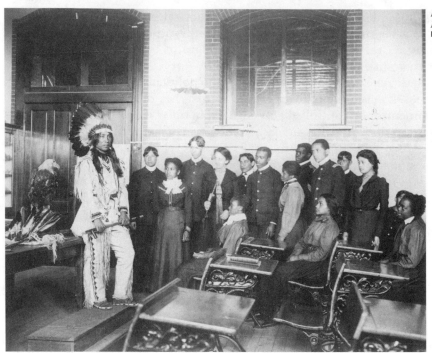

of opportunity. It divided the United States into two increasingly different sections: the southern states, in which black slavery became the basis of the economy, and the northern states, which chose to make slavery against the law.

A minority of whites in the North insisted that slavery and freedom could not exist together in a free country and demanded that slavery be **abolished**, even if this meant war with the South. A much larger number of northern whites believed that freedom and equality of opportunity needed to be protected for white people only, but they were afraid that black slavery would eventually take away their economic freedom. If, for example, the slave system of the South were allowed to spread into the frontier regions of the West, poor and middle-income whites could no longer look to the western frontier as a land of equality and opportunity where people could better their position in life. Rather, whites would have to compete with unpaid slave labor, a situation that they believed would degrade their work and lower their social status.

Abraham Lincoln was able to become president of the United States by appealing to both the white idealists who saw slavery as an injustice to African-Americans and to the larger numbers of northern whites who saw slavery as a threat to themselves. Lincoln's argument was that if black slavery continued to spread westward, white freedom and equality would be threatened. Lincoln also believed that basic ideals such as freedom and equality of opportunity had to apply to *all* people, black and white, or they would not last as basic American values.

When Lincoln won the presidency in 1860, the southern states left the Union and tried to form a new nation of their own based on slavery. A Civil War between the North and South resulted, which turned out to be the bloodiest and most destructive of all the nation's wars. When the North was finally victorious, black slavery ended in the United States.

However, African-Americans were not readily assimilated into the larger American culture. Most remained in the South, where they were not allowed to vote and were legally segregated from whites. Black children were not allowed to attend white public schools, for example, and many received an inferior education that did not give them an equal opportunity to compete in the white-dominated society. Many former slaves and their families became caught in a cycle of poverty that continued for generations. Although conditions were much worse in the segregated South, blacks continued to be the **victims** of strong racial prejudice in the North, as well as in the South.

The Civil Rights Movement of the 1950s and 1960s

This state of affairs remained unchanged until the United States Supreme Court declared in 1954 that racially segregated public schools did not provide equal educational opportunities for black Americans and were therefore illegal. Black leaders throughout the United States were greatly encouraged by this decision. They decided to try to end racial segregation in all areas of American life.

The most important of these leaders was Martin Luther King, Jr., a black Protestant minister with a great gift for **inspiring** his people. From the late 1950s until his **assassination** by a white gunman in 1968, King led thousands of African-Americans in nonviolent marches and demonstrations against segregation and other forms of racial discrimination.

Martin Luther King, Jr.'s 2nd visit to Memphis, AFL-CIO Local 1773, 1968   **AFL-CIO News**

Ethnic and Racial Assimilation in the United States   153

King's goal was to bring about greater assimilation of black people into the larger American culture. His ideals were largely developed from basic American values. He wanted greater equality of opportunity and "Freedom now" for his people. He did not wish to separate his people from American society but rather to gain for them a larger part in it.

Some black leaders, such as Malcolm X, urged a rejection of basic American values and complete separation of blacks from the white culture. Malcolm X believed that American values were nothing more than "white man's values" used to keep blacks in an inferior position. He believed that blacks must separate themselves from whites, by force if necessary, and build their own society based on values that they would create for themselves. Because he saw Christianity as a "white" religion, Malcolm turned to a faith based on Islam, and he became a leader of the "black Muslim" faith (founded in 1930). The great majority of American blacks, however, shared Martin Luther King, Jr.'s Protestant religious beliefs and his goal of assimilation rather than separation. Most African-Americans continued to look to King as their leader.

Largely as a result of King's activities, two major **civil rights** laws were passed during the 1960s that removed racial segregation from public facilities in the South and also removed the **barriers** that had prevented black people from voting in that region.

Race Relations after the Civil Rights Movement

The civil rights laws of the 1960s helped to bring about a significant degree of assimilation of blacks into the larger American culture. Most important, the laws eventually helped to reduce the amount of white prejudice toward black people in all parts of the country. The number of African-Americans attending the nation's colleges and universities, holding elective public office, and earning higher incomes increased dramatically in the late 1960s and 1970s. In 1984 and 1988, Jesse Jackson, a black leader who had worked with King in the 1960s, became the first African-American to run for president of the United States. Although he did not win, he received significant national attention and greatly influenced the policies of the Democratic party.

African-Americans are now mayors of major cities and members of Congress; they hold offices in all levels of government—local, state, and national. They are sports and entertainment heroes, university professors, medical doctors, lawyers, entrepreneurs, and reporters. There is now a sizable black middle class, and there are a number of wealthy African-Americans. More than 80 percent of whites now say that they would vote for a black for President, someone like General Colin Powell, for example. Powell was President Bush's Chairman of the Joint Chiefs of Staff, the senior military leader in the United States.

The bad news is that there is still a **gulf** between the races. Although African-Americans represent about 13 percent of the population, they are grossly underrepresented in Congress. The median income of a married black man working full time is 23 percent behind a married white man. Segregation and discrimination are against the law, but residential patterns create largely segregated neighborhood schools in many urban areas. Half the whites in the United States live in the suburbs, but only a fourth of the blacks. Many blacks are trapped in cycles of poverty, unemployment, violence, and despair in the inner city. They are the most frequent victims of violent crime, and as many as one in five young males now have a criminal record. Over 40 percent of all black children live in poverty and many have only one parent. Seventy percent of black children are born to unmarried women. Some point to the destruction of the family structure as the cause of many of the social problems that African-Americans now face. (See chart on page 168.)

Who is to blame? In a recent poll, 44 percent of blacks said the problems are due to white discrimination against them. Only 21 percent of whites agree. Some African-Americans have given up on ever having equal treatment within a society dominated by whites. There has been a renewed interest in Malcolm X, three decades after his death. In 1993, Spike Lee, a black film director, made a movie about the life of Malcolm X and his separatist ideas. In the '90s, Louis Farrakhan, a new black Muslim leader, advocated that blacks separate themselves from the hostile white culture instead of trying to become a part of it. In the fall of 1995, Farrakhan and others organized the "Million Man March" of African-American men and boys in Washington, D.C. The goal of the march was to gather together responsible fathers and sons who would demonstrate positive role models for African-Americans, and who would inspire people to take leadership roles and make a difference in their home communities.

The Million Man March, October, 1995, Washington, DC **National Park Service, National Capital Area**

Although some view Farrakhan as an extremist, his angry voice has a certain appeal to many African-Americans. Many young blacks, in particular, are searching for a separate African-American identity, one that will recognize the contributions that their black culture has made, and one that will **validate** the black culture as an equal alternative to the white. Since they did not live through the civil rights battles of the 1960s, the progress achieved and the status that African-Americans now have in the white society are not as real to them as the inequalities they believe they experience. They have no memory of the segregated buses, parks, restaurants, even restrooms and drinking fountains, of the pre–civil rights South.

Back in the 1830s, de Tocqueville predicted trouble between blacks and whites in the United States:

> *These two races are fastened to each other without intermingling; and they are unable to separate entirely or to combine. Although the law may abolish slavery, God alone can* **obliterate** *the traces of its existence.*

Nathan Glazer, an expert on assimilation, believes that blacks in the United States have had more difficulty being accepted by the white majority than have other racial and ethnic groups such as Hispanics, Native American Indians, and Asians. Therefore, racial and cultural separatism is a stronger force with them than with other minority groups. There has been no separatist leader of other ethnic or racial minority groups with the broad emotional appeal that Malcolm X and Louis Farrakhan have had with black Americans.

Although slavery was abolished in the 1860s, its **legacy** continues. Fortunately, however, people of good faith, both black and white, are working together to achieve harmony and equality between the races.

A Universal Nation

As we have noted, the dominant culture and its value system, established by the early settlers, had its roots in white, Protestant, western Europe. In the late 1800s and early 1900s, millions of immigrants came from eastern and southern Europe, bringing cultural traditions perceived by the dominant culture as quite different. By the 1920s, Americans had decided that it was time to close the borders to mass immigration, and the number of new immigrants slowed to a **trickle**. In spite of the worries of those in the dominant culture, the new immigrants did assimilate to life in the United States. They greatly enriched the cultural diversity of the nation, and they ultimately did not cause major changes to its system of government, its free enterprise system, or its traditional values.

In 1965, the United States made important changes in its immigration laws, allowing many more immigrants to come and entirely eliminating the older laws' bias in favor of white European immigrants. As a result, the United States is now confronted with a new challenge—taking in large numbers of new immigrants who are nonwhite and non-European. About 90 percent are from Asia, Latin America, and the Caribbean. In addition to the large numbers of legal immigrants, for the first time the United States has significant numbers of illegal immigrants.

Newly naturalized Americans take the oath of citizenship during a naturalization ceremony at the Federal Court in Washington, DC   R. Ellis, Congressional Quarterly

Many worry about what the impact will be on the American society. Can the American economy expand enough to offer these new immigrants the same opportunities that others have had? What will be the effect on the traditional value system that has defined the United States for over 200 years?

Many Americans see wonderful benefits for their country. Ben Wattenberg, a respected expert on American culture, believes that the "new immigration" will be of great help to the nation. According to Wattenberg, something very important is happening to the United States: It is becoming the first universal nation in history. Wattenberg believes that the United States will be the first nation where large numbers of people from every region on earth live in freedom under one government. This diversity, he says, will give the nation great influence and appeal to the rest of the world during the 21st century.

Perhaps the United States will be described not as a "melting pot" or a "salad bowl" but as a "**mosaic**"—a picture made up of many tiny pieces of different colors. If one looks closely at the nation, the individuals of different colors and ethnic groups are still distinct and recognizable, but together they create a picture that is uniquely American. "E Pluribus Unum"—the motto of the United States from its beginning—means one composed of many: "Out of many, one."

■ ■ ■ ■

Cherry Blossom Festival, Washington, DC
National Park Service, National Capital Area

Ethnic and Racial Assimilation in the United States   157

New Words

mingle to mix together

corrupt dishonest; immoral; bad

abolish to end; to do away with

victim someone who suffers because of other people's actions

inspire to encourage in someone the ability to act

assassination the murder of a leader

civil rights rights such as freedom and equality that belong to citizens regardless of race, religion, sex, or other factors

barrier something placed in the way in order to prevent people from moving forward

gulf an area of division or difference; something separating people

validate to confirm; to show that something is valid or right

obliterate to destroy completely; to eliminate completely so that there are no signs that it was ever there

legacy a lasting result; something passed on by someone else

trickle a small number or quantity; a small stream of liquid

mosaic a picture or design that is put together from many small pieces of glass or stone

A. Vocabulary Check

Complete the sentences using words or phrases from the New Words list.

1. Although slavery had ended in the North by the late 1700s, it was not _____ in the rest of the country until during the 1860s.

2. Black people in the 1950s and early 1960s did not have the same freedom and equality as whites in the South; they had to fight for their _____ _____.

3. Before black people could move forward, the _____ that had prevented them from voting had to be removed.

4. Martin Luther King, Jr. was able to _____ his followers to demonstrate against segregation.

5. King was the most important black leader in America from the late 1950s until his _____ by a white gunman in 1968.

6. Unfortunately, the _____ of slavery continues in the United States, and there are still problems between the races.

7. Although racial prejudice is really at an all-time low, many African-Americans feel that there is still a _____ that separates them from most white Americans.

8. Many young African-Americans are looking for ways to _____ the black culture as being an equal alternative to the white.

9. Jews have been the _____ of persecution in many countries.

10. People who come to the United States from many different countries have _____, and many have married persons of a different national origin.

11. Many of the big city political bosses of the late 1800s and early 1900s were _____; they stole money from the city governments.

12. Immigration by white Europeans has now slowed to a _____; 90 percent of the immigrants now come from Asia, Latin America, or the Caribbean.

13. Perhaps the United States is really more of a _____ than a "melting pot" or a "salad bowl."

14. No one would really want to _____ the rich diversity of cultures living together in the United States.

B. Comprehension Check

Write the letter of the best answer according to the information in the chapter.

_____ 1. Scholars who see the United States as a "salad bowl" emphasize
    a. the great extent of racial and ethnic assimilation in the United States.
    b. the many differences between racial and ethnic groups in the United States.
    c. the rapid growth of the population of the United States.

_____ 2. In American society, there are some members of ethnic groups (such as some Jews and Hispanics) that are bicultural; they feel that
    a. they are fully assimilated into American society.
    b. they do not belong at all to American society.
    c. they belong to American society, but at the same time they are separate from it.

_____ 3. Which of the following was *not* a characteristic of the dominant American culture during the early decades of the nation's history?
    a. Catholic
    b. western European
    c. middle class

_____ 4. Which of the following was *true* about the political bosses in northeastern cities during the late 19th and early 20th centuries?
   a. They were more afraid of new immigrants than were other Americans.
   b. They were more cruel to new immigrants than were other Americans.
   c. They were more helpful to new immigrants than were other Americans.

_____ 5. Today, ethnic groups in the United States
   a. have no feeling of belonging to an ethnic group (such as Irish, Italian, Polish) whatsoever.
   b. are assimilated into the dominant culture in varying degrees, often depending on how similar their culture is to the majority.
   c. all feel much more a part of their ethnic group than a part of the dominant culture.

_____ 6. What was the *main* reason that most northern whites disliked slavery?
   a. It went against their religious beliefs.
   b. It went against the U.S. Constitution.
   c. It threatened their own economic opportunities.

_____ 7. After the Civil War, African-Americans in the South lived in a social system where
   a. many continued to be slaves.
   b. segregation was legal.
   c. there was racial discrimination, but no laws separated them from whites.

_____ 8. In 1954, the U.S. Supreme Court declared that African-Americans in the United States
   a. could not be denied their right to vote for racial reasons.
   b. could not be forced to attend racially segregated public schools.
   c. could not be denied freedom of speech, press, or religion.

_____ 9. On which of the beliefs listed below did Malcolm X *disagree* with Martin Luther King, Jr.?
   a. Black people should be assimilated into the larger American society.
   b. Black people were not treated fairly by the larger American society.
   c. Black people must gain their freedom now, not in the distant future.

_____ 10. Which of these statements *is* true?
   a. Most young African-Americans today have little interest in learning about the black culture, and they identify fully with the white culture.
   b. Racial prejudice, segregation, and discrimination are at an all-time high in the United States today.
   c. Using the word *mosaic* to describe the American culture suggests a positive image.

C. Questions for Discussion

1. This chapter describes the dominant American culture as being white, English-speaking, Protestant, and middle class. How would you describe the dominant culture of your country?

2. What ethnic groups in your country have significantly different characteristics from the dominant culture? How well are they assimilated into your society? Are there any laws that either permit or forbid discrimination? Is your country more a "melting pot," a "salad bowl," or a "mosaic"? Why?

3. What is your country's policy on immigration? Is immigration encouraged or discouraged? Does your country permit "guest" workers? Are there language classes or government programs to help new immigrants assimilate? Do immigrants usually intermarry with natives of your country? Do they become citizens?

4. What is the official language of your country? Is there more than one official language? What other languages are spoken in your country? Do most people know more than one language? Does language separate groups in your country in any way?

5. What are the advantages to having a multicultural society in the 21st century? What are the disadvantages?

 D. Cloze Summary Paragraph

This paragraph summarizes the chapter. Fill in each blank with any word that makes sense.

The people of the ___United___ States are from a _____ variety of ethnic

groups _____ represent many races, nationalities, _____ religions.

Some of these _____ have assimilated completely into _____ main

culture while others _____ not. The more the _____ differed from the

characteristics _____ the dominant culture—which _____ white,

English-speaking, Protestant, _____ middle class—the less _____

group assimilated, generally. In _____ late 1800s and early _____

large groups of immigrants _____ from southern and eastern _____

countries. Although they were _____ different, they were assimilated

_____ the rapidly growing economy _____ the help of political _____. African-Americans, however, have had _____ difficulty assimilating. Slavery ended _____ the 1860s, but there _____ legal segregation in the _____ until the civil rights _____ of the 1960s. Although _____ progress has been made, _____ are still inequalities between _____ races. Now, new immigrants _____ Asia, the Caribbean, and _____ America are bringing both _____ and new opportunities for _____ United States, as the _____ century begins.

 E. Think, Pair, Share

Do you agree or disagree with these statements? Draw a circle around your response; then share your answers with a partner and another pair of students.

1. I would emigrate to another country if I could have a better life there for myself and my family.   **agree**   **disagree**

2. Foreigners who come from any country in the world are welcomed in my country.   **agree**   **disagree**

3. My government should encourage refugees from other countries to settle in my country.   **agree**   **disagree**

4. My family would not object if I chose to marry someone of another nationality.   **agree**   **disagree**

5. My family would not object if I chose to marry someone of another race.   **agree**   **disagree**

6. It is important to maintain your own language and cultural traditions even if you have left your country.   **agree**   **disagree**

7. People are really basically the same all over the world.   **agree**   **disagree**

8. People who are very different from the dominant culture (race, religion, or ethnic background) have as high a status as anyone else in my country.   **agree**   **disagree**

9. Every person in the world should learn to speak at least one foreign language.   **agree**   **disagree**

10. I believe that my children will have a higher standard of living than I had growing up.   **agree**   **disagree**

F. Small Group Discussion

Recent immigrant from Central America studies English **Eugene Gordon**

Unlike most countries, the United States does not have an official language. While English is widely understood to be the language of government, commerce, and most education, the people who wrote the Constitution purposely did not declare any one language as the official language. In the 1980s and 1990s, however, a number of states passed laws making English the official language of their states, and numerous bills were introduced into Congress to make English the official language of the whole nation.

1. Why do you think the founding fathers omitted the designation of an official language?

2. What are the possible consequences of one official language to speakers of other languages?

3. Do you think that most immigrants to the United States recognize the value of knowing English?

THE TOP LANGUAGES USED AT HOME (other than English)
(Total speakers over 5 years old)

	1980			1990	
1.	Spanish	11,116,194	1.	Spanish	17,345,064
2.	Italian	1,618,344	2.	French	1,930,404
3.	German	1,586,593	3.	German	1,547,987
4.	French	1,550,751	4.	Chinese	1,319,462
5.	Polish	820,647	5.	Italian	1,308,648
6.	Chinese	630,806	6.	Tagalog	843,251
7.	Philippine	474,150	7.	Polish	723,483
8.	Greek	401,443	8.	Korean	626,478

Source: Census Bureau, 1980 and 1990.

Ethnic and Racial Assimilation in the United States   163

G. Understanding Charts and Graphs: Small Group Discussion

The following chart shows some of the occupations that have high percentages of blacks, females, and Hispanics. Today, minorities make up 23 percent of the total workforce. (About 24 percent of the total population are African-Americans or Hispanics.) Women hold nearly half of the managerial and

THE JOB MARKET BY RACE AND GENDER

A look at where women and minorities have made the greatest gains in the working world the past decade, and which occupations have high percentages of females, blacks and Hispanics:

Selected occupations with high percentages of blacks:

Occupation	%
Baggage porters & bellhops	36%
Nursing aides & orderlies	29%
Barbers	28%
Correctional officers	27%
Social workers	24%
Statistical clerks	23%

Occupations experiencing large increases in the percentage of blacks over past 10 years:

Occupation	%
Airplane pilots & navigators	650%
Dentists	311%
Radio, TV, Appliance sales	188%
Civil engineers	180%
Barbers	173%
Authors	155%

Selected occupations with high percentages of females:

Occupation	%
Dental hygienists	100%
Family child-care providers	99%
Secretaries	99%
Pre-K & kindergarten teachers	98%
Licensed practical nurses	95%
Bookkeepers	92%

Occupations experiencing large increases in the percentage of females over past 10 years:

Occupation	%
Insulation workers	733%
Aerospace engineers	339%
Telephone line repairers	241%
Firefighting	200%
Forestry, logging	119%
Dentists	115%

Selected occupations with high percentages of Hispanics:

Occupation	%
Agricultural graders & sorters	59%
Supervisors, farm workers	35%
Tailors	32%
Cleaners & servants, private	31%
Butchers & meat cutters	25%
Upholsterers	25%

Occupations experiencing large increases in the percentage of Hispanics over past 10 years:

Occupation	%
Dental hygienists	1,350%
Grader, dozer operators	513%
Religious workers	508%
Financial sales	480%
Forestry, logging	417%

Note: Numbers are rounded

Source: 1994 Current Population Survey, Bureau of Labor Statistics   Analysis by Barbara Pearson, USA TODAY

professional positions but only 5 percent of the senior management positions (vice-president and above).

Answer these questions using the information on the chart on the opposite page.

1. Of the occupations with high percentages of African-Americans, which one do you think requires the most education?

2. Of the occupations with the largest increases in the percentage of blacks, which two would probably not require a college education?

3. Looking at the graphs for female workers, what generalizations can you make about the kinds of jobs that women hold in the United States? What differences are there in the percentages of women in occupations with high percentages of females compared to the occupations with high percentages of blacks and Hispanics?

4. What generalizations can you make about the kinds of jobs that are experiencing large increases in the percentages of females?

5. What generalizations can you make about the kinds of jobs that have high percentages of Hispanics?

6. How would you compare the level of education needed to do the jobs that are experiencing large increases in percentages of each of the three groups?

7. Are there any jobs in your country that are traditionally held by females? by particular ethnic groups?

New Americans studying English   **Children's Bureau, Department of Health and Human Services. Photographer: Dennis Brack**

 ## H. Ask Americans

Ask several Americans to tell you about their ethnic backgrounds.

1. What nationalities were your ancestors?

2. When did your ancestors immigrate to America?

3. Does anyone in your family still speak the language of the "old" (original) country?

4. Does your family maintain contact with any relatives in the old country?

5. What family customs or traditions from the old country do you observe?

I. Understanding Affirmative Action: Ask Americans

What should be the role of Americans today in addressing past injustices to blacks? That is a major question still being debated by many Americans today. After the Civil Rights laws were passed in the mid-1960s, the government began *affirmative action* programs to redress racial inequalities. Companies and universities were expected to take affirmative action and set quotas to recruit African-Americans into jobs and educational programs in proportion to their representation in the population. For example, if 10 percent of the population were black, then 10 percent of the employees or students should be black. Many universities offered black students scholarships and sometimes made adjustments in their admission standards to attract a larger percentage of black students.

As a result of many court cases and executive orders by Presidents Johnson and Nixon, affirmative action was extended to cover other ethnic and racial minorities and also women. So much progress has been made that many Americans now believe that affirmative action has achieved its goals. There is now a debate over the future of affirmative action. Should African-Americans and other minorities be given preferential treatment in being admitted to college, in being hired or promoted on their jobs, and in other ways? Should women be given preferential treatment?

Ask several Americans the following questions:

1. Should minorities receive special consideration in applying for admission to universities and colleges? Should women?

2. Should minorities receive preferential treatment in being hired for a job? In being promoted? Should women?

3. Are African-Americans and other minorities treated equally with whites in the United States today? Are women treated equally with men?

4. Would you vote for a qualified African-American (or member of another minority) if that person were to run for president? Would you vote for a woman?

5. All in all, do you feel that anti-minority feeling is on the rise in America today, is diminishing, or is about the same as it has been?

 J. Observing the Media

How are ethnic and racial minorities and women represented in the media? Watch national and local news broadcasts, and count the number of women and minorities reporting the news. What percentages do you find? If you are in the United States, watch TV commercials and count the racial and ethnic minorities. How do the numbers compare with the news reporters? Market research shows that most of the shopping in the United States is done by women. How are women and men pictured in ads on TV? Look at magazine ads. How many minorities do you see? How about the ratio of women to men? What conclusions can you draw from these observations?

VIEWS ON AFFIRMATIVE ACTION

More Americans approve of affirmative action programs for women . . .

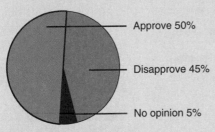

Approve 50%

Disapprove 45%

No opinion 5%

. . . than for minorities

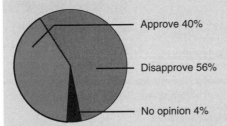

Approve 40%

Disapprove 56%

No opinion 4%

Source: The Gallup Organization's Feb 24–28 national telephone poll of 1,003 adults

THE CHANGING FACE OF THE WORKFORCE

The number of women and minorities in the workforce has grown substantially since 1964, when the Civil Rights Act was passed and affirmative action began taking hold. Much of the shift is due to changes in the economy and more households headed by women. But efforts by the government and employers have also been big factors, experts say.

1964
Total employed 69.3 million

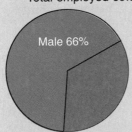

Male 66%

Race composition

White	89.3%
Black/other	10.7%

1994
Total employed 130 million

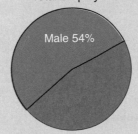

Male 54%

Race composition

White	85.5%
Black	10.4%
Hispanic	8.8%
Other races	4.1%

Note: Hispanics can be of any race.

Source: The Gallup Organization's Feb 24–28 national telephone poll of 1,003 adults

The state of black America: Gains but still lagging

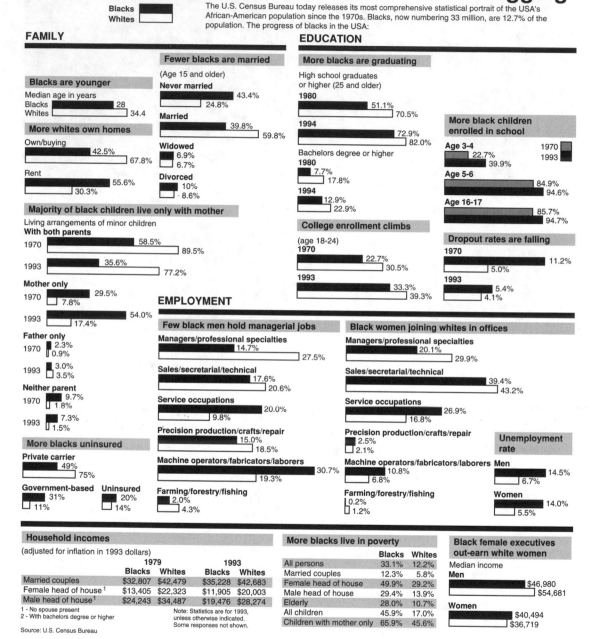

Blacks ▮
Whites ▯

The U.S. Census Bureau today releases its most comprehensive statistical portrait of the USA's African-American population since the 1970s. Blacks, now numbering 33 million, are 12.7% of the population. The progress of blacks in the USA:

FAMILY

Blacks are younger
Median age in years
Blacks — 28
Whites — 34.4

More whites own homes
Own/buying
Blacks 42.5%
Whites 67.8%
Rent
Blacks 55.6%
Whites 30.3%

Majority of black children live only with mother
Living arrangements of minor children
With both parents
1970 — 58.5% / 89.5%
1993 — 35.6% / 77.2%
Mother only
1970 — 29.5% / 7.8%
1993 — 54.0% / 17.4%
Father only
1970 — 2.3% / 0.9%
1993 — 3.0% / 3.5%
Neither parent
1970 — 9.7% / 1.8%
1993 — 7.3% / 1.5%

More blacks uninsured
Private carrier
49% / 75%
Government-based
31% / 11%
Uninsured
20% / 14%

Fewer blacks are married
(Age 15 and older)
Never married
43.4% / 24.8%
Married
39.8% / 59.8%
Widowed
6.9% / 6.7%
Divorced
10% / 8.6%

EDUCATION

More blacks are graduating
High school graduates or higher (25 and older)
1980 51.1% / 70.5%
1994 72.9% / 82.0%
Bachelors degree or higher
1980 7.7% / 17.8%
1994 12.9% / 22.9%

College enrollment climbs
(age 18-24)
1970 22.7% / 30.5%
1993 33.3% / 39.3%

More black children enrolled in school
Age 3-4 1970 22.7% / 1993 39.9%
Age 5-6 84.9% / 94.6%
Age 16-17 85.7% / 94.7%

Dropout rates are falling
1970 11.2% / 5.0%
1993 5.4% / 4.1%

EMPLOYMENT

Few black men hold managerial jobs
Managers/professional specialties 14.7% / 27.5%
Sales/secretarial/technical 17.6% / 20.6%
Service occupations 20.0% / 9.8%
Precision production/crafts/repair 15.0% / 18.5%
Machine operators/fabricators/laborers 30.7% / 19.3%
Farming/forestry/fishing 2.0% / 4.3%

Black women joining whites in offices
Managers/professional specialties 20.1% / 29.9%
Sales/secretarial/technical 39.4% / 43.2%
Service occupations 26.9% / 16.8%
Precision production/crafts/repair 2.5% / 2.1%
Machine operators/fabricators/laborers 10.8% / 6.8%
Farming/forestry/fishing 0.2% / 1.2%

Unemployment rate
Men 14.5% / 6.7%
Women 14.0% / 5.5%

Household incomes
(adjusted for inflation in 1993 dollars)

	1979 Blacks	1979 Whites	1993 Blacks	1993 Whites
Married couples	$32,807	$42,479	$35,228	$42,683
Female head of house[1]	$13,405	$22,323	$11,905	$20,003
Male head of house[1]	$24,243	$34,487	$19,476	$28,274

1 - No spouse present
2 - With bachelors degree or higher

Source: U.S. Census Bureau

Note: Statistics are for 1993, unless otherwise indicated. Some responses not shown.

More blacks live in poverty

	Blacks	Whites
All persons	33.1%	12.2%
Married couples	12.3%	5.8%
Female head of house	49.9%	29.2%
Male head of house	29.4%	13.9%
Elderly	28.0%	10.7%
All children	45.9%	17.0%
Children with mother only	65.9%	45.6%

Black female executives out-earn white women
Median income
Men $46,980 / $54,681
Women $40,494 / $36,719

© 1995 USA TODAY. Reprinted with permission.

K. Suggestions for Research and Oral Reports

1. Examine the chart on page 168 comparing blacks and whites, and find the information listed below. Then get a copy of the latest U.S. census data in a recent almanac, and find out how closely other minorities compare to whites in:
   a. annual income of two-parent families
   b. annual income of one-parent families
   c. home ownership
   d. high school graduation
   e. college attendance/graduation

2. Find out how many African-American and other minority men and women are holding political office in the United States.

3. In recent years, the United States has begun to question its open-door policy on immigration and acceptance of refugees. Look for articles in magazines and newspapers on this subject. What is the general opinion expressed in most of these articles?

 L. Suggestions for Further Reading

- Harriet Beecher Stowe, *Uncle Tom's Cabin*
- Claude Brown, *Manchild in the Promised Land*
- Eldridge Cleaver, *Soul on Ice*
- William Faulkner, *Light in August*
- Michael Novak, *The Rise of the Unmeltable Ethnics: Politics and Culture in the Seventies*
- Arthur P. Davis and Saunders Redding, Eds., *Cavalcade: Negro American Writing from 1760 to the Present*
- Lani Guinier, *The Tyranny of the Majority*
- Robert Nemiroff, *To Be Young, Gifted, and Black: A Portrait of Lorraine Hansberry In Her Own Words*
- Richard Wright, *Black Boy*
- Richard Wright, *Native Son*
- Ronald Takaki, *Strangers from a Different Shore: A History of Asian-Americans*
- Malcolm X with Alex Haley, *The Autobigraphy of Malcolm X*
- W. E. B. DuBois, *The Souls of Black Folk*
- Julia Alvarez, *How the Garcia Girls Lost Their Accents*

 M. Recommended Movies

- *Malcolm X*
- *Mississippi Burning*
- *Roots*
- *West Side Story*
- *Fried Green Tomatoes*

Graduation day at Fairleigh Dickinson University   **Ken Karp**

CHAPTER 9

Education in the United States

Americans regard education as the means by which the inequalities among individuals are to be erased and by which every desirable end is to be achieved.

George S. Counts

Before You Read

1. What do you know about the system of education in the United States? How many years do students go to school before entering college?

2. What are the differences between public and private schools in the United States?

3. What do American universities look for when admitting students? What qualities do they want the students to have?

4. What role do you think individual freedom, self-reliance, and equality of opportunity play in the educational system of the United States?

The Establishment of Public Schools in America: de Tocqueville's Observations

As might be expected, educational institutions in the United States reflect the nation's basic values, especially the ideal of equality of opportunity. From elementary school through college, Americans believe that everyone deserves an equal opportunity to get a good education.

From the beginning, when Americans established their basic system of public schools in 1825, they **reaffirmed** the principle of equality by (1) making schools open to all classes of Americans, and (2) financing the schools with tax money collected from all citizens. Those who favored these public schools believed that these institutions would help reduce social class distinctions in the United States by educating children of all social classes in the same "common schools," as they were known at the time.

When Alexis de Tocqueville arrived in the United States in 1831, he found a great deal of enthusiasm about the new and growing public elementary schools. The mayor of New York City gave a special dinner for de Tocqueville, during which a **toast** was offered in honor of "Education—the extension of our public schools—a national blessing."

Because he was a French aristocrat, de Tocqueville at first shared the fears of some wealthy Americans who believed that universal education would be a danger rather than a national blessing. He eventually decided, however, that the tendency of public education to encourage people to seek a higher status in life was in harmony with, not in conflict with, the customs of American society. The ideal of equal opportunity for all regardless of family background was much stronger in the United States than in France.

De Tocqueville also noted that American public education had a strong practical content that included the teaching of **vocational** skills and the duties of citizenship. Thus, public education not only gave Americans the desire to better themselves, but it also gave them the practical tools to do so. Moreover, the material abundance of the United States provided material rewards for those who took full advantage of the opportunity for a public education.

During the next century and a half, public schools in the United States were expanded to include secondary or high schools (grades 9–12) and colleges and universities, with both undergraduate and graduate studies.

The Educational Ladder

Americans view their public school system as an educational ladder, rising from elementary school to high school and finally college undergraduate and graduate programs. Most children start school at age five, by attending

Georgetown University, Washington, DC

kindergarten, or even at age three or four by attending pre-school programs. Then there are six years of elementary school and usually two years of middle school (or junior high school), and four years of high school. Not all school systems have kindergarten, but all do have twelve years of elementary, middle school, and senior high school. School systems may divide the twelve years up differently—grouping sixth, seventh, and eighth graders into middle school, for example. After high school, the majority of students go on to college. Undergraduate studies lead to a bachelor's degree, which is generally what Americans mean when they speak of a "college* **diploma**." The bachelor's degree can be followed by professional studies, which lead to degrees in such professions as law and medicine, and graduate studies, which lead to master's and doctoral degrees. American public schools are free and open to all at the elementary and secondary level (high school), but public universities charge tuition and have competitive entrance requirements.

The educational ladder concept is an almost perfect reflection of the American idea of individual success based on equality of opportunity and on "working your way to the top." In the United States there are no separate educational systems with a higher level of education for the wealthy and a lower

---

* The word *college* is used in several different ways. It is generally used instead of *university* to refer to the education after high school, as in the expressions "go to college," and "get a college education." It is also used to refer to the school, as in "Where do you go to college?" Often people use the word *college* to refer to a small school that does not offer graduate degrees, and *university* for large schools that offer both undergraduate and graduate degrees. Universities often call the divisions within them *colleges*, as in "the College of Arts and Sciences" of Georgetown University.

level of education for the masses. Rather, there is one system that is open to all. Individuals may climb as high on the ladder as they can. The abilities of the individuals, rather than their social class background, are expected to determine how high each person will go.

Although the great majority of children attend the free public elementary and high schools, some choose to attend private schools. There are a number of private religious schools, for example, that are associated with particular churches and receive financial support from them, though parents must also pay tuition. The primary purpose of these schools is usually to give religious instruction to children, which cannot be done in public schools. The most numerous of these, the Catholic schools, have students whose social class backgrounds are similar to the majority of students in public schools.

There are also some **elite** private schools, which serve mainly upper-class children. Students must pay such high **tuition** costs that only wealthier families can afford them. Parents often send their children to these schools so that they will associate with other upper-class children and maintain the upper-class position held by their parents, in addition to getting a good education.

Unlike private religious schools, elitist private schools do conflict with the American ideal of equality of opportunity. These schools often give an extra educational and social advantage to the young people whose families have the money to allow them to attend. However, because these schools are relatively few in number, they do not displace the public school as the central educational institution in the United States. Nor does the best private school education protect young people from competition with public school graduates for admission to the best universities in the nation.

Students graduating from a Catholic high school JoAnn Crandall

The American Ways

There is another area of inequality in the American education system. Because of the way that schools are funded, the quality of education that American students receive in public schools varies greatly. More than 90 percent of the money for schools comes from the local level (cities and counties), primarily from property taxes. School districts that have middle class or wealthy families have more tax money to spend on education. Therefore, wealthier school districts have beautiful school buildings with computers and the latest science equipment, and poorer school districts have older buildings with less modern equipment. The amount of money spent on education may vary from $7,000 per child in a wealthy suburb to only $1,200 per child attending an inner-city school, or one in a poor rural area. Although the amount of money spent per child is not always the best indicator of the quality of education the child receives, it certainly is an important factor.

Attending an American University

Money is also increasingly a factor in a college education. All university students must pay tuition expenses in the United States. Because tuition is much lower at public universities than at private ones, wealthy students have more choices. There are a number of financial aid programs in the form of loans and scholarships available at both public and private schools. However, the expenses of buying books and living away from home make it increasingly difficult for many students to attend even the less expensive public universities.

Ironically, it may be the middle-class family that suffers the most from the rising tuition costs. The family income may be too high to qualify for financial aid, but not high enough to afford the $15,000 to $35,000 per year (or more) needed for a private college education. At present, 80 percent of all college students attend public universities, where expenses are usually closer to $10,000 a year. Many students must work during their college years to help meet even these costs. A number of students who cannot afford to go away to college attend community college programs for two years in their hometowns. These two-year programs often feed into the state university systems and offer educational opportunities to large numbers of students who ordinarily would not be able to attend a university.

Despite its costs, the percentage of Americans seeking a college education continues to grow. In 1900, less than 10 percent of college-age Americans entered college. Today, over 60 percent of Americans ages 25 to 39 have taken some college courses, and over 20 percent of all Americans have attended four years or more. There are about 15 million students attending college now, about six times more than 50 years ago, and there are roughly 3,000 different colleges and universities to choose from. Today, many parents who were not able to attend college when they were young have the satisfaction of seeing their sons and daughters attend.

Even the formerly elitist private universities have yielded a great deal to public pressure for greater equality of opportunity in education. Harvard, a private university considered by many to be one of the nation's most prestigious, provides a good example. Before World War II, the majority of Harvard students

came from elite private preparatory schools. Now, the majority of them come from public high schools. As equality of opportunity came to Harvard, the competition that accompanies it also increased dramatically. Before World War II, Harvard admitted about 90 percent of those who applied. Now, Harvard admits only about 16 or 17 percent of its applicants.

The Money Value of Education

As we have seen in earlier chapters, the American definition of success is largely one of acquiring wealth and a high material standard of living. It is not surprising, therefore, that Americans value education for its **monetary** value. The belief is widespread in the United States that the more schooling people have, the more money they will earn when they leave school. The belief is strongest regarding the desirability of an undergraduate university degree, or a professional degree such as medicine or law, following the undergraduate degree. The money value of graduate degrees in "nonprofessional" fields such as art, history, or philosophy is not as great.

In recent years, there has been a change in the job market in the United States. In the past, it was possible to get a high-paying factory job without a college education. Workers with skills learned in vocational schools or on the job could do work that did not require a college education. These were among the jobs that new immigrants were often able to obtain. Increasingly, however, the advent of new technologies has meant that more and more education is required to do the work. Many of the new jobs in the United States either require a college education, even a graduate degree, or they are low-paying jobs in the service sector of the economy, such as fast-food restaurants, small stores, and hotels.

Educating the Individual

American schools tend to put more emphasis on developing critical thinking skills than they do on acquiring quantities of facts. American students are encouraged to express their own opinions in class and think for themselves, a reflection of the American values of individual freedom and self-reliance. The goal of the American education system is to teach children how to learn and to help them reach their maximum potential.

The development of social and interpersonal skills may be considered as important as the development of intellectual skills. To help students develop these other important skills, schools have added a large number of **extracurricular** activities (activities outside classroom studies) to daily life at school. These activities are almost as important as the students' class work. For example, in making their decisions about which students to admit, colleges look for students who are "well-rounded." Grades on high school courses and scores on tests like the SAT (Scholastic Aptitude Test) are very important, but so are the extracurricular activities. It is by participating in these activities that students demonstrate their special talents, their level of maturity and responsibility, their leadership qualities, and their ability to get along with others.

Some Americans consider athletics, frequently called *competitive sports*, the most important of all extracurricular activities. This is because many people believe it is important for young people, particularly young men, to learn how to compete successfully. Team sports such as football, basketball, and baseball are important because they teach students the "winning spirit." At times, this athletic competition may be carried to such an extreme that some students and their parents may place more importance on the high school's sports program than its academic offerings.

Student government is another extracurricular activity designed to develop competitive, political, and social skills in students. The students choose a number of student government officers, who compete for the votes of their fellow students in school elections. Although these officers have little power over the central decisions of the school, the process of running for office and then taking responsibility for a number of student activities if elected is seen as good experience in developing their leadership and competitive skills, and helping them to be responsible citizens.

Athletics and student government are only two of a variety of extracurricular activities found in American schools. There are clubs and activities for almost every student interest—art, music, drama, debate, foreign languages, photography, volunteer work—all aimed at helping the student to become more successful in later life. Many parents watch their children's extracurricular activities with as much interest and concern as they do their children's intellectual achievements in the classroom.

Racial Equality and Education

The most significant departure from the ideal of equality of opportunity in education has occurred in the education of African-Americans. As we saw in the previous chapter, after the Civil War in the 1860s, the southern states developed a social and legal system that segregated the former black slaves from the white population in all public **facilities**, including schools. Black people in the southern states were **prohibited** by law from attending schools with whites. Blacks had separate schools, that were inferior to the white schools by almost any measure.

In a test case in 1896, the Supreme Court of the United States stated that racial segregation in public schools and other public facilities in the southern states did not **violate** the Constitution. Equality of opportunity was such an important American value that the Supreme Court had to pretend that the separate black schools and other facilities were equal to those of whites, when everyone knew that they were not. The Supreme Court invented what is called the *separate but equal doctrine* to justify racial segregation in public schools and other public facilities in the southern states. One Supreme Court Justice strongly disagreed. Justice John Marshall Harlan believed that the decision violated the nation's highest law and its basic values. "Our Constitution is color-blind," he said, "and neither knows nor tolerates classes among its citizens."

Fifty-eight years later a more modern Supreme Court agreed with Justice Harlan. In a historic decision in 1954, it held that laws that forced black students to go to racially segregated schools violated the U.S. Constitution because such schools could never be equal. The opinion of the Court was that "to separate [black school children] from others... solely because of their race generates a feeling of inferiority... that may affect their hearts and minds in a way unlikely ever to be undone."

Although segregated schools were not legal after 1954, they continued to exist in the South until the passage of the Civil Rights bills of the mid-1960s. In the late 1960s and 1970s, a series of court decisions forced the nation to take measures to integrate all of its schools, both North and South. In the North, there had been no legal segregation of schools. However, in both the South and the North, the neighborhood schools reflected the makeup of the races who lived in the neighborhood. Thus, the residential patterns were often the source of the problem, particularly in urban areas. The public schools in the inner city were composed predominantly of African-American students and often shared the neighborhood problems of high crime rates and other forms of social disorder. These schools were clearly unequal to those in the predominantly white, middle-class neighborhoods in the suburbs.

For the next 20 years, Americans tried various methods to achieve racial balance in the public schools. The most **controversial** method used to deal with unequal neighborhood schools was the busing of school children from their home neighborhoods to schools in more distant neighborhoods in order to achieve a greater mixture of black and white children in all schools. Black children from

Children in a school bus **Stephen Capra**

the inner city were bused to schools in predominantly white middle-class neighborhoods, and students living in the middle-class neighborhoods were bused into the poorer black neighborhood schools. As a result, some children had to ride the bus for an hour each way, going to and from school. Most students did not like it, and neither did their parents. Many school districts have now abandoned **mandatory** busing, and they allow children to attend the school in their own neighborhood, even if it is predominantly black or white. Some school districts have established "magnet" schools in black neighborhoods to attract white children who want to participate in special programs offered only at the magnet school.

Three out of five American schools are still 90 percent white. In schools where African-Americans and other minorities are the majority, more than half the students come from low-income homes, in contrast to one in 25 of the majority white schools. There is no clear agreement among Americans as to whether or not busing has succeeded in increasing equal opportunity in the field of public education, although most would agree that equality is certainly a goal that should be pursued. It is doubtful that American parents would have tolerated the amount of busing that has taken place if the ideal of equality of opportunity were not so strong in the American culture.

A new question dealing with racial and ethnic equality in education was brought to the Supreme Court in the late 1970s. The question dealt with the admissions policies of professional schools, such as medical and law schools, which are attached to many of the nation's universities. Some of these schools have attempted to do more than treat all applicants equally. Many have tried in recent years to make up for past discrimination against blacks and other minorities by setting aside a certain number of places specifically for applicants from these groups, taking *affirmative action*. Schools set quotas for minimum numbers of minority students that must be admitted to their programs, even if that meant lowering somewhat the academic standards for admission of these students.

This could be seen as special treatment rather than equal opportunity. However, many professional school administrators believed that because of discrimination against these groups in the past, equality now demanded that certain limited numbers of minority students be given some extra advantage in the selection of new professional students.

These minority quotas were challenged by a white student, Allen Bakke, who was denied admission to the medical school at the University of California at Davis, California. He claimed that the medical school had admitted some nonwhite minority students less qualified than he. The U.S. Supreme Court in the famous *Bakke Case* of 1978 agreed that he had been denied an equal opportunity for admission. In a rather complicated decision, the Court held that a professional school could not set aside a certain number of places to be filled only by minority students. Such quotas were a denial of equal educational opportunity. Professional schools, however, could give some extra consideration to nonwhite minority applicants, but the Court was forbidding them to carry this practice too far.

The Increasing Responsibilities of Public Schools

Americans place the weight of many of their ideals, hopes, and problems on the nation's public school system. Some observers believe they have placed more responsibilities on the public schools than the schools can possibly handle. For example, public schools are often expected to solve student problems that result from the weakening of family ties in the United States. Rising divorce rates have resulted in an increasing number of children in the public schools who are raised by only one parent. Studies have shown that these children are more likely to have problems at school than are children raised in families with two parents.

The class graduating from high school in 2001 has many children that are "at risk" for having problems at school:

- Minority enrollment levels range from 70 percent to 96 percent in the nation's 15 largest school systems.
- One of four children live below the poverty level as childhood poverty has reached its highest level since the 1960s.
- Fifteen percent are physically or mentally handicapped.
- Fourteen percent are children of teenage mothers.
- Fourteen percent are children of unmarried parents.
- Ten percent have poorly educated, sometimes illiterate, parents.
- Between one-quarter and one-third have no one at home after school.
- Forty percent will live in broken homes [parents divorced] by the time they are 18 years old.
- Twenty-five percent or more will not finish school.

The education of new immigrant children provides the public school system with some of its greatest challenges. Many of the children come from countries where they have not had strong educational preparation, and their academic skills are below grade level. Others have come from school systems with standards similar to or more advanced than the American schools, and their academic adjustment is much easier. However, all these children must learn English. This means that they are trying to learn new concepts at the same time that they are struggling to learn a new language. Studies show that it takes five to seven years in order for them to be able to compete with English-speaking American children on an equal basis in classes where English is the language of instruction. There are some bilingual programs in areas where there is a large concentration of one language group, particularly Spanish speakers. However, in some school districts, there are children speaking anywhere from 50 to 115 different languages. It is not uncommon for a teacher to have children speaking five or six different native languages in one classroom.

At a time when enormous new **burdens** are being placed on the public schools, the nation finds itself faced with new limits on its material abundance. These limits have steadily reduced the amount of money available to the public schools as they try to deal with their rapidly growing problems.

Fort Lee High School, Fort Lee, NJ **Irene Springer**

The Standards Movement

Recently, international comparisons of education have revealed that, in general, American students do not perform as well in math, science, and other subjects as students from many other developed countries. Some believe this is because American standards for education may not be high enough. Traditionally, local community school districts have had responsibility for determining school curricula and selecting textbooks, with only limited state or national supervision. However, in the 1990s, both the states and the federal government have become more involved in determining school standards. The federal government has set national goals for education that include standards for early childhood, elementary, secondary, and adult education. Most major educational associations, such as national associations of teachers of science, or math, or language arts are also evaluating the current curricula and criteria for certification and developing new standards. To ensure that standards are met, many states now require students to pass a series of examinations in such subjects as reading, writing, mathematics, and civics before they can graduate from high school. There is also some discussion of national examinations, though that could be difficult to achieve, since Americans still believe in local control (and funding) of schools.

Multicultural Education

The changing populations of students in American schools has brought some changes in what is taught in the schools as well. Ethnic and racial minorities have criticized schools and textbooks for focusing too much on the literature and historical events of Anglo-Europeans or white males. They believe that schools have almost ignored the contributions of African-Americans, Latinos, and Native Americans. More seriously, some have charged that American history has been told from the **perspective** of Anglo-Europeans rather than exploring historical events from the various perspectives of those involved. For example, the frontier movement west has been presented more from the perspective of descendants of white settlers than from the perspectives of the descendants of the Native Americans who were moved in the process.

During the 1990s, schools began to examine seriously their curricula and to try to incorporate more varied cultural information and perspectives into education. These attempts to provide multicultural education have ranged from simply adding information and literature to the current textbooks and curricula to more sweeping attempts to **transform** the basic curriculum into one that is more reflective of the diversity of the students who will study it. At the most basic level, many schools celebrate African-American History Month or Hispanic Heritage Month, or they have international festivals that include dancing, singing, and foods from the nations from which the students have come. Many schools have adopted (1) history or social studies textbooks that include more information about African-Americans, Hispanic-Americans, and other minorities, and (2) American literature texts that include poetry and fiction written by Americans of all ethnic backgrounds. In some colleges, the traditional set of

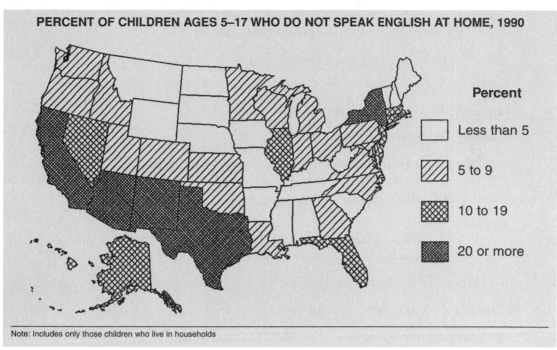

PERCENT OF CHILDREN AGES 5–17 WHO DO NOT SPEAK ENGLISH AT HOME, 1990

Percent

- Less than 5
- 5 to 9
- 10 to 19
- 20 or more

Note: Includes only those children who live in households

U.S. Department of Education; 1990 U.S. census data

Western great books, sometimes called *the canon*, has been replaced by a much broader set of literary texts, reflecting the experiences and backgrounds of the students who will be reading them.

Not all Americans support multicultural education, however. Some fear that replacing the Western civilization and literary traditions, which have been the basis of American education, with a much broader historical and literary discussion will result in **fragmentation** of American society. Schools have traditionally been the place where students of all ethnic, religious, and racial backgrounds have learned "American" history, literature, and values. With so many competing views of history or sets of values in the school, some fear that it will be difficult for the country to remain "American." It is a serious question: Can a country as diverse as the United States have schools that reflect that diversity and still retain a core national identity and culture?

■ ■ ■ ■

 New Words

reaffirm to affirm again; to state or declare again

toast an invitation to drink to honor someone or something; the words spoken before drinking

vocational preparing for (or connected with) a job

diploma an official paper showing that a person has successfully finished a course of study or passed an examination

elite serving the best or most important people in a social group

tuition money paid for instruction at a college or private school

ironically in a way that is not what would be expected

monetary having to do with money

extracurricular refers to activities outside regular academic class work (Note: *curriculum* means the course of study offered in a school. The plural is *curricula*.)

facilities a service or location provided so people can do something; public facilities include transportation services such as public buses, and places open to the public such as parks, restaurants, hotels, schools, etc.

prohibit to forbid by law; to prevent

violate to act against; to be against a law or rule

controversial causing much argument or disagreement

mandatory compulsory; something that must be done—one has no choice

burden a heavy load or responsibility; a duty that is hard to accomplish

perspective a specific point of view for making judgments

transform to change completely

fragmentation breaking or separating into small pieces

 A. Vocabulary Check

Complete the sentences using words or phrases from the New Words list.

1. In 1954, the Supreme Court ruled that segregation denied black children an equal opportunity to an education and it therefore _____ the Constitution.

2. In the past, many students who went to competitive schools such as Harvard received their high school education at _____ private schools that only the rich could afford.

3. Sports, clubs, and other _____ activities held after school help students get a well-rounded education.

4. Maintaining discipline and trying to teach children who come from broken homes and have severe problems are two of the numerous _____ the public schools are now expected to carry.

5. At a high school or college graduation ceremony, students receive their official _____.

6. Some Americans worry that if students do not study a core body of knowledge, they will not learn enough about "American" culture, and this could lead to the _____ of American society.

7. At the university level, there is no free system of public education; even universities supported by public funds charge students _____.

8. Decisions that cause people to disagree are _____.

9. Public education has many _____ problems; there never seems to be enough funding.

10. If you are asked if you still believe something and you say that you do, you are _____ your belief.

11. In order to integrate public schools, the courts ordered _____ busing; parents and children had no choice.

12. Something that is forbidden by law is _____.

13. Some Americans would like to see major changes in their public education system; they want to _____ it.

14. Before drinking an alcoholic beverage, it is customary to offer a _____ and ask people to drink in honor of someone or something.

15. Before the civil rights laws were passed, segregation of public _____ was legal in the South.

16. Those who are in favor of multicultural education believe that it is important to study history from the _____ of a number of cultures.

17. Some American high schools offer _____ education to prepare students to take jobs right after school; these students do not plan to attend college.

18. One would think that rising college costs might have the strongest effect on students from poorer families, but _____ it may be the middle-class students who are hit the hardest, since they may not be able to qualify for the financial aid they need.

B. Comprehension Check

Write the letter of the best answer according to the information in the chapter.

_____ 1. In the beginning of the chapter it is *implied* that some wealthier Americans opposed the first public schools in the United States because
    a. they cost too much money.
    b. they would weaken social class barriers.
    c. the rich believed that if people did not pay for their education, they would not value it.

_____ 2. De Tocqueville finally concluded that public education in the United States would
  - a. give Americans not only the desire but also the means to better their position in life.
  - b. not provide any practical training in vocational skills.
  - c. not work because people would have the desire to rise to a higher social class but they would be prevented from doing so by the aristocracy.

_____ 3. Which of these statements is *not* true?
  - a. American high school students have the choice of going to a free public school or a private one where they must pay tuition.
  - b. The American education system is based on strong principles of equality of opportunity—all students should have an equal opportunity to get a good education.
  - c. After 12 years of school, American students receive a bachelor's degree diploma at graduation.

_____ 4. Which of these statements *is* true?
  - a. Most of the money to pay for American public schools comes from local taxes.
  - b. Religious schools that serve middle-class students receive money from the national government, but elite private schools do not.
  - c. The national Department of Education determines the curriculum for all schools and sets the standards for high school graduation and college admission.

_____ 5. Since 1900, the percentage of young Americans who attend college has
  - a. increased enormously, from less than 10 percent to over 60 percent.
  - b. increased slightly, from about 10 percent to about 20 percent.
  - c. stayed about the same, at around 20 percent.

_____ 6. What most Americans like most about higher education is
  - a. its cultural value.
  - b. its monetary value.
  - c. its moral value.

_____ 7. Which of the following would *not* be considered an extracurricular activity?
  - a. a school baseball team
  - b. the student government of a school
  - c. a classroom research project

_____ 8. In 1896, the U.S. Supreme Court said that racially segregated schools and other public facilities
  - a. violated the principle of equality.
  - b. violated the U.S. Constitution.
  - c. did not violate the principle of equality or the U.S. Constitution.

_____ 9. Which of these statements is *not* true?

    a. Public schools that are mainly black or mainly white today usually are the result of the racial makeup of neighborhoods.

    b. Less than 50 percent of all American schools are 90 percent white.

    c. In the 15 largest school districts in the United States, at least 70 percent of the students are from nonwhite minorities.

_____ 10. Which of these statements *is* true?

    a. In the United States, all immigrant children attend bilingual programs until they learn English very well and are allowed to attend regular classes with native speakers.

    b. The "Standards Movement" has succeeded in establishing national standards for all the public schools in the United States.

    c. Multicultural education discusses history from the perspectives of all the ethnic groups involved, not just the Anglo-American.

 ## C. Questions for Discussion

1. Is education compulsory in your country? If so, how long is a child required by law to stay in school? Are there both public and private schools in your country? What are these schools like? What kind of school did you attend?

2. Are most schools in your country coeducational? Are women and men offered equal educational opportunities? Are all fields of education open to women?

3. What is the role of the teacher in your country? Is it possible for college teachers and students to be friends? Would a student ever be invited to a professor's home in your country? How strict is discipline in elementary or high schools? How do schools punish students who misbehave?

4. Are there extracurricular activities in high schools and colleges in your country? If so, what are they? Are they considered to be part of a student's education? Did you participate in nonacademic clubs or activities in high school in your country? Do universities place importance on these high school activities when admitting students?

5. Is it possible to raise your social class level by getting a college education in your country? Do universities charge tuition? How much money does it cost to get a college education? Are there any scholarships or student loans available for students who do not have enough money?

6. Are there enough universities in your country to educate most young people? Is it necessary to take a national examination to get into a university? Is there a lot of competition? Do universities take other personal qualities into account when admitting students, or do they only consider test scores? Does your government have a scholarship program to encourage students to study abroad?

D. Cloze Summary Paragraph

This paragraph summarizes the chapter. Fill in each blank with any word that makes sense.

From the time when ____*the*____ system of public education _____ established in America in _____, the ideal of equality _____ opportunity has been reaffirmed. _____ think of their public _____ system as an educational _____ that should give people _____ equal opportunity to climb _____ high as they wish. _____ though some children go _____ private schools, most attend _____ schools in their neighborhoods. _____ are many differences in _____ schools because funding comes _____ local taxes; the amount _____ money a school district _____ depends on the wealth _____ the people who are _____ the taxes. American college _____ must pay tuition to _____ all universities, even public _____ and the costs are _____. However, most Americans believe _____ can earn more money _____ they have a college _____. The American education system _____ to educate the individual, _____ students participate in extracurricular _____ to learn social skills. _____ schools face many challenges—_____ racial balance, providing better _____ for immigrant children who _____ not speak English well, _____ standards for academic achievement, _____ children from broken homes, _____ providing a multicultural education _____ all students.

E. Ask Americans

Find out how Americans feel about education. Ask several Americans the following questions, and record their answers.

1. Should there be prayer in the public school?

2. Should tax money be used to fund private schools?

3. Should poor children be given free lunches at school?

4. Should there be sex education in the schools? If so, should it be taught in elementary school, high school, or both?

5. How much exposure to drugs is there at the schools in your neighborhood? Is this a problem?

6. How important is a college education? Will it give you more status? Will you make more money with a college education?

7. Is which college you attend important, or are all colleges about the same?

8. What is the highest level of education your parents had? (What was the last grade completed or degree received?)

9. What is the highest level of education you have received? Do you expect to further your education?

F. Think, Pair, Share

What should be taught in public schools? What should be the priorities? Read the following list of areas that are covered in American schools, and decide which are the most important. Arrange the items in order from most important to least important by renumbering the sentences. Then share your list with a partner, and after that with another pair of students.

_____ 1. Developing students' moral and ethical character

_____ 2. Teaching students how to think

_____ 3. Preparing students who do not go to college for a job or career after graduation

_____ 4. Helping students to become informed citizens so that they will be adequately prepared to vote at age 18

_____ 5. Preparing students for college

_____ 6. Developing students' appreciation of art, music, and other cultural pursuits

_____ 7. Other (your opinion)

G. Small Group Discussion

Some American parents are so dissatisfied with the public schools that they are educating their children at home. "Home schooling" now provides education for about 1 percent of all children, but the trend is growing rapidly. Some public school educators agree that the current model for public schools needs to be changed, and they themselves have begun to create alternative schools, experimenting with class size, grouping, schedules, and curriculum. Perhaps most dramatic, they are transforming the roles of the teachers and the students, giving students much more power to decide what they want to learn.

Imagine that you could plan an ideal school. With your group, decide first whether it would be "home schooling" or an alternative school, and then describe your ideal school in detail. You may want to include the following points:

- Who would the students be? (age, social class, ethnicity)
- What kind of a building would you use?
- Would the school have a special emphasis? (science, music)
- What would the teachers be like? (age, experience, roles)
- Who would determine the curriculum?
- What about tests and homework?
- How would discipline be maintained?
- What would be the role of the parents?
- What special activities would the students have?
- What would a typical day be like?
- What do you think others would say about this school?

When your description is complete, share your new school with the rest of the class.

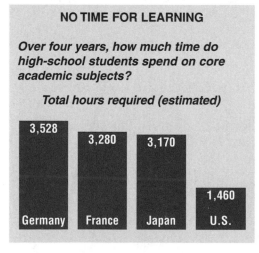

NO TIME FOR LEARNING

Over four years, how much time do high-school students spend on core academic subjects?

Total hours required (estimated)

Germany	France	Japan	U.S.
3,528	3,280	3,170	1,460

Source: Federally Funded Report
Appeared in Newsweek May 16, 1994

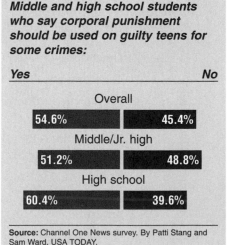

TEENS WOULDN'T SPARE THE ROD

Middle and high school students who say corporal punishment should be used on guilty teens for some crimes:

	Yes	No
Overall	54.6%	45.4%
Middle/Jr. high	51.2%	48.8%
High school	60.4%	39.6%

Source: Channel One News survey. By Patti Stang and Sam Ward, USA TODAY.

© 1995 USA TODAY. Reprinted with permission

H. People Watching

1. When is the "right" time to ask a question in an American classroom? Watch others and notice the following. (If you have difficulty finding the answers to these questions, ask a fellow student, or ask the teacher to explain when it is the right time for questions.)

   a. Is the teacher talking when students ask questions?
   b. How do students indicate that they have a question to ask?
   c. How does the teacher indicate that he or she is ready for questions?
      Does the teacher ask, "Are there any questions?"
      Does the teacher pause and look up from notes or from the blackboard?
   d. What other signals does a teacher send to indicate that questions are invited?

2. One of the most difficult things for students to understand is when an interview or an appointment with a teacher or professor is over. How do you know when the interview has ended? Watch a teacher and student in an interview or appointment, if possible, and see which of these are used to indicate that the appointment is over. If you cannot observe a teacher and student, perhaps you can watch another similar situation such as a job interview, a meeting with a counselor, or an appointment with a doctor. Look for the following:

   a. The teacher moves noticeably in the chair—maybe closer to the desk or toward the door.
   b. The teacher says, "Well…" or "It has been nice talking to you" or "I think you understand now.…"
   c. The teacher turns his or her attention to other business such as papers on the desk or a schedule of appointments.
   d. The teacher moves the chair back from the desk.

Laimute E. Druskis

I. Ask Yourself and Compare Your Answers with Americans

Schools around the world differ in their expectations of students. In some schools, students are expected only to listen and remember what their teachers say; in others, they are expected to ask questions. It's important to know these differences if you are going to be successful in a school in another country.

Answer the following questions, using **T** *(true) or* **F** *(false), to indicate how you think students should behave in your country. Record those answers in the first column. Then ask an American (preferably a student) for his or her opinion, and record those answers in a second column. What differences do you notice? Compare your answers with others in the class.*

	you	American student
1. Students should not ask questions; they should only answer them.	_____	_____
2. Students should rise when the teacher enters the classroom.	_____	_____
3. Asking a teacher questions challenges his or her authority.	_____	_____
4. Students should never address teachers by their first names.	_____	_____
5. Students should memorize everything their teachers assign; education is primarily memorizing books and teachers' lectures.	_____	_____
6. Male and female students should attend the same classes.	_____	_____

J. Suggestions for Writing and Making Oral Reports

1. Americans have always respected the few people who "worked their way through college," but now working while attending classes has become a necessity for more and more students. Because of rising tuition costs, more than 50 percent of full-time college students (between ages 16 and 24) now have to work in order to pay college expenses. (In 1972, only 35 percent held jobs.) These students work an average of 25 hours a week, while still carrying a full class schedule. What are the advantages and disadvantages of working while attending college?

2. What do you think the real value of education is? Is it monetary? Is it intellectual? Is it social? Write an essay explaining your views.

3. Many believe that there is significant gender bias in the American education system. Seventy percent of all public school teachers are female, but only 28 percent of the school principals and school superintendents (the school administrators) are female. Girls tend to get better grades in elementary and high school, but boys get more attention. Several studies have shown that teachers call on and praise boys in their classes two to three times more than girls. Some educators are now saying that separating male and female students may not be such a bad idea. Certainly women who attend all-female colleges seem to do better in the world of business. Only 4 percent of female college students graduate from women's colleges. These women make up one-third of the board members of the top businesses in the United States. List the advantages and disadvantages of females' attending coeducational schools. What advice would you give your daughter about attending college in the United States?

 ## K. Suggestions for Further Reading

- Ralph Waldo Emerson, *The American Scholar*
- Leonard Q. Ross, *The Education of Hyman Kaplan*
- Charles Silberman, *Crisis in the Classroom*
- Jonathan Kozol, *Savage Inequalities: Children in America's Schools*

 ## L. Recommended Movies

- *Stand and Deliver*
- *Mr. Holland's Opus*
- *Ferris Beuller's Day Off*
- *To Sir, with Love*

The García family celebrates graduation day at Seton Hall University   **Vivian García**

Mitchell Layton, Georgetown University Sports Information

The American Ways

CHAPTER 10

Leisure Time: Organized Sports, Recreation, and Television

The form and type of play and sports life which evolve in any group or nation mirror the development in other segments of the culture.

American Academy of Physical Education

Before You Read

1. How do you think Americans like to spend their leisure time?
2. What are the advantages and disadvantages of playing competitive sports? Why do you think Americans love American football so much?
3. What do you know about Americans' eating habits? What is "junk food"?
4. What is the impact of television on children?

Sports and American Values

Most social scientists believe that the sports that are organized by a society generally reflect the basic values of that society and attempt to strengthen them in the minds and emotions of its people. Therefore, organized sports have a more serious social purpose than spontaneous, unorganized play by individuals. This is certainly true in the United States, where the three most popular organized sports are football, basketball, and baseball. Nowhere are the ways and words of democracy better illustrated than in sports.

Organized sports are seen by Americans as an inspiring example of equality of opportunity in action. In sports, people of different races and economic backgrounds get an equal chance to excel. For this reason, notes sociologist Harry Edwards, Americans view organized sports as "a laboratory in which young men, regardless of social class, can learn the advantages and rewards of a competitive system." Although Edwards specifically mentions young men, young women also compete in organized sports without regard to their race or economic background. Women's sports are growing in popularity in the United States, and they now have more funding and support at the college level than in the past. The 1996 Olympics provided evidence of the increased interest in women's organized sports. American women won gold medals for several team sports—softball, basketball, soccer, and gymnastics.

Karen Warnock

The idea of competition is at the very heart of organized sports in the United States. Many Americans believe that learning how to win in sports helps develop the habits necessary to compete successfully in later life. This training, in turn, strengthens American society as a whole. "It is commonly held," says one sports writer, "that the competitive ethic taught in sports must be learned and **ingrained** in youth for the future success of American business and military efforts."

The competitive ethic in organized sports contains some elements of hard work—often called "**hustle**," "persistence," or "never quitting"—and of physical courage—being "tough" or having "**guts**." Slogans are sometimes used to drive home the competitive virtues for the young participants: "Hustle—you can't survive without it." "A quitter never wins; a winner never quits." "It's easy to be ordinary, but it takes guts to excel."

Amateur athletics, associated with schools and colleges, are valued for teaching young people traditional American values. Professional sports, in addition to their profit and entertainment purposes, are seen as providing an example to inspire the young to take part in organized sports. In the process of serving as an inspiration for traditional basic American values, organized sports have become part of what was referred to in Chapter 3 as "the national religion," a mixture of patriotism and national pride on the one hand with religious ideas and symbols on the other. Billy Graham, a famous American Protestant religious leader, once observed: "The Bible says leisure and lying around are morally dangerous... sports keep us busy.... There are probably more really committed Christians in sports, both collegiate and professional, than in any other occupation in America."

Competition Carried to an Extreme?

Although sports in the United States are glorified by many, there are others who are especially critical of the power of sports to corrupt when certain things are carried to excess. An excessive desire to win in sports, for example, can weaken rather than strengthen traditional American values.

Critics have pointed out that there is a long tradition of coaches and players who have done just this. Vince Lombardi, a famous professional football coach of the 1960s, was often criticized for stating that winning is the "only thing" that matters in sports. Woody Hayes, another famous football coach, once said: "Anyone who tells me, 'Don't worry that you lost; you played a good game anyway,' I just hate." Critics believe that such statements by coaches weaken the idea that other things, such as fair play, following the rules of the game, and behaving with dignity when one is defeated, are also important. Unfortunately, many coaches still share the "winning is the only thing" philosophy.

There is, however, also a tradition of honorable defeat in American sports. Sociologist Harry Edwards, for example, has pointed out that "The all-important significance of winning is known, but likewise, there is the **consoling** 'reward' of the 'honorable defeat.' Indeed, the 'sweetness' of winning is derived... from the knowledge of having defeated a courageous opponent who performed honorably."

When the idea of winning in sports is carried to excess, however, honorable competition can turn into disorder and violence. In one game, the players of two professional baseball teams became so angry at each other that the game turned into a large-scale fight between the two teams. The coach of one of the teams was happy about the fight because, in the games that followed, his team consistently won. He thought that the fight had helped to bring the men on his team closer together. Similarly, a professional football coach stated: "If we didn't go out there and fight, I'd be worried. You go out there and protect your teammates. The guys who sit on the bench, they're the losers." Both coaches seemed to share the view that if occasional fights with opposing teams helped to increase the winning spirit of their players, so much the better. Hockey coaches would probably agree. Professional hockey teams are **notorious** for the fights among players during games. Some hockey fans seem to expect this fighting as part of the entertainment.

Larry Fleming

There are some who criticize this violence in American sports, particularly football, perhaps America's favorite sport. From time to time, articles appear in newspapers or magazines such as *Sports Illustrated*, one of the nation's leading sports magazines, criticizing the number of injuries that have resulted from the extreme roughness of the game, increased by a burning desire to defeat one's opponent. Some people are particularly concerned about the injuries that high school players get in football games. The pressure to "hit hard" and win high school games is intense. In some parts of the country, especially in the South, boys start playing tackle football in elementary school, bringing the risks of competitive pressure to 9- and 10-year-olds.

Most Americans would probably say that competition in organized sports does more to strengthen the national character than to corrupt it. They believe that eliminating competition in sports and in society as a whole would lead to laziness and vice rather than hard work and accomplishment. One high school principal, for example, described the criticism of competitive sports as "the revolutionaries' attempt to break down the basic foundations upon which society is founded." Comments of this sort illustrate how strong the idea of competition is in the United States and how important organized sports are as a means of maintaining this value in the larger society.

Another criticism of professional sports is that the players and the team owners get too much money, while fans have to pay more and more for tickets to the games. Basketball, baseball, and football stars get multi-million-dollar contracts similar to rock singers and movie stars. Some have asked whether these players are athletes or entertainers. In 1994, when the baseball players went on strike during the season, history was made: for the first time in 90 years, there was no World Series. The players wanted no "cap," or limit, on the salaries they could earn; the owners refused to agree, but they also refused to reveal how much profit they make. The fans were the losers, and most people were **disgusted** by both the players and the owners. Sportscasters talked about how greed was spoiling the sport that is "as American as apple pie."

Recreation: A Time for Self-Improvement

Unlike organized sports, what is generally called **recreation** in the United States is not expected to encourage competition. For this reason, it is much more spontaneous and serves the individual's needs beyond the competitive world of work. Nevertheless, much can be learned about the values of Americans from an examination of the kinds of recreation in which they engage.

Many Americans prefer recreation that requires a high level of physical activity. This is true of the three fastest growing adult recreational sports: jogging or running, tennis, and snow skiing. It would seem that Americans carry over their belief in hard work into their world of play and recreation. The well-known expression "we like to work hard and play hard" is an example of this philosophy.

What began in the 1970s as the "physical fitness craze" has become a way of life for many. A number of people regularly work out at sports clubs—lifting

New York Marathon   **Marc P. Anderson**

weights, swimming, playing squash or racquetball, participating in aerobic exercise classes, or using exercise bikes, treadmills, rowing machines, or stair-steppers. Long-distance marathon races are so popular that the organizers often have to limit the number of people who can participate. In addition to the famous Boston and New York marathons, there are races in many other cities and even in small towns, drawing from several hundred to as many as 80,000 participants. Few of the people expect to win—most just want to finish the race. The races are usually open to all, young and old alike, even those in wheelchairs.

The high level of physical activity enjoyed by many Americans at play has led to the observation that Americans have difficulty **relaxing**, even in their leisure time. Yet the people who enjoy these physical activities often say that they find them very relaxing mentally because the activity is so different from the kind of activity they must do in the world of work, often indoor office work involving mind rather than body.

The interest that Americans have in self-improvement, traceable in large measure to the nation's Protestant heritage (see Chapter 3), is also carried over into their recreation habits. It is evident in the joggers who are determined to improve the distance they can run, and in the people who spend their vacation time learning a new sport such as sailing or deep-sea diving. The self-improvement motive, however, can also be seen in many other popular forms of recreation that involve little or no physical activity.

Interest and participation in cultural activities, which improve people's minds or skills, are also popular. Millions of Americans go to symphony concerts, attend

American Ballet Theater

The American Ways

live theater performances, visit museums, hear lectures, and participate in artistic activities such as painting, performing music, and dancing. Many Americans also enjoy hobbies such as weaving, needlework, candle making, wood carving, and other **handicrafts**. Community education programs offer a wide range of classes for those interested in anything from "surfing the net" (using the computer Internet) to gourmet cooking, learning a foreign language, writing, art, self-defense, and birdwatching.

The recreational interests of Americans also show a continuing respect for the self-reliance, and sometimes the adventure and danger, of frontier life. While some choose safe pastimes such as handicrafts, gardening, or "do-it-yourself" projects like building bookcases in their den, others are ready to leave home and take some risks. By the mid-1990s, *Newsweek* magazine noted that adventure travel had grown to "an $8 billion business, perhaps as much as a fifth of the U.S. leisure travel market." Millions of Americans have bought mountain bikes to explore the wilderness on their own. Many others are choosing to go white-water rafting, mountain climbing, rock climbing, sky diving, helicopter skiing, and bungee jumping. U.S. park officials complain about the number of people who take life-threatening risks in national parks and have to be rescued. "It is as if they are looking for hardship," one park official stated. "They seem to enjoy the danger and the physical challenge."

Not all Americans want to "rough it" while they are on their adventure holidays, however. *Newsweek* reports that there are a number of travelers in their 40s who want "soft adventure." Judi Wineland, who operates Overseas Adventure Travel says, "Frankly, it's amazing to us to see baby boomers seeking creature comforts." On her safari trips to Africa, she has to provide hot showers, real beds, and night tables. The American love of comfort, mentioned in Chapter 5, seems to be competing with their desire to feel self-reliant and adventurous.

Health and Fitness

Not all Americans are physically fit, or even try to be. The overall population is becoming heavier, due to poor eating habits and a **sedentary** lifestyle. Some studies estimate that less than half of Americans exercise in their leisure time. Experts say that it is not because Americans "don't know what's good for them"—they just don't do it. Compared to the beginning of the 1980s, three-quarters of Americans in the 1990s say that physical fitness is more important to them now than it was then. But the National Center for Health Statistics reports that the number of people who are at least 20 percent over their desirable weight has risen from one in four to one in three Americans.

Newspapers and magazines are full of information on nutrition and proper diet. Television news programs urge people to eat more vegetables and warn of the dangers of high-fat diets and high cholesterol levels—particularly heart disease and certain types of cancer. Since 1994 the government has required uniform labeling so that consumers can compare the fat and calories in the food they buy. Grocery stores are full of low-fat or fat-free cookies, crackers, bread, milk, margarine, mayonnaise, and even potato chips. Many Americans have switched to skim milk, but they still buy fancy, fat-rich ice cream. More than half of Americans say that they pay attention to the nutritional content of the food they eat, but they also say they eat what they really want whenever they feel like it. As one American put it, "Let's face it—if you're having chips and dip as a snack, fat-free potato chips and fat-free sour cream just don't taste as good as the real thing."

Experts say that it is a combination of social, cultural, and psychological factors that determine how people eat. A *Newsweek* article on America's weight problems refers to "the culture of **over-indulgence**

Nutrition Facts

Serving Size 1 Bag (21 g)

Amount Per Serving	
Calories 110 Calories from Fat 50	

	% Daily Value*
Total Fat 6g	9%
Saturated Fat 1.5g	8%
Cholesterol 0 mg	0%
Sodium 270mg	11%
Total Carbohydrate 13g	4%
Dietary Fiber 0g	0%
Sugars 1g	
Protein 1g	

Vitamin A 0%	●	Vitamin C 0%	
Calcium 0%	●	Iron	0%

* Percent Daily Values are based on a 2,000 calorie diet. Your daily values may be higher or lower depending on your calorie needs:

		Calories:	2,000	2,500
Total Fat	Less than		65g	80g
Sat Fat	Less than		20g	25g
Cholesterol	Less than		300mg	300mg
Sodium	Less than		2,400mg	2,400mg
Total Carbohydrate			300g	375g
Dietary Fiber			25g	30g

Calories per gram:
Fat 9   ●   Carbohydrate 4   ●   Protein 4

seemingly ingrained in American life. The land of plenty seems destined to include plenty of pounds as well," they conclude. Part of the problem is that Americans eat larger **portions** and often go back for second helpings, in contrast to how much people eat in many other countries. Another factor is Americans' love of fast food. Some estimates are that 50 percent of Americans eat pizza once every two weeks, a percentage that is no doubt quite a bit higher among high school and college students. Americans are consuming more and more hamburgers, french fries, and soft drinks at restaurants, not only because they like them but also because these foods are often the cheapest items on the menu. Another significant factor is Americans' busy lifestyle. Since so many women are working, families are eating a lot of fast food, frozen dinners, and restaurant "takeout." Some experts believe that Americans have really lost control of their eating; it is not possible to limit fat and calories when they eat so much restaurant and packaged food. It takes time to prepare fresh vegetables and fish; stopping at KFC (Kentucky Fried Chicken) on the way home from work is a much faster alternative. Often American families eat "on the run" instead of sitting down at the table together.

The Impact of Television

Ironically, as Americans have gotten heavier as a population, the image of a beautiful woman has gotten much slimmer. Marilyn Monroe would be overweight by today's media standards. Television shows and commercials feature actresses who are very **slender**. Beer and soft drink commercials, for example, often feature very thin girls in bikinis. As a result, many teenage girls have become insecure about their bodies and **obsessed** with losing weight. Eating disorders such as anorexia and bulimia are now common among young women.

Another irony is that although television seems to promote images of slender, physically fit people, the more people watch TV, the less likely they are to exercise. Television has a strong effect on the activity level of many Americans. Some people spend much of their free time lying on the couch watching TV and eating junk food. They are called "couch potatoes," because they are nothing but "eyes." (The small marks on potatoes are called "eyes.") Couch potatoes would rather watch a baseball game on TV than go play softball in the park with friends or even go to a movie. Cable and satellite TV bring hundreds of stations into American homes. By the mid-1990s, 60 percent of all homes had cable TV, offering an average of 50 to 100 channels 24 hours a day, and satellite dishes were becoming popular. (Satellite TV can bring in as many as 500 channels.) Many of the American TV channels are specialized—the weather channel, home shopping, CNN and other news networks, ESPN (sports), MTV (Music TV), HBO (Home Box Office), and various other movie channels, to name a few.

With so many programs to choose from, it is not surprising that the average family TV set is on six hours a day, and estimates are that children are watching TV programs and videotapes an average of four or five hours a day. Many adults are worried about the impact of so much television on the nation's children. They are not getting as much exercise as they should, but the effect on their bodies may not be as serious as the effect on their minds. Many children do not spend enough time reading, educators say. And some studies have shown that excessive watching of television by millions of American children has lowered their ability to achieve in school.

One effect of watching so much TV seems to be a shortening of children's **attention span**. Since the advent of the remote control device and the **proliferation** of channels, many watchers like to "graze" from one program to the next, or "channel surf"—constantly clicking the remote control to change from channel to channel, stopping for only a few seconds to see if something catches their attention.

And what do children see? Too much sex and violence, most Americans would say. In a recent study, 72 percent said that they believed there was too much violence on television. The American Psychological Association estimates that the average child will witness 8,000 made-for-TV murders before finishing elementary school. Children are also exposed to sexual situations on TV that are much more **explicit** than they were a generation ago. Some of the most popular TV shows feature their characters in stories about sex outside of marriage, or even unmarried characters choosing to have a baby. Many Americans worry about the effect of explicit sex (and violence) on the moral values of the young.

As an alternative, public television provides many educational shows, but most people, including children, spend the majority of their viewing time watching commercial television. In 1990, Congress passed a law requiring the entertainment industry to improve the quality of programs directed at children on commercial television. Unfortunately, most experts would probably say that the '90s brought few positive changes in children's programming. Indeed, some studies have discovered that there are even more violent acts committed on children's shows, many of them by cartoon characters, than there are on adult shows.

Some argue that parents are responsible for supervising their children's TV viewing. But how? Children are often watching television when their parents are either not in the room or even at home. In 1996, Congress, President Clinton, and entertainment executives began to explore the possibility of rating TV programs for their violent content. They planned for new TV sets to be equipped with a "V chip" that will be programmed to block the reception of programs unsuitable for children. Many parents think they can use the help in monitoring what their children see. The reality is that one in four families is headed by a single parent, and in two-thirds of two-parent families, both parents are working. Furthermore, nearly 50 percent of children between the ages of 6 and 17 have their own TV sets in their bedrooms. The possession of their own TV is an indication of both the material wealth and the individual freedom that many children have in the United States. We will explore these issues more in the next chapter.

The popularity of home computers and "surfing the net"—seeing what is on the Internet and the World Wide Web—has brought a whole new world of leisure-time activities to Americans. Some value the enormous educational opportunities it brings, while others prefer spending their time in "chat rooms" (having discussions with others "on-line"), communicating with friends or family via "E-mail," or playing the latest computer games. Computers are also extremely popular with children and teenagers, and this of course raises questions of where they are traveling on the net or the web and what they are seeing. Now parents have to worry about monitoring the computer in addition to monitoring the TV.

Leisure time in the United States offers something for everyone; the only complaint that most Americans have is that they do not have enough of it. Americans, like people everywhere, sometimes choose recreation that just provides rest and relaxation. Watching television, going out for dinner, and visiting friends are simply enjoyable ways to pass the time. As we have seen, however, millions of Americans seek new challenges involving new forms of effort even in their leisure time. "Their reward," states *U.S. News and World Report*, "is a renewed sense of **vitality**," a sense of a goal conquered and confidence regained in dealing with life's ups and downs.

■ ■ ■ ■

Roxane Fridirici

 **New Words**

ingrained fixed deep inside so that it is difficult to get out or destroy

hustle aggressive hard work

guts courage; determination

consoling giving comfort or sympathy to someone in times of disappointment or sadness

notorious known or famous for being or doing something bad

disgusted having a strong feeling of dislike caused by something unpleasant or by bad behavior

recreation amusement; a way of spending free time

relax to become less active and stop worrying; to unwind; to rest; to become less tight

handicrafts things made by hand

sedentary sitting a lot; not moving around much; lacking physical exercise

over-indulgence doing too much of something; eating or drinking too much (Note: *over* as a prefix means to do too much. *Indulge* is to give yourself permission to do something that you like to do, perhaps something that you know is not really good for you.)

portion the amount of each food on your plate; the quantity of food served to a person at a restaurant

slender thin, slim; not fat

obsessed thinking about something over and over, unable to get it our of your mind; worrying about something continuously and unnecessarily

attention span the amount of time you can concentrate on something before you lose interest or your attention wanders and you start thinking about or doing something else; the length of time a person's attention continues

proliferation a rapid increase in numbers; growing fast or spreading

explicit clear; expressed fully; shown in such a way that nothing is left to the imagination

vitality life; forcefulness of character or manner; energy and enthusiasm

A. Vocabulary Check

Fill in the crossword puzzle with words from the New Words list.

Across

2. the time spent concentrating on something
4. to rest, have fun
5. what you have to do to succeed in sports
7. life; enthusiasm
9. too much of a good thing
14. famous for something bad
16. sitting around not exercising
17. activities you do in your free time

Down

1. thinking about something constantly
3. everything is shown clearly
5. some things you make by hand
6. increasing quickly
8. has become a habit or belief deep inside
10. strongly disliked something
11. fearlessness; daring
12. a helping of food
13. comforting someone
15. thin

B. Comprehension Check

Write the letter of the best answer according to the information in the chapter.

_____ 1. Organized sports in a society
   a. are a poor reflection of the values of that society.
   b. are a good reflection of the values of that society.
   c. are leisure activities and games that tell us very little about the social values of a country.

_____ 2. Which of the following ideals is *at the very heart* of organized sports in the United States and is therefore the most important ideal expressed in organized sports?
   a. self-reliance
   b. self-denial
   c. competition

_____ 3. Which of these statements is *not* true?
   a. Billy Graham, a Protestant religious leader, has criticized American football for being too violent.
   b. Most Americans would probably agree that organized sports are an important way for young people to learn to compete.
   c. Organized sports are an example of the "national religion," the mixing of national pride and religious values.

_____ 4. Vince Lombardi, a famous professional football coach, expressed the view that
   a. sports help boys grow into men.
   b. a good football player makes a good soldier.
   c. winning is the only thing that matters.

_____ 5. Respected publications such as *Sports Illustrated* have stated that
   a. sports are good in general, but excessive violence in sports should be stopped.
   b. sports corrupts the American spirit and should be replaced with noncompetitive activities.
   c. many aspects of American culture, such as music and art, have been replaced by the love of sports.

_____ 6. Some of the fastest growing forms of recreation in the United States, such as jogging, reflect the attitude that
   a. a healthy body helps to maintain a healthy mind.
   b. contact with nature is good for the soul.
   c. it is good to work hard and to play hard.

_____ 7. Which of these statements is *not* true?
   a. Many Americans like to spend their leisure time learning new skills in order to improve themselves.

    b. The American respect for self-reliance can be
       popularity of "adventure travel," where people
       "rough it."

    c. Because of their active lifestyles, the number c
       weigh more than they should is decreasing.

_____ 8. According to the chapter, why do so many Americans have poor
      eating habits?
       a. They are unaware of the dangers of high-fat diets.
       b. The foods that they buy in the stores have no labels that give
          nutritional information.
       c. They are too busy to cook, and they eat a lot of fast food.

_____ 9. Which of these statements is *not* true?
       a. The majority of American homes have TV systems that can
          get 50 channels or more.
       b. Most Americans have such a busy lifestyle that they watch
          very little TV.
       c. American children watch a lot of television, and many even
          have their own TV in their room.

_____ 10. Which of these statements *is* true?
       a. Most Americans are not concerned about the level of violence
          on television.
       b. "Channel surfing" may lower a child's attention span.
       c. Children's television programs are educational and have
          much less violence than adult programs.

 C. Questions for Discussion

1. What organized sports are popular in your country? soccer? American-style
football? basketball? volleyball? baseball? hockey? Did you play any of these
in high school or college? Do boys and girls play the same sports? Can you
see college sports on TV, or only professional teams? Are sports used to
teach competition or cooperation?

2. What are popular forms of recreation in your country? running and jogging?
hiking? skiing? tennis? handicrafts? gardening? camping? How much
interest in cultural activities is there? What was the last cultural event that
you attended? What do you like to do in your leisure time? Do you think
leisure time is a good opportunity for self-improvement, or is it better to
just relax?

3. How would you compare the day-to-day level of physical activity of
people in your country with that of Americans? Do people in your
country walk or ride bicycles as often as they drive? What do you do to
keep physically fit?

4. How much concern do people in your country have about nutrition and eating a healthy diet? Do foods have labels that list the number of calories, the fat content, and other nutritional information? What is the daily diet like in your country?

5. Is there much sex and violence on television in your country? Is there much talk about possible harmful effects of television on children? How much TV did you watch when you were a child? What effect do you think that TV had on you? How many TV channels do most homes in your country get? What has your experience with computers been? Have you tried "surfing the net"?

 D. **Cloze Summary Paragraph**

This paragraph summarizes the chapter. Fill in each blank with any word that makes sense.

Organized sports in the ___United___ States reflect the values _____ the American people. Americans _____ in equality of opportunity _____ sports, but competition is _____ most important value. They _____ that participation in sports _____ healthy and important because _____ teaches young people how _____ compete successfully. The emphasis _____ winning can sometimes lead _____ violence in sports. Many _____ view their leisure time _____ an opportunity for self-improvement, _____ they frequently seek recreational _____ such as running, tennis, _____ skiing, which require a _____ level of physical activity. _____ and artistic activities are _____, and many Americans like _____ attend community education classes. _____ travel and do-it-yourself projects _____ some Americans a feeling _____ self-reliance. However, many Americans _____ not get enough exercise, _____ many have poor eating _____. Although they know high-fat _____ are bad for them, _____ eat too much fast _____ and portions that are _____ big. Couch potatoes watch _____ lot of TV, and _____ children do, too. Many _____ worry about the sex _____ violence that children see. _____ many parents work, it _____ difficult to supervise what _____ watch. Although all Americans do _____ to rest and relax, _____ spend some of their _____ time in activities that _____ them.

E. Think, Pair, Share

How do you prefer to spend your leisure time? Read the following list of leisure-time activities and decide which things you enjoy most. Imagine that you had a whole weekend free and you could spend it doing any of the activities on the list. What would you most like to do? List that as number 1. Put the rest of the items in order of importance of things you would like to do on your free weekend. Share your list with your partner and then with another pair of students.

_____ 1. Go on a hike
_____ 2. Read a good book
_____ 3. See a movie
_____ 4. Play tennis
_____ 5. Work on your car
_____ 6. Have dinner at a nice restaurant
_____ 7. Watch TV
_____ 8. Go to a friend's house
_____ 9. Have a friend visit you

_____ 10. Go swimming
_____ 11. Listen to records
_____ 12. Attend a concert
_____ 13. Have a family picnic
_____ 14. See a play
_____ 15. Visit a museum
_____ 16. Go shopping
_____ 17. Go to a game
_____ 18. Other (you name it)

F. Ask Americans

Interview several Americans of different ages and ask them the following questions about TV. Record their answers.

1. On an average day, about how much time do you spend watching TV?

2. Do you think you spend too much time or too little time watching television?

3. How would you describe your feelings overall about the television programming now being offered? Would you say that you are very satisfied, somewhat satisfied, somewhat dissatisfied, or very dissatisfied?

4. As far as sexually oriented material on television is concerned, do you think there is far too much, somewhat too much, about the right amount, somewhat too little, or far too little?

5. There has been a good deal of discussion lately about television programs that show violence—that is, gunplay, fist fights, and the like. Do you think there is a relationship between violence on TV and the crime rate in the United States?

6. Here are some statements about TV commercials. For each statement, please tell me whether you agree or disagree.
   • Commercials are a fair price to pay for the entertainment you get.
   • Commercials are (generally/ordinarily) in poor taste and very annoying.
   • I prefer to watch shows without commercials, even if I have to pay for them.
   • I don't mind commercials because they give me time to go to the kitchen to get something to snack on.

 G. Test a Hypothesis: Small Group Work

Some people say that Americans don't have any culture. By that they probably mean that the United States has not been a country long enough to have developed its own art forms, traditions, music, dance, or theater—what we usually refer to as the fine arts.

Let's test that hypothesis. If you are living in the United States, find out about your local community. Are there libraries? Museums? Theaters where concerts and plays are performed? Check the entertainment section of your local newspaper to see if any of the following are scheduled:

• Ballets or other dance performances
• Art or other exhibitions
• Symphony concerts

- Other concerts or musical performances
- Lectures
- Operas
- Plays

Are the performers or the artists Americans, or are they from another country? Are they performing works created by an American, or someone from another country? For example, if there is a play scheduled, is it being performed by American actors? Was the play written by an American playwright?

Make a list of these performances or exhibitions, and indicate the nationality of both the artist who is performing the work and the artist who created it. What do you conclude?

 ## H. Suggestions for Research and Oral Reports

1. One weekend ritual among American homeowners is taking care of the lawn—seeding it, weeding it, mowing it. Some would say that Americans have an obsession with having a beautiful lawn. Consider the following facts about the United States:

Maryanne Kearny Datesman

- Lawns occupy more land than any single crop, including wheat, corn, or tobacco.
- In Western cities, as much as 60 percent of water is used for lawns, and as much as 30 percent in Eastern cities.
- Of the 34 major pesticides commonly used on lawns, 32 have not been tested for their long-term effects on humans and the environment.

Look through home and garden magazines for articles and advertisements about lawn care. What products are advertised? What advice is given about caring for the lawn? What do you think about all this? Is there such an emphasis on lawns in your country? What is the impact on the environment?

2. Look in American newspapers and magazines for articles on health, nutrition, and physical fitness. List the titles of the articles you find. What are Americans concerned about today? How does this compare to your country? Visit an American grocery store and list the "low-fat," "fat-free," "reduced fat or calories," "light," and "diet" products. What color are many of the packages?

3. Some visitors to the United States are surprised to find that many public places are "non-smoking" areas and that some Americans are almost hostile to smokers. In most American restaurants, you will be asked, "Smoking or "non-smoking?"—indicating which section of the restaurant you wish to sit in. Recently, the U.S. government has published studies of the dangers of "second-hand smoke"—lung cancer, respiratory infections, and asthma, especially for children whose parents smoke at home. Many state and local governments have passed laws that prohibit smoking in most workplaces and public buildings, forcing people to go outside to smoke. Whose rights should be protected—the smokers, or the non-smokers? Write your opinions in an essay about whether or not smoking should be banned in the workplace and other public buildings.

4. Do you think that adults should prevent children from watching movies or television programs that show explicit sex or violence? If so, whose responsibility is it? Parents? Those who create the movies and TV shows? The government? Write an essay about how society should deal with this issue, or have a class debate.

 I. Ask Americans / Ask Yourself

The weekend is traditionally considered the time to forget the week's work and to have fun. Many Americans even refer to their Friday night's activities as TGIF. See if you can find out what TGIF means. Ask Americans what this stands for and what it means to them. Then ask them the following question, and compare their answers with the poll that follows.

Here is a list of things some people look for in their leisure activities. Please read down the list and for each one tell me how important it is to you in your leisure activities—very important, somewhat important, not too important, or not at all important?

- Amusement/entertainment
- The chance to learn new things
- Companionship
- Creativity
- Cultural enrichment
- Excitement

- Exercise
- Having time to yourself
- Help other people
- Meet new people
- Relaxation
- Spend time with your family

Question: Now I'll give you a list of things some people look for in their leisure activities. Please read down the list and for each one tell me how important it is to you in your leisure activities—very important, somewhat important, not too important, or not at all important?

Very important to you in your leisure activities

Spend time with your family	65%
Relaxation	58%
Companionship	56%
Having time to yourself	55%
The chance to learn new things	37%
Amusement/entertainment	33%
Help other people	32%
Creativity	29%
Meet new people	26%
Exercise	25%
Excitement	24%
Cultural enrichment	20%

Source: Survey by the Roper Organization (*Roper Reports* 93–10), October 16–23, 1993.

What would Americans do if they had four extra hours each day? Ask several Americans the following question and compare their answers with the poll. What would *you* do with four extra hours a day?

Question: I'd like you to imagine a situation in which you had four extra hours every day to do whatever you wanted to do. Which two or three of these things do you think you would do more of with those extra four hours?

Would do more of with four extra hours a day

Reading	32%
Spending more time with family	29%
Exercising or playing sports	15%
Sleeping	15%
Watching television	13%

Note: Not all categories shown.
Source: Surveys by the Roper Organization (*Roper Reports* 93–5), April 17–24, 1993.

J. Understanding a Map

*Look at the following consumer map that shows where jogging is popular, and read the explanation. Decide whether the statements that follow are true or false. Write **T** for true or **F** for false.*

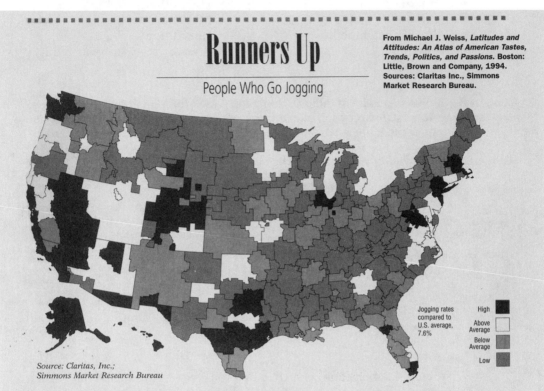

Runners Up

People Who Go Jogging

From Michael J. Weiss, *Latitudes and Attitudes: An Atlas of American Tastes, Trends, Politics, and Passions.* Boston: Little, Brown and Company, 1994. Sources: Claritas Inc., Simmons Market Research Bureau.

Jogging rates compared to U.S. average, 7.6%

High
Above Average
Below Average
Low

Source: Claritas, Inc.; Simmons Market Research Bureau

THE running revolution that erupted in the 1970s today has slowed to a walk as bad-kneed baby boomers have settled into middle age and cellulite. But a hearty corps of Americans still lace up their Nikes to jog along streets, ravines, and school tracks, and not all are brawny jocks or student athletes, cutting class for an afternoon jaunt. In fact, there's plenty of evidence that the majority of the nation's joggers are workaholic professionals who want a quick, high-aerobic form of exercise that can be squeezed into their time-compressed schedules.

As the map above shows, joggers tend to live in areas where they can run year-round, either outdoors in Sunbelt communities —

like Houston or San Diego — or in the nation's big cities, where abundant health clubs and Ys offer indoor tracks. The highest proportion are college-educated singles in their twenties and thirties who hold well-paying jobs in business, finance, or entertainment services.

Although jogging does not carry the same cachet as, say, sailing or skiing — writer Alison Lurie defined a high-status sport as one "that requires a great deal of expensive equipment or an expensive setting or both" — joggers are more likely to play upper-middle-class sports like tennis and racquetball rather than pursue such proletariat activities as bowling and billiards. Indeed, when they're not doing laps

after work, joggers are a fairly civilized lot, enjoying jazz, theater, and gourmet cooking. By contrast, the nation's sedentary souls in the map's dark gray areas spend more of their time watching TV; their idea of exercise is gardening or fishing.

While jogging critics may think that all that roadwork is excessive if not downright obsessive, joggers counter that they run to maintain their equilibrium. One poll found that their favorite food was not popcorn or yogurt, as one might expect, but high-fat, artery-hardening ice cream. Joggers are heavy consumers of Ben & Jerry's, Häagen-Dazs, and Frusen Gladje, reflecting their ethic: Work hard, run hard, eat guilt-free.

_____ 1. Joggers are usually very busy people who want to get a lot of exercise in a short amount of time.

_____ 2. Jogging is only popular in areas of the country that have a year-round warm climate.

_____ 3. There are a higher than average number of joggers in New York City, Boston, Washington, D.C., San Francisco, Los Angeles, Chicago, Miami, and Houston.

_____ 4. Most big cities have clubs where people can run indoors.

_____ 5. Jogging is a high-status sport in the United States.

_____ 6. Most joggers watch a lot of TV and enjoy gardening and fishing.

_____ 7. Some people think that joggers are obsessive about running.

_____ 8. Joggers are very careful about what they eat and they avoid high-fat foods such as gourmet ice cream.

 K. Suggestions for Further Reading

- Jim Bouton, *Ball Four*
- Jerry Kramer and Dick Schaap, *Distant Replay*
- George Plimpton, *The Paper Lion*
- J. W. Loy, Jr., and G. S. Kenyon, Eds., *Sport, Culture and Society*
- Michael Novak, *The Joy of Sports*
- Ernest Hemingway, "The Short, Happy Life of Francis Macomber"
- Frank Deford, *Arthur Ashe: Portrait in Motion*

 L. Recommended Movies

- *Hoop Dreams*
- *Field of Dreams*
- *The Natural*

Leisure Time: Organized Sports, Recreation, and Television   **217**

Rhoda M. Sommer, her husband Donald Friedman, and their children Aaron and Whitney   **Rhoda M. Sommer**

CHAPTER 11

The American Family

The American has fashioned anew the features of his family institutions, as he does everything else about him.

Max Lerner

Before You Read

1. Who lives in a typical American household?
2. What changes have occurred in the American family since the 1950s?
3. How have the traditional American values affected family relationships?
4. What are "family values"?

Family Structures

What is the typical American family like? If Americans are asked to name the members of their families, family structure becomes clear. Married American adults will name their husband or wife and their children, if they have any, as their "immediate family." If they mention their father, mother, sisters, or brothers, they will define them as separate units, usually living in separate households. Aunts, uncles, cousins, and grandparents are considered "extended family."

The structure of the American family has undergone enormous changes since the 1950s. Traditionally, the American family has been a nuclear family, consisting of a husband, wife, and their children, living in a house or apartment. Grandparents rarely live in the same home with their married sons and daughters, and uncles and aunts almost never do.

In the 1950s, 70 percent of American households were the "classic" American family—a husband, wife, and two children. The father was the "breadwinner" (the one who earned the money to support the family), the mother was a "homemaker" (the one who took care of the children and did not work outside the home), and they had two children under the age of 18. If you say the word "family" to Americans, this is probably the picture that comes to their minds.

Yet, in reality, in the 1990s, only 8 percent of American households consist of a working father, a stay-at-home mother, and two children under 18. An additional 18 percent of households consist of two parents who are both working and one or more children under the age of 18 living at home. That means that a total of only 26 percent of households in the United States consist of two parents and their children. The remaining households consist of the following: 30 percent are married couples without children; 8 percent are single parents and their children; 11 percent are unmarried couples and others living together. And, perhaps most startling, in 25 percent of the households, there is someone living alone.

What has happened to the traditional American family, and why? Some of the explanation is **demographic**. In the 1950s, men who had fought in World War II had returned home, married, and were raising their families. There was a substantial increase (or "boom") in the birth rate, producing the "baby boomers." A second demographic factor is that today young people are marrying and having children later in life. Some couples now choose not to have children at all. A third factor is that people are living longer after their children are grown, and they often end up alone. And, of course, there is a fourth factor—the high rate of divorce. But numbers alone cannot account for the dramatic changes in the family. Understanding the values at work in the family will provide some important insights.

The Emphasis on Individual Freedom

Americans view the family as a group whose primary purpose is to advance the happiness of individual members. The result is that the needs of each individual take **priority** in the life of the family. In contrast to that of many other cultures, the primary responsibility of the American family member is not to advance the family as a group, either socially or economically, nor is it to bring honor to the family name. This is partly because the United States is not an aristocratic society.

Family name and honor are less important than in aristocratic societies, since equality of opportunity regardless of birth is considered a basic American value. Moreover, there is less emphasis on the family as an economic unit because the American family is rarely self-supporting. Relatively few families maintain self-supporting family farms or businesses for more than one generation. A farmer's son, for example, is very likely to go on to college, leave the family farm, and take an entirely different job in a different location.

The American desire for freedom from outside control clearly extends to the family. Americans do not like to have controls placed on them by other family members. They want to make independent decisions and not be told what to do by grandparents or uncles or aunts. For example, both American men and women expect to decide what job is best for them as individuals. Indeed, young Americans are encouraged by their families to make such independent career decisions. What would be best for the family is not considered to be as important as what would be best for the individual.

A June wedding at Chautauqua, NY **Trish Mortellaro**

Marriage and Divorce

Marriages are not "arranged" in the United States. Young people are expected to find a husband or wife on their own; their parents do not usually help them. In fact, parents are frequently not told of marriage plans until the couple has decided to marry. This means that parents have little control, and generally not much influence, over whom their children marry. Americans believe that young people should fall in love and then decide to marry someone they can live happily with, again evidence of the importance of an individual's happiness. Of course, in reality this does not always happen, but it remains the ideal, and it shapes the views of **courtship** and marriage among young Americans.

Over the years, the value placed on marriage itself is determined largely by how happy the husband and wife make each other. Happiness is based primarily on companionship. The majority of American women value companionship as the most important part of marriage. Other values, such as having economic support and the opportunity to have children, although important, are seen by many as less important.

CATCHING UP

Divorces per 100 marriages 25 years ago and at last report

	1970	LATEST
UNITED STATES	42.3	54.8
SWEDEN	23.4	44.1
DENMARK	25.1	44.0
ENGLAND, WALES	16.2	41.7
CANADA	18.6	38.3
FRANCE	12.0	31.5
HUNGARY	25.0	31.0
NETHERLANDS	11.0	28.1
GREECE	5.0	12.0
ITALY	5.0	8.0

USN & WR Basic Data—The Population Council, June 1995

If the couple is not happy, the individuals may choose to get a divorce. A divorce is relatively easy to obtain in most parts of the United States. Most states have "no-fault" divorce. To obtain a no-fault divorce, a couple states that they can no longer live happily together, that they have "**irreconcilable differences**," and that it is neither partner's fault.

The divorce rate rose rapidly in the United States after the 1950s, but it had leveled off by the 1990s. Approximately one out of every two marriages now ends in divorce. Often children are involved. The great majority of adult Americans believe that unhappy couples should not stay married just because they have children at home, a significant change in attitude since the 1950s. Most people do not believe in sacrificing individual happiness for the sake of the children. They say that children actually may be better off living with one parent than with two who are constantly arguing. Divorce is now so common that it is no longer socially unacceptable, and children are not embarrassed to say that their parents are divorced. However, sociologists are still studying the long-term psychological consequences of divorce.

The Role of the Child

The American emphasis on the individual, rather than the group, affects children in a **contradictory** way. On the one hand, it may cause them to get more attention and even have more power than they should. On the other hand, because most children have mothers who are working outside the home, they may not get enough attention from either parent. Worse yet, parents who feel guilty for not having enough time with their children may give them more

Ready to go trick-or-treating on Halloween   JoAnn Crandall

material things to **compensa** for the lack of attention. Stud show that both parents are now spending less time with their children, due to work habits and a busy lifestyle.

In general, American families tend to place more emphasis on the needs and desires of the child and less on the child's social and family responsibilities. In the years since World War II, so much stress has been placed on the psychological needs of children that the number of experts in this field has increased enormously. Child psychologists, **counselors**, and social workers are employed to help children with problems at school or in the family. Many books on how to raise children have become best sellers. Sometimes these books offer conflicting advice, but almost all of them share the American emphasis on the development of the individual as their primary goal.

Some Americans believe that the emphasis on the psychological needs of the individual child have been carried too far by parents and experts alike. Dr. Benjamin Spock, the most famous of the child-rearing experts, finally concluded that "what is making the parent's job most difficult is today's child-centered viewpoint." Many **conscientious** parents, said Spock, tend to "keep their eyes exclusively focused on their child, thinking about what he needs from them and from the community, instead of thinking about what the world, the neighborhood, the family will be needing from the child and then making sure that he will grow up to meet such obligations." Although Americans may not agree on how best to **nurture** and discipline their children, they still hold the basic belief that the major purpose of the family is the development and welfare of each of its members as individuals.

Equality in the Family

Along with the American emphasis on individual freedom, the belief in equality has had a strong effect on the family. Alexis de Tocqueville saw the connection clearly in the 1830s. He said that in aristocratic societies inequality extends into the family, particularly to the father's relationship to his children. The father is accepted as ruler and master. The children's relations with him are very formal, and love for him is always combined with fear. In the United States, however, the democratic idea of equality destroys much of the father's status as ruler of the family and lessens the emotional distance between father and children. There is less formal respect for, and fear of, the father. But there is more affection expressed toward him. "The master and constituted [legal] ruler have **vanished**," said de Tocqueville; "the father remains."

What de Tocqueville said of American fathers and children almost two centuries ago applies to relations between parents and children in the United States today. There is much more social equality between parents and children than in most aristocratic societies or societies ruled by centuries of tradition. This can be witnessed in arguments between parents and their children, and in the considerable independence granted to teenagers. In fact, some Americans are worried that there is too much democracy in the home. Since the early 1960s, there has been a significant decline in parental authority and children's respect for their parents. This is particularly true of teenagers. Some parents seem to have little or no control over the behavior of their teenage children, particularly after they turn 16 and get their drivers' licenses.

On the other hand, Americans give their young people a lot of freedom because they want to teach their children to be independent and self-reliant. American children are expected to "leave the nest" at about age 18, after they graduate from high school. At that time they are expected to go on to college (many go to another city) or to get a job and support themselves. By their mid-20s, if children are still living with their parents, people will suspect that something is "wrong." Children are given a lot of freedom and

Leaving the nest   **Maryanne Kearny Datesman**

equality in the family so that they will grow up to be independent, self-reliant adults. Today, however, many young people are unable to find jobs that support the lifestyle they have grown up with, and they choose to move back in with their parents for a time. These young people are sometimes called "boomerang kids," because they have left the nest once but are now back again.

Four Stages of Marriage Relationships

The idea of equality also affects the relationships between husbands and wives. Women have witnessed steady progress toward equal status for themselves in the family and in society at large. According to Letha and John Scanzoni, two American sociologists, the institution of marriage in the United States has experienced four stages of development.* In each new stage, wives have increased the degree of equality with their husbands and have gained more power within the family.

Stage I: Wife as Servant to Husband   During the 19th century, American wives were expected to be completely obedient to their husbands. As late as 1850, wife beating was legal in almost all the states of the United States. Although both husbands and wives had family duties, the wife had no power in family matters other than that which her husband allowed her. Her possessions and any of her earnings belonged to her husband. During the 19th century, women were not allowed to vote, a restriction that in part reflected women's status as servant to the family.

Stage II: Husband-Head, Wife-Helper   During the late 19th and early 20th centuries, opportunities for women to work outside the household increased. More wives were now able to support themselves, if necessary, and therefore were less likely to accept the traditional idea that wives were servants who must obey their husbands. Even though the great majority of wives chose not to work outside the home, the fact that they might do so increased their power in the marriage. The husband could no longer make family decisions alone and demand that the wife follow them. The wife was freer to disagree with her husband and to insist that her views be taken into account in family decisions.

Even though the wife's power increased, the husband remained the head of the family. The wife became his full-time helper by taking care of his house and raising his children. She might strongly argue with him and sometimes convince him, but his decision on family matters was usually final.

This increase in equality of women in marriages reflected increased status for women in the society at large and led to women's gaining the right to vote in the early 20th century.

---

* Scanzoni, Letha Do, and John Scanzoni. *Men, Women, and Change*. New York, N.Y.: McGraw-Hill, Inc., 1981.

The husband-head, wife-helper marriage is still found in the United States. Economic conditions in the 20th century, however, have carried most marriages into different stages.

Stage III: Husband-Senior Partner, Wife-Junior Partner

During the 20th century, more and more wives have taken jobs outside the home. In 1940, for example, only 14 percent of married women in the United States held jobs outside the home. In the 1990s, more than 60 percent do. When married women take this step, according to Scanzoni, their power relative to that of their husbands increases still further. The wife's income becomes important in maintaining the family's standard of living. Her power to affect the outcome of family decisions is greater than when her duties were entirely in the home.

Although she has become a partner, however, the wife is still not an equal partner with her husband, since his job or career still provides more of the family income. He is, therefore, the senior partner and she is the junior partner of the family enterprise. Even though she has a job, it has a lower priority than her husband's. If, for example, the husband is asked to move to advance his career, she will give up her job and seek another in a new location.

In the United States today, many marriages are probably the senior-partner/junior-partner type, since the majority of women have jobs outside the home. The main reason seems to be that it has become increasingly difficult for families to maintain their standard of living on just one income. It is also due to the desire of American women for greater economic opportunity.

Stage IV: Husband-Wife Equal Partners

Since the late 1960s, a growing number of women have expressed a strong dissatisfaction with any marriage arrangement where the husband and his career are the primary considerations in the marriage. By the end of the 1970s, for example, considerably less than half of the women in the United States (38 percent) still believed that they should put their husbands and children ahead of their own careers. In the 1990s, most American women believe that they should be equal partners in their marriages and that their husbands should have equal responsibility for child care and household chores.

In an equal-partnership marriage, the wife pursues a full-time job or career that has equal importance to her husband's. The long-standing division of labor between husband and wife comes to an end. The husband is no longer the main provider of family income, and the wife no longer has the main responsibilities for household duties and raising children. Husband and wife share all these duties equally. Power over family decisions is also shared equally.

The reality of life in the United States is that although most American women now have an equal say in the decisions affecting the family, they generally earn less than men for the same work. Also, most women are still spending more time taking care of the children, cooking, and cleaning house than their husbands are. Many women are **resentful** because they feel like they have two full-time jobs—the one at work and the one at home. In the

This husband does more than half the cooking   **Maryanne Kearny Datesman**

1980s, women were told they could "have it all"—fast-track career, husband, children, and a clean house. Now, some women are finding that lifestyle **exhausting** and unrewarding. Some young women are now choosing to stay at home until their children start school, but many others who would like to cannot afford to do so.

Juggling two careers and family responsibilities can be as difficult for men as it is for women, especially if there is truly an equal division of duties. American fathers are often seen dropping the kids off at the baby sitter's or taking a sick child to the doctor. Some businesses are recognizing the need to accommodate families where both parents work. They may open a day-care center in the office building, offer fathers "paternity leave" to stay home with their new babies, or have flexible working hours. Unfortunately, these benefits are still the exception. While young couples strive to achieve equality in their careers, their marriages, and their parenting, society at large still lacks many of the structures that are needed to support them.

The Role of the Family in Society

The American ideal of equality has affected not only marriage but all forms of relationships between men and women. Americans gain a number of benefits by placing so much importance on achieving individual freedom and equality within the context of the family. The needs and desires of each member are given a great deal of attention and importance. However, a price is paid for these benefits. American families are less **stable** and lasting than those of most cultures. The high rate of divorce in American families is perhaps the most important indicator of this instability.

The American attitude toward the family contains many contradictions. For example, Americans will tolerate a good deal of instability in their families, including divorce, in order to protect such values as freedom and equality. On the other hand, they are strongly attached to the idea of the family as the best of all lifestyles. In fact, the great majority of persons who get divorces find a new partner and remarry. Studies show consistently that more than 90 percent of Americans believe that family life is an important value.

What is family life? We have seen that only 26 percent of the households are the "typical" American family—a father, mother, and children. Many of these are really "step families," or "**blended** families." Since most divorced people remarry, many children are living with a stepmother or stepfather. In a "blended" family, the parents may each have children from a previous marriage, and then have one or more children together—producing "yours," "mine," and "ours." Such families often result in very complicated and often stressful relationships. A child may have four sets of grandparents instead of two, for example. Blending families is not easy, and, sadly, many second marriages fail.

In addition to traditional families and blended families, there are a number of single parents, both mothers and fathers (more mothers), raising their children alone. Many of the single mothers are divorced, but some have never married. Indeed, by the mid-1990s, a startling one-third of all new babies were born to single mothers. Sometimes single parents and their children live with the grandparents for economic and emotional support. There are all sorts of

Three generations of a multi-ethnic family   **Maryanne Kearny Datesman**

arrangements. In recent years, some gay and lesbian couples have created fa...
units, sometimes adopting children, and some have sought to have single-sex
marriages recognized by law. The definition of "family" has become much
broader in the '90s. The majority of Americans would now define it as "people
who live together and love each other."

Sociologists and psychologists tell us that the family is the best place for children to learn moral values and a sense of responsibility. Beginning in the early 1990s, experts began to voice concern over what was happening to many children in

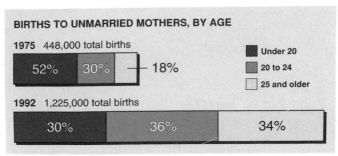

BIRTHS TO UNMARRIED MOTHERS, BY AGE

1975 448,000 total births

52% 30% — 18%

Under 20
20 to 24
25 and older

1992 1,225,000 total births

30% 36% 34%

USN & WR Basic Data—National Center for Health Statistics

America. Today, the state of the American family is frequently discussed, not
only by experts but by the press, elected officials, and the general public. The
majority of Americans believe that the institution of the family and "family
values" are both in deep trouble, and they are asking the schools to provide
more moral education than in the past. But if you ask Americans how their own
families are, most will tell you they are generally happy with their family life.

Family Values

In *Values and Public Policy*, Daniel Yankelovich reports on surveys done on
family values. There are 11 points that a majority of Americans agree are "family
values." Yankelovich classifies six of them as "clearly traditional":

- Respecting one's parents
- Being responsible for one's actions
- Having faith in God
- Respecting authority
- Married to the same person for life
- Leaving the world in better shape

The other five are "a blend of traditional and newer, more expressive values":

- Giving emotional support to other members of the family
- Respecting people for themselves
- Developing greater skill in communicating one's feelings
- Respecting one's children
- Living up to one's potential as an individual

The ideal of the American family is group cooperation to help achieve the
fulfillment of each individual member, and shared affection to renew each member's

emotional strength. Families can be viewed as similar to churches in this regard. Both are seen by Americans as places where the human spirit can find **refuge** from the highly competitive world outside and renewed resources to continue the effort. Although in many cases churches and families do not succeed in the task of spiritual renewal, this remains the ideal of church and family in America.

New Words

demographic statistics (numbers) and other information about the population of an area and the changes over time (includes information on age, income, marriages, divorces, and so on.)

priority having the position of most importance; the matter that has first place and therefore must be considered first

courtship the time two people spend getting to know each other and deciding if they want to marry

irreconcilable differences differences people cannot agree about; having such different opinions that people cannot solve their problems

contradictory involving evidence or facts that seem to contradict each other (seem to speak against each other); two facts that seem opposite, yet both are true

compensate to make up for; to provide some payment for a loss

counselor a person who has studied psychology and is trained to help people with their personal problems

conscientious trying hard to do the right thing

nurture to care for and feed; to provide love, guidance, and education for children so that they can be healthy; to take care of a person's physical or emotional needs

vanish to disappear completely

resentful having feelings of anger; feeling that one is not being treated fairly

exhausting extremely or completely tiring; making a person so tired that he or she cannot function normally

juggling trying to keep several objects up in the air at the same time; trying do several activities at one time

stable firm and strong; unchanging

blended mixed together; combined to make something new

refuge a safe place

 A. Vocabulary Check

Complete the sentences using words or phrases from New Words list.

1. Many _____ American mothers would like to stay at home with their young children, but they have to work to make ends meet.

2. _____ a career and family responsibilities is very stressful and often leaves little time for people to relax and enjoy life.

3. Many young mothers who work have an _____ lifestyle— they work all day at their jobs and then come home and work nights and weekends to take care of their families and homes.

4. Women whose husbands do not help with housework and child care may become very _____.

5. Most Americans would probably agree that fathers, as well as mothers, should be able to _____ their children.

6. Sometimes a demanding career can be a _____, even though a parent would like to have more time to spend with the children.

7. Parents who do not have enough time for their children may feel guilty and then try to _____ by giving their children material gifts.

8. The value of individual freedom may produce _____ results—children may have more power and get more consideration of their needs and desires, while they really get less of their parents' time.

9. _____ families may be a source of stress, as parents try to cope with raising each other's children as well as their own.

10. Some families choose to visit a _____ to get help with their problems.

11. Couples who have _____ _____ may be able to get a divorce quite easily and quickly.

12. In the United States, _____ is the time that young people in love get to know each other better and decide if they want to get married.

13. Although marriage is not very _____ in the United States, most Americans still believe that it is an important institution in society.

14. Families have traditionally provided an important _____ from the competitive stresses of American society.

15. _____ studies show that young Americans are now waiting longer to get married and have children.

16. In spite of all its problems, the institutions of marriage and the family will certainly never _____.

B. Comprehension Check

Write **T** *if the statement is true and* **F** *if it is false according to the information in the chapter.*

_____ 1. Most Americans picture the traditional "classic" family as a married couple with two children.

_____ 2. The majority of American households still consist of this "classic" family.

_____ 3. One American household in four now consists of someone living alone.

_____ 4. "Baby boomers" are young people who are in their twenties.

_____ 5. Americans usually consider what is best for the whole family first and what is best for them as individuals second.

_____ 6. Americans believe that the family exists primarily to serve the needs of its individual family members.

_____ 7. Most Americans believe that marriages should make both individuals happy and that if they cannot live together happily, it is better for them to get a divorce.

_____ 8. American parents generally think more about the individual needs of their children than they do about what responsibilities the child will have to the society as a whole.

_____ 9. Although Americans believe in democracy for society, they generally exercise strict control over their children, particularly teenagers.

_____ 10. The amount of equality between husbands and wives has remained pretty much the same since de Tocqueville visited the United States in the 1930s.

_____ 11. If an American wife works outside the home, she is likely to have more power in the family than a married woman who does not work.

_____ 12. In the *husband-senior partner, wife-junior partner* type of marriage, the husband and wife both work, have equal power and influence in making family decisions, and divide the family duties equally.

_____ 13. In most American families, the father does just as much housework and child care as the mother.

_____ 14. Having faith in God and respecting authority are two of the traditional American family values.

_____ 15. Although one out of every two marriages end in divorce, Americans still believe strongly in the importance of marriage and the family.

C. Questions for Discussion

1. How would you describe the typical family in your country? Who lives in household? Do several generations usually live together? How many children are there? What do you think is the ideal number of children to have? What are the roles of the family members? How much freedom do teenagers have? When can a teenager get a driver's license? Would you give your children the same amount of freedom as you had as a teenager?

2. Which type of marriage is most common in your country? Which of the four types do you think is the best for men? for women? for the children? Which type of marriage does your family have? Which do you think is the ideal? Why?

3. In your country, what do people have to do to get a divorce? What happens to people who divorce there? How are they treated? Do they usually remarry? If two people are unhappy, should they get a divorce? What if they have children? Under what circumstances would you get divorced?

4. Should mothers with small children work? In your country, who takes care of the children of working mothers? Are there day-care centers? Do other members of the family do the baby-sitting? What was your experience growing up? Did you have a baby sitter? Would you leave your child in a day-care center?

5. If there is true equality between the sexes, husbands should be able to choose to stay at home while their wives go to work. Do you agree? Do "househusbands" exist in your country? Can men nurture children as well as women can? Would you ever want this kind of relationship?

 ## D. Cloze Summary Paragraph

This paragraph summarizes the chapter. Fill in each blank with any word that makes sense.

The traditional American family _____*has*_____ undergone many changes

since _____ 1950s. Now only 26 percent _____

American households consist of _____ and their children.

Americans _____ the primary purpose of _____

family is to advance _____ happiness of individual family

_____. This stress on individual _____ means that (1) unhappy marriages _____ end in divorce, and (2) _____ emphasis is placed on _____ needs of the child _____ on the child's responsibility _____ others. The American belief _____ equality results in democratic _____ within the family, both _____ parents and children and _____ husbands and wives. American _____ have progressed through four _____, from the wife as _____ servant, to the wife _____ a completely equal partner _____ her husband. The role of _____ wife within the family, _____ her equality with her _____, have increased as women _____ taken jobs outside the _____. Unfortunately, this emphasis on _____ freedom and equality has _____ stress on the American _____. Half of all marriages end _____ divorce, and when parents _____ again, blending two families _____ be difficult. Also, when _____ parents work, there is _____ enough time for the _____. However, in spite of _____ problems, Americans still believe _____ family values, and they _____ the family as a _____ from their competitive society.

E. Small Group Discussion

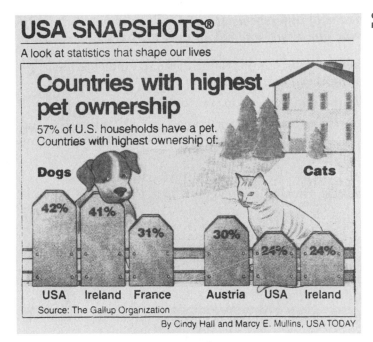

USA SNAPSHOTS®

A look at statistics that shape our lives

Countries with highest pet ownership

57% of U.S. households have a pet.
Countries with highest ownership of:

Dogs

42% USA
41% Ireland
31% France

Cats

30% Austria
24% USA
24% Ireland

Source: The Gallup Organization

By Cindy Hall and Marcy E. Mullins, USA TODAY

Many Americans have pets that they consider to be part of the family. Some studies have shown that owning a pet lowers a person's blood pressure and helps to reduce stress. Do you have a pet? Are pets popular in your country? What are the advantages and disadvantages of having a pet? Share your experiences with pets with others in your group.

The dog enjoys a ride in the family's old convertible   JoAnn Crandall

F. Ask Americans

Interview several Americans of different ages and ask them about their families. Ask each one the following questions, and record their answers.

1. Who are the members of your family? Name them and indicate their relationship to you (mother, sister, etc.).
2. Who lives in your household? Where do your other relatives live?
3. How often do you see your parents? Your grandparents? Your sisters and brothers? Your aunts, uncles, and cousins? Do you write or telephone any of them regularly?
4. What occasions bring your relatives together (birthdays, holidays, weddings, births, deaths, trips)? Have you ever been to a family reunion?
5. Do you feel you have a close family? Why?
6. Who would you ask for advice if you had a serious personal problem?
7. Who would take care of you if you became ill?
8. What obligations and responsibilities do you feel you have toward your family?
9. What duties and responsibilities do you believe a child has toward his or her family?
10. On a scale of 1 to 10, with 10 as "most important," how important are the opinions of the members of your immediate family concerning:

   - Whom you marry
   - Where you live
   - Where you go to school
   - What job you take
   - How you spend your money

G. Ask Yourself

Do you agree or disagree with each of the following statements? Put a check under the number that indicates how you feel.

+2 = Strongly agree
+1 = Agree
 0 = No opinion
-1 = Disagree
-2 = Strongly disagree

	+2	+1	0		

1. Arranged marriages are better than marriages where the couple have met and dated on their own. ____ ____ ____

2. It is very important for my family to approve of the person I marry. ____ ____ ____ ____ ____

3. If my parents disapproved of my choice, I would still marry that person if we were very much in love. ____ ____ ____ ____ ____

4. A woman's place is in the home. ____ ____ ____ ____ ____

5. Married women with small children should not work. ____ ____ ____ ____ ____

6. Men should be able to be "househusbands" and let their wives work to support them. ____ ____ ____ ____ ____

7. Husbands and wives should share equally the work of taking care of the house and the children. ____ ____ ____ ____ ____

8. Unhappy couples should stay married for the sake of the children. ____ ____ ____ ____ ____

9. Married couples who choose not to have children are selfish. ____ ____ ____ ____ ____

10. Equality between a husband and wife causes divorce. ____ ____ ____ ____ ____

Read the above statements to several Americans, and ask them if they agree or disagree. Compare your answers with theirs.

H. People Watching

It has been said that in most societies children are spectators watching adults interact. They are learning what it means to be an adult in their society. In American society, however, the adults are usually the spectators who are watching the children.

Observe American adults interacting with children in the following places:

- In restaurants
- On a playground or at a sports event
- At the movies
- On the street
- At home (If you are unable to visit an American home, watch American TV shows that have children as characters.)

Record your observations. You may wish to write up these observations as a report and present it to the class. What differences did you observe in the way children are treated in other countries?

I. Proverbs and Sayings

Ask Americans to explain these proverbs and sayings to you. Then ask them for other examples of sayings about men, women, children, or the family.

1. The hand that rocks the cradle rules the world.
2. As the twig is bent, so grows the tree.
3. That child is a chip off the old block.
4. A man may work from sun to sun, but a woman's work is never done.
5. Behind every successful man, there is a woman.
6. Blood is thicker than water.

J. Think, Pair, Share

Working mothers often feel that they have two full-time jobs—one outside the home, for which they get paid, and the other inside the home, for which they do not get paid. The job at home is being "household manager." Most working American women still have the major responsibility for managing the household—cooking, cleaning, shopping, and seeing that the children are cared for—even if their husbands help them with some of the household duties. What do you think husbands with working wives should do around the house? Should married women work? What if they have children?

Write your answers to these questions and discuss them with your partner. Then share your answers with another pair of students.

K. What's Your Opinion? Small Group Discussion

Some people are surprised to learn that Americans get less vacation time than workers in other countries. American companies offer an average of only two weeks paid vacation, compared to some other countries. For example, in France, Germany, Italy, Spain, and the United Kingdom, companies offer an average of four weeks or more.

A recent *USA Today* article examines how Americans' leisure time is being redefined from "time to relax" to "time to accomplish other non-work-related tasks." One in ten Americans now claim that they have no free time, and four in ten say that they constantly feel rushed. (These are the people that you are likely to see doing their grocery shopping at midnight.) Baby boomer families where both the husband and wife work are particularly affected. Although there has been a social revolution since the 1950s, the workplace is still organized pretty much the same, as if husbands had jobs and wives stayed at home taking care of the family.

Part of the problem is that "this nation lives—or thinks it should—by the Puritan work ethic: Somehow, it's not The American Way to complain about an excess of work, only about a lack of it." Another explanation is the desire for material wealth—"the need for bigger paychecks to satisfy bigger consumer needs."

People get caught up in a cycle of work-and-spend, and luxuries become neces. In order to get more free time, people must make a painful choice: "Do I want work less but have less money?" Only 14 percent of Americans would answer "Y

Look at the following poll. [How would you answer each poll question?] Idea how much time should people work each day? How much vacation time shou they get each year? How do people keep from getting caught in the work-and-spend cycle?

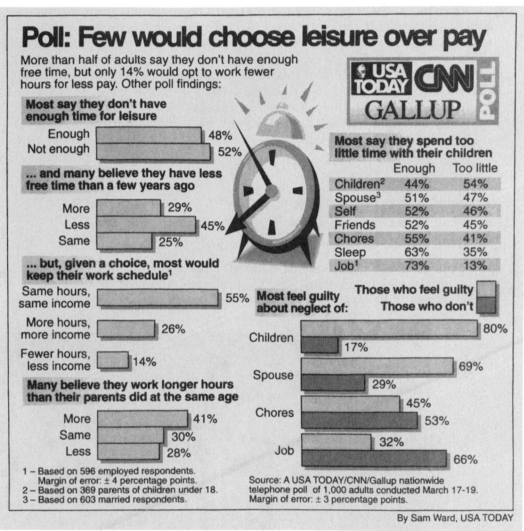

Poll: Few would choose leisure over pay

More than half of adults say they don't have enough free time, but only 14% would opt to work fewer hours for less pay. Other poll findings:

USA TODAY CNN GALLUP POLL

Most say they don't have enough time for leisure

Enough	48%
Not enough	52%

... and many believe they have less free time than a few years ago

More	29%
Less	45%
Same	25%

... but, given a choice, most would keep their work schedule[1]

Same hours, same income	55%
More hours, more income	26%
Fewer hours, less income	14%

Many believe they work longer hours than their parents did at the same age

More	41%
Same	30%
Less	28%

Most say they spend too little time with their children

	Enough	Too little
Children[2]	44%	54%
Spouse[3]	51%	47%
Self	52%	46%
Friends	52%	45%
Chores	55%	41%
Sleep	63%	35%
Job[1]	73%	13%

Most feel guilty about neglect of:

Those who feel guilty / Those who don't

Children	80%	17%
Spouse	69%	29%
Chores	45%	53%
Job	32%	66%

1 – Based on 596 employed respondents.
Margin of error: ± 4 percentage points.
2 – Based on 369 parents of children under 18.
3 – Based on 603 married respondents.

Source: A USA TODAY/CNN/Gallup nationwide telephone poll of 1,000 adults conducted March 17-19. Margin of error: ± 3 percentage points.

By Sam Ward, USA TODAY

L. Ask Americans

The role of the elderly is one that most foreigners cannot understand about American life. Some have heard that all the elderly are in nursing homes, but this is not true. Actually, only one in four Americans spends any time in a nursing home, and the average stay is two years. It is generally the sick and the disabled who require nursing-home care at the end of their lives. Americans generally try to live on their own as long as possible, choosing to be independent and self-reliant. Eighty percent of the care of the elderly is done by family members. Working mothers with children under 18 who must care for elderly parents are called "the sandwich generation," because they must be a parent to both their children and their own dependent parents. However, as the baby boomers age, adult children who are taking care of their parents are themselves getting older and older.

To try to understand how Americans feel about being old and what they plan to do with their lives when they are old, ask several Americans who are not yet 65 the following questions:

1. What do you hope to do when you retire?
2. Where do you plan to live?
3. Would you move in with your children? Under what conditions?
4. What do you think life will be like when you are 65 or older?
5. Are you afraid of growing old? Are you looking forward to growing old?

If you are able to, you may wish to visit a nursing home or a retirement community for older Americans. Many retirement communities now have different kinds of living arrangements, from independent living in homes and

Maryanne Kearny Datesman

apartments, to assisted living in buildings with private rooms and meals ⸮ in a common dining room, to nursing homes that offer full-time care by d⸮ and nurses. Why do you think that many older people choose to live apart f their grown children? Think about the description of the family presented in chapter. What evidence do you see of the American values of equality in the family and the emphasis on individual freedom?

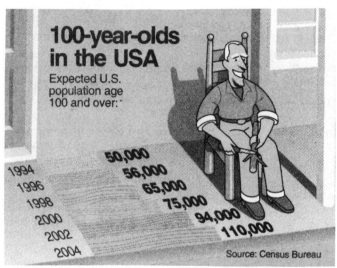

100-year-olds in the USA

Expected U.S. population age 100 and over:⸰

1994   50,000
1996   56,000
1998   65,000
2000   75,000
2002   94,000
2004   110,000

Source: Census Bureau

By Scott Boeck and Bob Laird, *USA TODAY*, May 22, 1995

M. Suggestions for Writing

It is sometimes difficult for young people to find someone to marry. Young adults are expected to find their own husbands or wives themselves, but it is often difficult for them to meet others, especially if they are not in college. Families play a very minor role in getting young people together. Some young adults have turned to computer dating or putting advertisements in the newspapers. These new services are designed to help people meet "Mr. or Miss Right." Men and women are asked to fill out questionnaires about themselves—their interests, hobbies, likes and dislikes—and they also indicate the qualities they are looking for in a husband or wife. Couples are then matched by the computer, and each person receives a list of names of people to contact for a date.

Imagine that you are writing an ad for the newspaper or explaining to a computer service what kind of person you would like to meet (and perhaps marry). What things about yourself would be important for your date to know? What qualities would you want your date to have?

Write an ad describing yourself and the kind of person you would like to meet, or choose one of the following composition topics:

1. Qualities I Want My Husband/Wife to Have
2. The Pros and Cons of Computer Dating
3. How to Find the Perfect Mate
4. Courtship in My Country
5. The Real Me

Vivian Garcia

♥♥

Love Is In the Air Dating Service- Singles Profile Form

♥♥

Characteristics of Your Ideal Mate:

Age Preference:
☐ From ___ to ___
☐ Does not matter

Smoke:
☐ Yes
☐ No
☐ Does Not Matter

Ethnic Background:
☐ African-American
☐ Asian
☐ Latin
☐ Native American
☐ White
☐ Other-(Please specify)_____

Religion:
☐ Catholic
☐ Jewish
☐ Mormon
☐ Protestant
☐ None
☐ Other
(Please Specify)_____
_____

Education:
☐ High School or equivalent
☐ Jr. College
☐ 4-year College/University
☐ Masters
☐ Ph.D or greater

Appearance:
☐ Extremely attractive
☐ Fairly attractive
☐ Average
☐ Does not matter

Occupation:
☐ Professional
☐ Technical
☐ Arts/entertainment
☐ Other (Please specify)

Interests:
(Check all that apply)
☐ Outdoor activities
☐ Movies
☐ Music
☐ Dancing
☐ Sports
☐ Theater
☐ Other
(Please Specify)_____
_____

♥♥

Personal Information:

Name_____   Age_____ ☐Male ☐Female

Address_____   Phone- Home_____
_____   Work_____

City_____ Zip_____   Height_____ Weight_____

Occupation_____   Marital Status_____
                                           (Never married, divorced,
Education_____   separated, widowed)

N. Suggestions for Further Reading

- Letha and John Scanzoni, *Men, Women, and Change*
- Laura Ingalls Wilder, *Little House on the Prairie*
- Louisa May Alcott, *Little Women*
- Tennessee Williams, *The Glass Menagerie*
- Thornton Wilder, *Our Town*
- Willa Cather, *My Antonia*
- Robert S. and Helen M. Lynd, *Middletown*
- Betty Friedan, *The Feminine Mystique*
- Robert Bly, *Iron John*
- Joe Starita, *The Dull Knifes [sic] of Pine Ridge: A Lakota Odyssey*
- Jade Snow Wong, *Fifth Chinese Daughter*
- Maxine Hong Kingston, *The Woman Warrior*

O. Recommended Movies

- *Father of the Bride*
- *My Family, Mi Familia*
- *Kids*
- *When Harry Met Sally*

Dad and daughter dancing at a family wedding
Maryanne Kearny Datesman

Astronaut Michael Gernhardt appears to be floating in space while attached to the robot arm of the Endeavour during a six-hour space walk Saturday, Sept. 16, 1995   **AP Photo/NASA**

CHAPTER 12

American Values at the Crossroads: The United States in the 21st Century

The sole certainty is that tomorrow will surprise us all.

Alvin Toffler

Before You Read

1. What are the major historical events that have shaped the United States in recent years?

2. What is the status of the United States in the world today?

3. What are some of the problems that Americans face now?

4. What do you think will happen to the American values in the 21st century?

Factors That Affect American History

As the 21st century begins, the nations of the world are caught up in a whirlwind of change. While the global information network brings us closer together, the distance between the "haves" and the "have nots" seems to be widening. Where does the United States stand now? What will be its role in the new century? What will happen to this country and these people who have **championed** the values of individual freedom, self-reliance, equality of opportunity, competition, material wealth, and hard work? As the futurist Alvin Toffler has predicted, only one thing about the future is certain—we will all be surprised. Who, for example, would have predicted the disintegration of the Soviet Union in the early 1990s? And what does fate now have in store for the remaining "super power"? Since we cannot predict the future, we can only reflect on what has held the United States together for the last 200 years and guess about where Americans' traditional values may lead the nation in the future. There are several factors that should be kept in mind.

First, the United States has always had a racially and ethnically diverse population. Sometimes these people get along well together, and sometimes they do not. At times there has been great suspicion and even hatred between people of different races and national origins. But even in the darkest times, there have always been individuals who held up the ideals stated in the Declaration of Independence:

> *We hold these truths to be self-evident, that all men are created equal, that they are endowed by their Creator with certain unalienable rights, that among these are Life, Liberty and the pursuit of Happiness. That to secure these rights, Governments are instituted among Men, deriving their just powers from the consent of the governed.*

Second, although Americans have traditionally had a strong distrust of their government, they have also had a strong faith in its design. Over a period of more than 200 years, they have amended the United States Constitution only 26 times. The first 10 amendments, the Bill of Rights, were added two years after the Constitution itself, and the last amendment was in 1971, lowering the voting age from 21 to 18. The framework of the political system was designed to protect the freedom and the individual rights of the citizens. Americans believe that this system has successfully carried the nation from the 18th century through the 20th, and that it will still protect them in the 21st century.

Third, the right of free speech and the existence of a free press have meant that all people have the right to express their opinions, and that everything from public policy to private concerns such as abortion or sexual preference can be openly discussed and debated. The result is that all the problems of the country are displayed for the rest of the world to see. The bad news is that there are a lot of problems. The good news is that there are also large numbers of indiv who are sincerely concerned about society's problems and are working hard solve them. Because Americans believe so strongly in the freedom and the wor of the individual, they have traditionally had an optimistic faith in the ability o individuals eventually to invent creative solutions to all the nation's problems.

Fourth, in spite of the image of the United States and some of the actions that the government has taken, there is a long tradition of **isolationism**. President George Washington declared in 1796: "It is our true policy to steer clear of permanent alliances with any portion of the foreign world." The spirit of isolationism persists even today, as Americans continue to debate what being a "world power" means. Most people are not in favor of the United States becoming a "world policeman," for example. Americans are very reluctant to see the United States become involved in international military actions unless they are convinced that there is some national interest to be protected, or that there is some great humanitarian need. Americans are also **skeptical** about international economic alliances, wanting to be sure that self-interests are protected before commitments are made to other countries. (This is why there has been so much debate about NAFTA.) Most Americans are more interested in what is happening close to home than what is happening in the rest of the world. They want to know how events, national or international, will affect them personally.

Korean War Memorial, Washington, DC **National Park Service. National Capital Area**

Fifth, the United States, like all countries, goes through different political and economic phases that have a strong effect on the mood of the people. When the economy is in good shape, people are naturally more optimistic about the state of their country and life in general. Pollsters are continually taking the emotional temperature of the American citizens. "What do you think about the future?" they ask. "Are you better off now than you were four years ago?" As the mood swings back and forth from optimistic to pessimistic, or from liberal to conservative, the underlying traditional values have so far remained intact. At times, Americans may talk about some values more than others, but when times get tough, many are likely to say that it is because the American people (and their government) have strayed too far from these traditional values. Interestingly enough, pollsters find that there is really no statistically significant difference in the attitudes and values of young people, the middle-aged, or the older generation.

20th-Century Challenges to American Values

If we take a brief look at the 20th century, we can see these five factors at work in history. In the first two decades, there was mass immigration from southern and eastern European countries, at times as many as a million people per year— 1 percent of the total population. By the early 1920s, many believed that the United States could no longer handle so many new immigrants, and by 1924, immigration laws had slowed the number to about 150,000 a year. Industry was growing, and the country had many manufacturing jobs for new immigrants. About a third of them, however, did not find the better life they were seeking, and they eventually left the United States and went back home.

After World War I—"the war to end all wars"—the United States enjoyed economic prosperity during the "Roaring Twenties." The stock market crash of 1929 ushered in the Great Depression of the 1930s, and it was not until World War II that the economy turned around. The need for weapons created new factory jobs, many of them filled by women. When the soldiers came back home in 1945, many young women quit their jobs, got married, and started their families. The large number of babies born in the 20 years after the war, from the mid-1940s to the mid-1960s, produced the "baby boom"—a **bulge** in the population that is now resulting in "the graying of America."

Many Americans look back on the 1950s as an age of economic prosperity and national stability. They nostalgically reminisce about a time when fathers were working, mothers were at home with their children, and life seemed less complicated. There was another side to the 50s, however. The Cold War with the Soviet Union was in full swing, leading to fears of a **nuclear holocaust** and the communist takeover of the world. There was so much fear of communism that a senator, Joseph McCarthy, was able to almost **single-handedly** create a climate that posed a serious threat to free speech in the United States. In televised hearings in the Senate, McCarthy accused a number of Americans of being communist traitors. Some of these people were writers and film makers in

Hollywood. Today, some people in the entertainment industry may fear censorship of any kind because they still remember the McCarthy era.

There were two other problems in the 1950s that had to be dealt with in t. 1960s: poverty and segregation. About one-fourth of the population lived in poverty. In the 1960s, President Johnson pushed through a plan called "The Great Society" that significantly enlarged the welfare programs begun during the Depression in the 1930s. Johnson declared a "war on poverty," and over the next two decades, the percentage of poor people did drop. However, these programs began to create an expectation that the government, not the individual, should solve social problems.

The second problem was the continued legal segregation in the South. Although the Supreme Court ruled in 1954 that segregation in public schools was unconstitutional, it was not until the Civil Rights movement of the 1960s that segregation ended. The nonviolent Civil Rights demonstrations of the 1960s led to the eventual passage of laws to protect the rights of black Americans, and there was much talk about the value of equality of opportunity. Quota systems were enacted to try to improve the education level and job opportunities for African-Americans, and gains were made. For example, in 1940, only 11 percent of blacks between the ages of 25 and 29 had completed high school, compared to 39 percent of whites. Today, the percentages are about the same for both races—82 percent and 85 percent, respectively.

The 1960s are most often remembered as a decade of violence and unrest. Popular leaders were assassinated: President Kennedy in 1963, Malcolm X in 1965, Martin Luther King, Jr., and Bobby Kennedy in 1968. After the death of King, there were riots in a number of big cities. Some feared the rioting would bring the country to the **brink** of a racial civil war, but fortunately this did not happen.

John F. Kennedy, President 1961–1963   **JFK Library**

The War in Vietnam and the Watergate Scandal

The other major event in the 1960s was the American involvement in Vietnam. After Kennedy's death, President Johnson vastly increased the number of American troops in Vietnam in order to prevent the Vietnamese communists from taking control of the country. He believed that communism would spread throughout Southeast Asia if it succeeded in Vietnam. Eventually, it could threaten Japan, the Philippines, and even Hawaii. This was called the "**domino** theory"; if one nation fell to communism, it would cause others to fall, like a line of dominoes. Since the United States had had success in stopping communism from spreading from North Korea to South Korea, a policy of trying to contain communism developed. The United States tried sending advisors to South Vietnam, followed by more and more troops. By 1966, the struggle in Vietnam had become a major American war.

Initially, most Americans agreed with the action. But even so, there was stronger opposition to the Vietnam War than to any previous American war in the 20th century. As the war dragged on and more Americans were wounded or killed, the opposition to the war grew. Many of the opponents of the war

Memorial to women who served in the war in Vietnam, Washington, DC **National Park Service. National Capital Area**

The Watergate building, Washington, DC **Maryanne Kearny Datesman**

attacked it as immoral. On the other side, feelings were just as strong. There were those who believed that the United States had a moral obligation to fight against communism, defend freedom, and make the world safe for democracy. Their message to anti-war protestors was "America—love it or leave it!" However, the anti-war movement may have made many Americans who originally supported the war more doubtful about their beliefs.

In 1975, North Vietnam conquered South Vietnam. Most Americans had been brought up believing that the United States had never lost a war. Now it seemed that for the first time, this had happened. Was the nation losing its strength? If it was, was this because it was losing faith in its traditional values? These were the kinds of troubling questions that Vietnam raised in the minds of many Americans.

In addition to the defeat in Vietnam, the 1970s brought the Watergate **scandals** and the forced **resignation** of President Richard Nixon in 1974. Men paid by President Nixon's reelection committee were arrested for breaking into the national headquarters of the opposition Democratic party (in the Watergate building)* in order to place illegal listening devices on the telephones and to photograph Democratic party documents. President Nixon repeatedly denied any knowledge of the break-in and tried to cover up the involvement of his staff. Eventually, a Senate investigation revealed the truth, and he was forced to resign.

---

* Because the break-in occurred in the Watergate building, the scandal became known as "Watergate." Since then, problems that presidents have had have sometimes been named "——gate." For example, when some of President Bill Clinton's appointees revealed that they had not paid proper taxes for nannies they had employed in their homes, the press referred to the affair as "Nannygate."

The failure of the Vietnam War effort and the resignation of President Nixon in **disgrace** made many Americans pessimistic about their country. Furthermore, in the late 1970s, there was an economic recession and an oil crisis. As Americans waited in line for gas for their cars, they wondered what had happened to the abundant resources they had always taken for granted. For the first time since the Depression of the 1930s, average Americans faced the possibility that their future standard of living might actually go down, instead of up. In 1979, President Jimmy Carter **gloomily** observed, "The **erosion** of our confidence in the future is threatening to destroy the social and political fabric of America... The symptoms of this crisis of the American spirit are all around us."

This was not the message that Americans wanted to hear, however, and in 1980 they elected Ronald Reagan president. *Time* magazine chose President Reagan as its "man of the year" and said of him: "intellectually, emotionally, Reagan lives in the past." One of President Reagan's basic beliefs was that the United States should return as much as possible to its pre-1930 ways, when business institutions were strong and government institutions were weak. Reagan had made his personal fortune in the years of America's greatest economic expansion, 1945 to 1965. He believed that there was no reason why Americans could not have the same opportunity in the 1980s to get rich; the United States could be as wealthy and strong as it ever had been in the past. As president, Reagan took two major actions to bring this about. First, he lowered taxes—the largest tax cut in American history. Then he increased the government's spending on military weapons—the greatest increase in history. The result was the largest national debt in history—$2.6 trillion dollars by the time he left office in January of 1989. The debt had almost tripled in less than a decade.

On one hand, the 1980s was the decade when there was the longest economic growth ever, inflation and interest rates dropped, and more than 19 million new jobs were created. But it was also the decade when the rich got richer, the poor got poorer, and the middle class got **squeezed**. And the United States went from the largest money lender to the biggest borrower on earth.

The 1990s began as the decade when the bills had to be paid and the United States needed to find long-term solutions to social problems such as poverty, the breakdown of the family, violent crime, and the problems in the education system. In the mid-1990s, the Republicans gained control of both Houses of Congress for the first time in 40 years, and the mood of the country was definitely more conservative. Once again, there was talk of balancing the budget. But what government programs should be cut? Welfare? School lunches for poor children? Defense? Social Security? Health benefits for the elderly and the poor? In the 21st century, Americans will have to make tough choices, particularly as the baby boomers grow older, start to retire, and draw Social Security* benefits.

---

* Social Security is a government retirement system. Almost all working Americans and their employers contribute to the Social Security fund, which is administered by the government and distributed to retired citizens.

The Need for New National Values

As the 21st century begins, a number of leaders in politics, education, and other professions believe that the United States must adopt some new values to go along with the older traditional ones. What new values should Americans adopt? This is a very difficult question to answer. Certainly, a greater value should be placed on the conservation of natural resources; Americans should learn to use less and waste less. But conservation has never been a strong value to Americans, who have believed that their country offered an endless, abundant supply of natural resources. Recently, progress has been made—more and more Americans are recycling their paper, cans, bottles, and other goods—but old wasteful habits die hard. Furthermore, the need to protect the environment may conflict with the need for jobs, as in the Northwest, where conservationists battle lumber companies that want to cut down ancient redwood trees. A belief in the value of conservation is still weak compared with other American values; it can become stronger only as Americans see the need for it more clearly.

Redwood trees **Roxanne Fridirici**

In addition, Americans may need to place a stronger value on cooperation on a national scale to achieve important national objectives. The American idea of the national good has never been based on national cooperation but rather on the freedom of the individual, maintaining those conditions that provide the greatest freedom and prosperity for the individual. It is far more difficult for Americans to accept shared sacrifice for the common good and well-being of the entire country. For example, although the majority of Americans believe that it is extremely important to balance the national budget and reduce the deficit, they do not want to see cuts in government programs that benefit them personally.

The American value of competition also hinders the development of a spirit of national cooperation. Competition sometimes encourages feelings of suspicion rather than the mutual trust that is necessary for successful national cooperation. Although Americans often cooperate successfully on the local level—in neighborhood groups and churches, for example—they become suspicious when the national government becomes involved. For example, on the national level, they may see themselves as part of an interest group that is competing with other interest groups for government funds. A request by the national government for shared sacrifice may be seen as **coercive** and destructive rather than voluntary and constructive. However, the demands of the 21st century may compel Americans to place a greater value on national cooperation to solve problems that affect them all, directly or indirectly.

The United States: The First Universal Nation?

One of the other challenges that the United States faces is the absorption of a new wave of immigrants that began in the mid-1970s. As a result of the Vietnam War and events that followed, large numbers of refugees from Southeast Asia came to the United States in the 1970s and 1980s. In the 1980s and 1990s, there were large numbers of immigrants from Mexico, Central and South America, and the Caribbean, some seeking political freedom, others looking for jobs and economic well-being. The hope of finding "the American Dream" still attracts them. As a result of the geographic location of the United States and immigration policies favoring family reunification, these populations have been growing more rapidly than those coming from other parts of the world.

We have already discussed some of the **ramifications** of the arrival of more than one million new immigrants into the United States per year. Sometimes nations reach a "**saturation point**" where they cannot take in more people from other countries and still function well. From time to time, the United States has chosen to limit the number of new immigrants it permits, just as many other countries have done. Some Americans believe that as the 21st century begins, the United States may have again reached one of those saturation points when it can no longer comfortably absorb millions of new immigrants. Some politicians have played on these fears and have spoken out against immigration. In the 1996 presidential primaries, while seeking the Republican nomination, Pat Buchanan actually suggested building a wall along the U.S.–Mexican border to keep out illegal immigrants.

On the other hand, many recognize that new immigrants bring new life and energy into the United States. As the baby boomers get older, these immigrants may be an important source of youth and vitality for the nation. Perhaps most importantly, the diversity of ideas and cultures in the United

By courtesy of Statue of Liberty National Monument

States may be one of its great sources of strength as it moves into the 21st century. Ben Wattenberg, an expert in American culture, believes that the United States has an advantage because it is becoming a microcosm of the world—it may be the first "universal" nation, where people from every race, religion, culture, and ethnic background live together in freedom, under one government. Because Americans have come from so many different countries, people all over the world can identify with the United States and its values. The popularity and influence of American culture may be one indication that this is happening. "People all over the world," says Wattenberg, "listen to our music, read our books, watch our tapes.... American culture—for all its ills and all its glory—has become the only broad-based global culture there is."

Much of American culture, however, is not admired in many parts of the world. American movies, television, and videotapes are often thought to have too much sex, violence, and loud music. Foreign observers also note the high divorce rates, the level of violent crime, and other negative facets of American life. Many conclude that Americans carry their favorite value of individual freedom too far, to the edge of social **chaos**. Wattenberg agrees that the United States still has serious problems that it must solve, but he does not believe that the country is really declining. Wattenberg believes that a nation made up of people from around the world, whose culture has worldwide appeal, is not a nation in decline.

However, the American people and their values have reached another historic crossroads. Americans can be certain of only one thing—that the rapid pace of change will continue. How Americans respond to these changes is a question that can be answered only as events of the 21st century unfold.

■ ■ ■ ■

New Words

champion to support strongly; to fight for; to defend

isolationism a policy that a country should not concern itself with the affairs of other countries, avoiding international agreements

skeptical suspicious; doubting; distrustful

bulge a sudden increase that does not last

nuclear holocaust a nuclear war in which there would be mass destruction and death ("holocaust" refers to the loss of many lives, especially by burning)

single-handedly done by one person working alone; without help from others

brink at the edge of; on the verge of, or near something dangerous or unpleasant

domino a small black rectangle of wood with white spots used for playing games; *domino effect* refers to one event causing another (chain reaction), as when dominoes are lined up on edge so that when one is pushed over, it knocks over the next, and the next, until they are all down

scandal some action taken that is morally wrong and offensive to others; public discussion of such behavior

resignation formal notice (usually a letter) that someone is giving up, or leaving, a job or position

disgrace shame; loss of honor and respect; public dishonor

gloomily darkly; with little hope or cheerfulness

erosion gradual wearing away or disintegration

squeeze to put pressure on; to cause financial problems

coercive using force to make people do something they do not want to do

ramification effect; consequence; result

saturation point the point at which nothing more can be absorbed; completely filled up; to be so full that nothing more can be accepted or contained

chaos complete disorder and confusion

A. Vocabulary Check

Complete the sentences using words or phrases from the New Words list.

1. Baby boomers, born after World War II, are responsible for a
   _____ in the population.

2. Watergate was the biggest political _____ in recent United
   States history.

3. Richard Nixon left the presidency in _____ because of his
   role in Watergate.

4. It was the first time in U.S. history that a president had submitted his
   _____.

5. Watergate and the loss of Vietnam had a number of _____
   for the American society.

6. There was an _____ of confidence in the moral leadership of
   American presidents after Watergate.

7. Many Americans became _____ about what the president
   and other government leaders were telling them, as a result of the
   Watergate scandal.

8. President Carter _____ predicted that the United States
   would continue to suffer economic hardships in the late 1970s.

9. Some Americans saw Carter's call for conservation and sacrifice as
   _____, and many were slow to cooperate.

10. Martin Luther King, Jr., almost _____ inspired thousands of
    African-Americans to demonstrate peacefully for their civil rights.

11. After the assassination of Martin Luther King, Jr., racial tensions in the
    United States were so high that many feared the country was on the
    _____ of a racial war.

12. Many conscientious white leaders _____ the cause of black
    civil rights and worked for peaceful integration in the South.

13. Although many blacks made important economic gains in the late 1960s
    and the 1970s, in the 1980s they started to be _____ again
    financially, along with others in the middle class.

14. Because the United States has been so active on the international scene, it
    may be hard to believe that there has also been a long-standing historical
    tradition of _____.

15. There can be no winners in a war that turns into a _____
    _____.

16. Some Americans believe that the country has once again reached a
    _____ _____ and should begin limiting the
    number of immigrants permitted to enter the United States.

17. If there are not enough common cultural ties to join people together in a country, there will probably be disagreements and even _____.

18. In the most popular game of _____, players must match the numbers (the white dots) of one of their pieces with one of the pieces already on the table.

 B. Comprehension Check

Write the letter of the best answer according to the information in the chapter.

_____ 1. Which of these statements is *not* true?
   a. People of different national origins have always gotten along well in the United States.
   b. The U.S. Constitution has been amended 26 times.
   c. The tradition of isolationism goes back to 1796.

_____ 2. Which decade do Americans remember nostalgically as a time when the economy was strong and there was national stability?
   a. the 1950s
   b. the 1960s
   c. the 1970s

_____ 3. Which president tried to fight poverty with government programs called "the Great Society"?
   a. Kennedy
   b. Johnson
   c. Reagan

_____ 4. The majority of American people were discouraged mainly by
   a. the immorality of the Vietnam War.
   b. failing to win the Vietnam War.
   c. the amount of money wasted in the Vietnam War.

_____ 5. Which of these events did *not* cause most Americans to become pessimistic about the future?
   a. Nixon was involved in the Watergate scandal.
   b. In the late 1970s, there was an oil crisis.
   c. Reagan cut taxes and increased spending on military weapons.

_____ 6. Which of these statements about President Reagan is *not* true?
   a. He believed that the national government should play a stronger role.
   b. He believed that business should be free from most government regulation.
   c. He believed that Americans should be able to get rich in the 1980s, as he had done after World War II.

_____ 7. In the 1980s,
   a. there was little economic growth.
   b. inflation and interest rates rose.
   c. the rich got richer and the poor got poorer.

_____ 8. In the 1990s,
   a. the Democrats regained control of Congress for the first time in 40 years.
   b. the mood of the country by the middle of the decade had become much more liberal.
   c. Congress had to deal with huge budget deficits from the 1980s.

_____ 9. Which of the following is *not* one of the values that works against a spirit of national cooperation in the United States?
   a. individual freedom
   b. competition
   c. hard work

_____ 10. Which of these statements is *not* true?
   a. The hope of finding the "American Dream" still attracts immigrants to the United States.
   b. Ben Wattenberg is pessimistic about the future of the United States and sees evidence of a nation in decline.
   c. Although some Americans believe that the country may have reached the saturation point, others believe that the United States needs the youth and vitality new immigrants bring.

C. Questions for Discussion

1. What do you think will happen to the balance of power in the world during the next 10 years? What countries are gaining influence? What role do you think your country will have in the 21st century? What role do you think the United States should play in international affairs?

2. How has your country changed in your lifetime? What is happening to your traditional cultures? What elements of American culture are popular in your country? What are the advantages and disadvantages of having a "global culture"?

3. How would you compare your country's policies on conservation with those of the United States? Is conservation important in your country? Are there any serious shortages? What plans does your country have to serve its energy needs in the future?

4. How does the government of your country encourage national cooperation? Does your government set national priorities for industrial development or agricultural production? How much control over the economy does your government have?

5. In general, what do you think about the American values presented in this book? What values do you think Americans should change? Are there any values in your country that you think should be changed?

6. Are you basically optimistic about the future? Why, or why not?

D. Cloze Summary Paragraph

This paragraph summarizes the chapter. Fill in each blank with any word that makes sense.

We can only guess _____*about*_____ the future of the _____ States, but there are _____ generalizations we can make _____ its past: the consistent _____ and racial diversity of _____ population, the stability of _____ form of government, the _____ debate of its problems, _____ historical tradition of isolationism, _____ the continuity of its _____ traditional values. The 20th _____ provided many challenges _____ the United States and _____ value system, particularly equality _____ opportunity. Some believe that _____ the future there should _____ less emphasis on individual _____ and more emphasis on _____ to solve national problems. _____ United States has become _____ microcosm of the world, _____ it may become the _____ "universal nation" as the _____ century begins.

E. Small Group Discussion

April 22, 1995 was the 25th anniversary of Earth Day. *USA Today* published a report on the state of the environment in the United States and conducted polls to see what Americans thought about environmental issues. Twenty-four percent said that they believed the United States had made a "great deal" of progress since the first Earth Day in 1970. Only 35 percent said that

LITTLE BY LITTLE, OUR WATERS ARE LOOKING LESS LIKE ART AND MORE LIKE TRASH.

You can help protect our water by using natural lawn care products, less toxic household cleaners and by recycling used motor oil.

Call 1-800-504-8484 and we'll send you more on how you can help protect our rivers, lakes and oceans forever.

CLEAN WATER. IF WE ALL DO A LITTLE WE CAN DO A LOT.

NRDC Natural Resources Defense Council   AC Japan Ad Council   Ad Council A Public Service of This Publication   EPA

NRDC Symbol, Japan Ad Council Symbol, Ad Council Symbol, EPA Symbol

environmental problems need "additional, immediate, drastic action," while 48 percent said "some additional actions" are required. Interestingly, 48 percent said they "trust the federal government more than private business to handle environmental issues."

What is the state of the environment in your country? What are the issues? Do you think that progress has been made in protecting the environment during your lifetime? Are things getting better, or worse? Look at the chart on the following page from *USA Today* and make comparisons with your country.

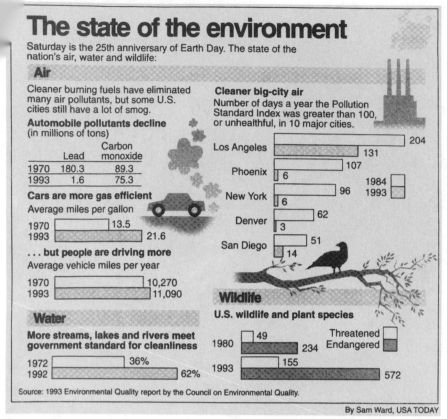

The state of the environment

Saturday is the 25th anniversary of Earth Day. The state of the nation's air, water and wildlife:

Air

Cleaner burning fuels have eliminated many air pollutants, but some U.S. cities still have a lot of smog.

Automobile pollutants decline
(in millions of tons)

	Lead	Carbon monoxide
1970	180.3	89.3
1993	1.6	75.3

Cars are more gas efficient
Average miles per gallon

1970	13.5
1993	21.6

. . . but people are driving more
Average vehicle miles per year

1970	10,270
1993	11,090

Water

More streams, lakes and rivers meet government standard for cleanliness

1972	36%
1992	62%

Cleaner big-city air
Number of days a year the Pollution Standard Index was greater than 100, or unhealthful, in 10 major cities.

Los Angeles	204 / 131
Phoenix	107 / 6
New York	96 / 6
Denver	62 / 3
San Diego	51 / 14

1984 / 1993

Wildlife

U.S. wildlife and plant species

Threatened / Endangered

1980	49 / 234
1993	155 / 572

Source: 1993 Environmental Quality report by the Council on Environmental Quality.

By Sam Ward, USA TODAY

F. Ask Americans

Find out what Americans think about the future. Ask several Americans the following questions, and record their answers. On the basis of your findings, do you think Americans are basically optimistic or pessimistic about the future?

1. Do you think America's best days are behind it or in the future?

2. What do you think your chances are of achieving "the good life"?
   Very good
   Fairly good
   Not very good
   Not good at all

3. Thinking now of your parents when they were your age, would you say you are better off financially than they were or not?

4. When you are older, do you expect to own more possessions than your parents do now, about the same, or less?

5. Do you agree or disagree with the following statements:

- Young people can no longer take for granted that they will be able to live better than their parents.
- People like me don't have much of a chance to be successful in life.

6. Now, thinking of your children when they get to be your age, would you say they will be better off financially than you are now or not as well off?

7. Where do you think the truly important work in solving our country's problems will be done in the next 10 years or so—the government or private organizations?

8. At the present time, do you think environmental protection laws and regulations have gone too far, not gone far enough, or struck about the right balance?

9. Which of these two statements comes closer to your own feelings?
   - We need to relax our environmental laws in order to achieve economic growth.
   - We need to maintain present environmental laws in order to preserve the environment for future generations.

10. There is still a controversy over energy needs and protecting the environment. Some people say that an adequate supply of energy is worth any risks to the environment. Others feel that it is better to risk not having enough energy than to risk spoiling the environment. Which side are you on? Are you more on the side of adequate energy or more on the side of protecting the environment?

 G. Think, Pair, Share

Do you agree or disagree with these statements? Circle your answers and share them with your partner. Then discuss your answers with another pair of students.

1. Nuclear power plants are basically safe and are good sources of energy for the future.	**agree**	**disagree**
2. Science and technology do more to improve the overall quality of life than do religion and philosophy.	**agree**	**disagree**
3. Protecting the environment is more important than industrial development.	**agree**	**disagree**
4. I expect to have more material possessions than my parents do now.	**agree**	**disagree**
5. I am confident that my children will have as good a life as mine or better.	**agree**	**disagree**
6. I am basically optimistic about the future.	**agree**	**disagree**

H. Ask Americans

Ask several Americans what they are concerned about. Record their answers, and then compare them with the poll that follows.

What are the serious problems facing the United States today? On a scale of zero to ten, how serious is each of these:

_____ Drug abuse

_____ The economy

_____ Federal deficit

_____ Health care system

_____ The job situation

_____ Moral values of society

_____ Public education system

_____ Violent crime

_____ Welfare system

Question: **On a scale of zero to ten, how serious do you feel...**

	Extremely serious problem for the country	Moderately serious	Not that serious
Violent crime	66%	28%	5%
Drug abuse	57%	31	11
Federal deficit	49%	35	13
Moral values of society	48%	33	18
Welfare system	45%	39	14
Health care system	39%	39	21
Public education system	34%	42	23
The economy	26%	48	24
The job situation	25%	44	29

Source: Survey by the Gallup Organization, September 14–17, 1995.

Reprinted by permission from *The American Enterprise*, a Washington-based magazine of politics, business and culture (1-800-596-2319)

I. Suggestions for Writing and Oral Reports

1. In 1995, about 20 years after the fall of Saigon to the North Vietnamese, Robert McNamara, the U.S. Secretary of Defense during the war in Vietnam, wrote a book about his experiences. He confessed that the United States could have or should have withdrawn in 1963 (after the assassination of the president of South Vietnam), in 1964 or 1965 (when the United States realized that South Vietnam could not defend itself), or in 1967 (when the CIA—Central Intelligence Agency—reported that bombing North Vietnam would not work). Instead, Presidents Johnson and Nixon hid the truth from the American public, using concepts like the domino theory, and 58,196 Americans were eventually killed or reported missing in action. Today, Americans still try to make sense of a war that bitterly divided their nation and devastated Southeast Asia. What experience has your country had with war? Is war ever justifiable? Under what circumstances do you think that your country should go to war? What should be the role of the United Nations in keeping peace?

2. If you were the leader of your country, what would be your priorities? Imagine that you are running for office, and write a campaign speech. Present the challenges now facing your country, and explain what you would do if you were elected. How would you deal with today's problems? What would your vision be for the future?

J. Have a Panel Discussion: Small Group Work

There is an ongoing debate about whether or not to limit immigration to the United States. What are some of the positive contributions that immigrants bring to a country? What are some of the negatives? Divide the class into groups to study various aspects of this issue. Each group should examine a different aspect and then appoint a spokesperson for the group. That person will be on a panel made up of one representative from each group. Members of the group should help their spokesperson to prepare his or her presentation, and then should be available to offer additional ideas and support during the panel discussion. (The following information is on the United States, but you may choose to discuss the pros and cons of immigration in your country or on a worldwide basis.) After each group has presented its information, as a class decide what a good immigration policy might be.

Aspects to consider:

1. Contributions immigrants make. For example, *Time* magazine profiled a Haitian refugee named Berenice Belizaire, who is a student at Massachusetts Institute of Technology. The writer points out that immigrant energy really revitalized New York City in the 1980s. Immigrants brought business to the New York stores, and they started many new businesses of their own. "They added far more to the local economy than they removed; more important,

they reminded enlightened New Yorkers that the city had always worked best as a vast, noisy, dreamy hothouse for the cultivation of new Americans."

2. Problems immigrants bring.

3. How natives feel about immigrants.

4. What governments must do to help immigrants.

5. Famous immigrants.

6. Special problems refugees have and what must be done to address them.

7. Immigration laws and regulations.

 ## K. Final Project

Analyze some aspect of American culture and find specific examples of the six values covered in this text. You may not find examples of all six in what you analyze, but there should be mention of at least two or three of the values.

You may wish to analyze an American movie, a TV show, commercials on TV, advertisements in newspapers or magazines, some current event on the news, the results of interviews or conversations you have with Americans about their beliefs, or observations you have made about how Americans behave. You may choose any aspect of life in the United States that you have observed.

If you prefer, you may approach the assignment from a different direction—you may choose a value and then describe how you have observed that value existing in American life, with specific examples. You may also wish to contrast this value with your own culture and how things are done differently. When you have finished your analysis, prepare a short speech to report your findings to the rest of the class.

The six traditional values, again, are:

Individual freedom—the freedom of individuals to meet their own individual needs and to do what they want

Self-reliance—being able to take care of themselves and not depend on others for support

Equality of opportunity—having an equal chance to succeed, regardless of being male or female or being part of some racial or ethnic minority

Competition—having to compete with others for success, not expecting to be given something

Material wealth—seeing possessions as the mark of having status in the society and as the natural reward for hard work

Hard work—the belief that everyone should work hard, sometimes putting in very long hours, to be successful

L. What's Your Opinion? Small Group Discussion

Theodore H. White, a well-known political analyst, has said that the problem the United States has is "trying to do everything for everybody." Ever since the early 1960s, he says, Americans have been making promises—

> ...promises to save the cities, promises to take care of the sick, the old, the universities.... Many of our problems flow out of American goodwill, trying to do everything for everybody.... In the 1960s we exploded with goodwill as blacks, who had been denied equality, rightfully demanded it. We could afford it, and we should have done what we did. But we have ended up pushing equality and other ideas to absurd limits as we sought perfect equality rather than realistic equality of opportunity.... We have to choose what we can do; we have to discipline our goodwill.*

Contrast this view with that expressed by Martin Luther King, Jr., in his "I Have a Dream" speech. In 1963, on the 100th anniversary of the Emancipation Proclamation that freed the slaves in the southern states that had left the Union, there was a huge civil rights march in Washington, D.C. Martin Luther King, Jr., delivered his famous speech on the steps of Lincoln Memorial to several hundred thousand marchers. In the speech, he spoke of the journey of the African-Americans from slavery into freedom, and the need to continue the journey so that they could one day have equality with the whites, and be truly free from prejudice and discrimination.

The "I Have a Dream" speech is one of the finest in the English language, and one that you should hear. If you are in the United States, your university or town library probably has a videotape of it, or you may purchase an audio- or videotape from the Martin Luther King, Jr., Center in Atlanta, Georgia. The speech concludes with a quote from the Declaration of Independence and an old African-American folk song. Here are some excerpts:

> Five score years ago, a great American, in whose symbolic shadow we stand today, signed the Emancipation Proclamation.... But one hundred years later, the Negro still is not free....One hundred years later, the Negro is still anguished in the corners of American society and finds himself in exile in his own land. And so we have come here today to dramatize a shameful condition.
>
> In a sense, we have come to our nation's capital to cash a check. When the architects of our republic wrote the magnificent words of the Constitution and the Declaration of

---

* White, Theodore H. "America's Problem: 'Trying to Do Everything for Everybody.'" *U.S. News and World Report.* 5 July 1982, 59-60.

Martin Luther King, Jr. **AFL/CIO News**

Independence, they were signing a promissory note to which every American was to fall heir. This note was a promise that all men—yes, Black men as well as white men—would be guaranteed the inalienable rights of life, liberty, and the pursuit of happiness.

It is obvious that America has defaulted on this promissory note insofar as her citizens of color are concerned.... Now is the time to make real the promises of democracy.... Now is the time to make justice a reality for all of God's children....

I say to you today, my friends, even though we face the difficulties of today and tomorrow, I still have a dream. It is a dream deeply rooted in the American dream.... I have a dream that my four little children will one day live in a nation where they will not be judged by the color of their skin, but by the content of their character.... I have a dream today.

I have a dream that one day this nation will rise up and live out the true meaning of its creed: "We hold these truths to be self-evident, that all men are created equal."... [One day] all of God's children, Black men and white men, Jews and Gentiles, Protestants and Catholics, will be able to join hands and sing in the words of the old Negro spiritual: "Free at last! Free at last! Thank God Almighty. We are free at last."

Now that you have finished this book, what do you think the "American Dream" is? How can Americans protect it for future generations? How much can and should a nation do to ensure equality of opportunity for its people?

M. Suggestions for Further Reading

- Robert Woodward and Carl Bernstein, *All the President's Men*
- Alvin Toffler, *The Third Wave*
- Alvin Toffler, *Future Shock*
- George Orwell, *1984*
- Aldous Huxley, *Brave New World*
- Theodore Roszak, *The Making of a Counter Culture*
- Nathan McCall, *Makes Me Wanna Holler: A Young Black Man in America*
- Studs Terkel, *Race: How Blacks and Whites Think and Feel about the American Obsession*
- Peter Bimelow, *Alien Nation: Common Sense About America's Immigration Disaster*

N. Recommended Movies

- *"I Have a Dream" Speech*
- *El Norte*
- *All the President's Men*

Greater Houston Convention & Visitors Bureau

Bibliography

Aaron, Henry J., Thomas E. Mann, and Timothy Taylor, eds. "Introduction." *Values and Public Policy*. Washington, D.C.: The Brookings Institution, 1994.

Alger, Horatio. *Mark the Match Boy, or Richard Hunter's Ward*. Philadelphia: John C. Winston Company, 1897.

Alger, Horatio. *Tony the Tramp, or Right Is Might*. New York: The New York Book Company, 1909.

"America's Heartland: The Midwest's New Role in the Global Economy. *Business Week*. 11 July 1994, 116–124.

"America's Immigrant Challenge." *Time* Magazine. Special Issue, Fall 1993, 3–12.

Becker, Carl L. *The Declaration of Independence: A Study in the History of Political Ideas*. New York: Vintage Books, 1958.

"Been There, Done That" [Adventure Travel]. *Newsweek*. 19 July 1993, 42–49.

Blackman, Ann. "Lowell's Little Acre: Gateway for Immigrants." *Time* Magazine. Special Issue, Fall 1993, 34.

"Breaking the Divorce Cycle." *Newsweek*. 13 January 1992, 48–53.

Brogan, D. W. *The American Character*. New York: Alfred A. Knopf, 1944.

Brogan, Hugh. *Tocqueville*. London: Fontana, 1973.

Brookheser, Richard. "We Call All Share American Culture." *Time* Magazine. 31 August 1992, 74.

Burns, James MacGregor. *Cobblestone Leadership: Majority Rule, Minority Power*. Norman: University of Oklahoma Press, 1990.

Burns, James MacGregor. *Deadlock of Democracy: Far-Party Politics in America*. Englewood Cliffs, N.J.: Prentice-Hall, 1963.

Carlson, Margaret. "And Now, Obesity Rights." *Time* Magazine. 6 December 1993, 96.

Carnegie, Andrew. *Autobiography of Andrew Carnegie*. Boston: Houghton Mifflin, 1920.

Carnegie, Andrew. *The Gospel of Wealth and Other Timely Essays*. Cambridge: Harvard University, Belknap Press, 1962.

Cash, W. J. *The Mind of the South*. New York: Alfred A. Knopf, 1960.

Cater, Douglass, ed. *Television as a Social Force: New Approaches to TV Criticism*. New York: Praeger, 1975.

Church, George. "Unions Arise—With New Tricks." *Time* Magazine. 13 June 1994, 56–58.

Church, George. "We're #1—And It Hurts." *Time* Magazine. 24 October 1994, 50-56.

"A Class of Their Own." *Time* Magazine. 31 October 1994, 52–61.

Counts, George S. *Education and American Civilization*. New York: Bureau of Publications, Teachers College, Columbia University, 1952.

Counts, George S. *Education and the Foundations of Human Freedom*. Pittsburgh: University of Pittsburgh Press, 1962.

"Crunching Numbers: New Data on How We Eat." *Consumer Reports*. July 1994, 491.

"Daughters of Murphy Brown" [Single Motherhood]. *Newsweek*. 2 August 1993, 58–59.

"The Dawn of Online Home Schooling." *Newsweek*. 10 October 1994, 67.

"Domesticated Bliss: New Laws Are Making It Official for Gay or Live-In Straight Couples." *Newsweek*. 23 March 1992, 62–63.

"Dying Dream." *Guardian Education*. 5 July 1994, 4–5.

"The '80s: A Final Reckoning." *Newsweek*. 1 March 1993, 49.

Ellwood, Robert S. "East Asian Religions in Today's America." *World Religions in America: An Introduction*, ed. Jacob Neusner. Louisville, Ky.: Westminster/John Knox Press, 1994.

Elson, John. "The Great Migration." *Time* Magazine. Special Issue, Fall 1993, 28–33.

"Endangered Family." *Newsweek*. 30 August 1993, 16–27.

"An Epidemic of Obesity." *Newsweek*. 1 August 1994, 62–63.

Esposito, John L. "Islam in the World and in America." *World Religions in America: An Introduction*, ed. Jacob Neusner. Louisville, Ky.: Westminster/John Knox Press, 1994.

Farrand, Max. *The Framing of the Constitution of the United States*. New Haven: Yale University Press, 1913.

"The Fight to Bear Arms." *U.S. News & World Report*. 22 May 1995, 28–37.

Fineman, Howard. "Throwing a Mighty Tantrum: The Lure of Third-Party Candidacies." *Newsweek*. 27 April 1992, 28.

Fineman, Howard. "The Virtuecrats." *Newsweek*. 13 June 1994, 31–36.

Fox-Genovese, Elizabeth. "Religion and Women in America." *World Religions in America: An Introduction*, ed. Jacob Neusner. Louisville, Ky.: Westminster/John Knox Press, 1994.

"Fractured Family Ties: Television's New Theme is Single Parenting." *Newsweek*. 30 August 1993, 50–52.

Frank, Jeffrey A. "Our Guns, Our Selves: Clinton's Common-Sense Message to Urban— and Rural—America." *Washington Post*, 12 February 1995, 5(C).

Friedan, Betty. *The Feminine Mystique*. New York: W. W. Norton, 1963.

Friedan, Betty. *The Second Stage*. New York: Summit Books, 1981.

Galbraith, John Kenneth. *American Capitalism: The Concept of Countervailing Power*. Classics in Economics Series. Boston: Houghton Mifflin, 1956.

Galbraith, John Kenneth. *The Affluent Society*. Boston: Houghton Mifflin, 1976.

Galbraith, John Kenneth. *The Culture of Contentment*. Boston: Houghton Mifflin, 1992.

Gates, David. "White Male Paranoia." *Newsweek*. 29 March 1993, 48–53.

Gelman, David. "The Violence in Our Heads." *Newsweek*. 2 August 1993, 48.

Gibbs, Nancy. "Angels Among Us." *Time* Magazine. 27 December 1993, 56–65.

Gibbs, Nancy. "The Vicious Cycle." *Time* Magazine. 20 June 1994, 24–33.

Gill, Sam. "Native Americans and Their Religions." *World Religions in America: An Introduction*, ed. Jacob Neusner. Louisville, Ky.: Westminster/John Knox Press, 1994.

Glazer, Nathan. "Multiculturalism and Public Policy." *Values and Public Policy*, ed. Henry J. Aaron, Thomas E. Mann, and Timothy Taylor. Washington, D.C.: The Brookings Institution, 1994.

Glazer, Nathan and Daniel P. Moynihan. *Beyond the Melting Pot: The Negroes, Puerto Ricans, Jews, Italians, and Irish of NYC.* Publications of the Joint Center for Urban Studies. Cambridge: M.I.T Press, 1963.

Gonzalez, David. "What's the Problem with 'Hispanic'? Just Ask a 'Latino.' " *New York Times*, 15 November 1992.

Gonzalez, Justo L. "The Religious World of Hispanic Americans." *World Religions in America: An Introduction*, ed. Jacob Neusner. Louisville, Ky.: Westminster/John Knox Press, 1994.

Greeley, Andrew M. "The Catholics in the World and in America." *World Religions in America: An Introduction*, ed. Jacob Neusner. Louisville, Ky.: Westminster/John Knox Press, 1994.

Greeley, Andrew M. "Religion and Politics in America." *World Religions in America: An Introduction*, ed. Jacob Neusner. Louisville, Ky.: Westminster/John Knox Press, 1994.

Green, William Scott. "Religion and Society in America." *World Religions in America: An Introduction*, ed. Jacob Neusner. Louisville, Ky.: Westminster/John Knox Press, 1994.

Handlin, Oscar. *Race and Nationality in American Life.* Boston: Little, Brown, 1957.

Henry, W. A. "Pride and Prejudice." *Time* Magazine. 28 February 1994.

Hinson, Hal. "Life, Liberty and the Pursuit of Cows: How the Western Defines America's View of Itself." *Washington Post*, 3 July 1994, 1(G), 6(G).

Hofstadter, Richard. *The American Political Tradition and the Men Who Made It.* New York: Vintage Books, 1954.

Hofstadter, Richard. *Social Darwinism in American Thought.* New York: G. Braziller, 1969.

"In Search of the Sacred." *Newsweek.* 28 November 1994, 52–55.

Jones, Malcolm. "The New Turf Wars: A Plague of Critics Bushwhacks the Venerable American Lawn." *Newsweek.* 21 June 1993, 62–63.

Kegley, Charles, and Eugene Wittkopf. *World Politics: Trend and Transformations*, 3d ed. New York: St. Martin's, 1989.

Kennedy, John F. *A Nation of Immigrants.* New York: Harper & Row, 1958.

"Kids Who Care: Everybody Wins When Students Volunteer to Help Out." *Better Homes and Gardens.* March 1992, 37–39.

King, Martin Luther, Jr. *I Have a Dream.* Littleton, Mass.: Sundance Publications, 1991.

Klein, Joe. "The Education of Berenice Belizaire." *Time* Magazine. 9 August 1993, 26.

Klein, Joe. "Whose Family? Whose Values? Who Makes the Choices?" *Newsweek.* 8 June 1992, 18–22.

Lasch, Christopher. *The Culture of Narcissism: American Life in an Age of Diminishing Expectations.* New York: W. W. Norton, 1978.

Lipset, Seymour Martin. *Continental Divide: The Values and Institutions of the United States and Canada.* New York: Routledge, 1990.

Lipset, Seymour Martin. *American Exceptionalism: A Double-Edged Sword.* New York: W. W. Norton, 1996.

"Losing Ground: New Fears and Suspicions as Black America's Outlook Grows Bleaker."
Newsweek. 6 April 1992, 20-22.

Lowi, Theodore. *The End of Liberalism: Republic of the United States*. New York:
W.W. Norton, 1969.

Lowi, Theodore, and Benjamin Ginsberg. *American Government: Freedom and Power*.
New York: W. W. Norton, 1994.

Macbay, Harvey. *Swim with the Sharks Without Being Eaten Alive*. New York: William
Morrow Company, 1988.

McCarroll, Thomas. "Executive Pay: The Shareholders Strike Back." *Time* Magazine.
4 May 1992, 46–48.

Malcolm X and Alex Haley. *The Autobiography of Malcolm X*. New York: Grove Publishers,
1966.

"Malcolm X." *Newsweek*. 16 November 1992, 66–71.

Mansbridge, Jane. "Public Spirit in Political Systems." *Values and Public Policy*,
ed. Henry J. Aaron, Thomas E. Mann, and Timothy Taylor. Washington, D.C.:
The Brookings Institution, 1994.

Marty, Martin E. "Protestant Christianity in the World and in America." *World Religions
in America: An Introduction*, ed. Jacob Neusner. Louisville, Ky.: Westminster/John
Knox Press, 1994.

Mason, Alpheus T. *In Quest of Freedom: American Political Thought and Practice*.
Englewood Cliffs, N.J.: Prentice-Hall, 1959.

Mason, Alpheus T., and Gordon E. Baker, eds. *Free Government in the Making: Readings
in American Political Thought*. New York: Oxford University Press, 1949.

Mathews, Jessica. "Immigration and the Press of the Poor." *Washington Post*,
21 November 1994, 25(A).

Morganthau, Tom. "America: Still a Melting Pot?" *Newsweek*. 9 August 1993, 16–23.

Morrow, Lance. "Family Values." *Time* Magazine. 31 August 1992, 22–27.

Nelan, Bruce W. "Not So Welcome Anymore." *Time* Magazine. Special Issue, Fall 1993,
10–12.

Neusner, Jacob, ed. "Introduction." *World Religions in America: An Introduction*.
Louisville, Ky.: Westminster/John Knox Press, 1994.

Nevins, Allan, and Henry Steele Commager. *America: The Story of a Free People*. Boston:
Little, Brown, 1942.

"A New Era of Segregation: Classrooms Still Aren't Colorblind." *Newsweek*. 27 December
1993, 44.

"Networks Under the Gun." *Newsweek*. 12 July 1993, 64–66.

"The Numbers Game." *Time* Magazine. Special Issue, Fall 1993, 14–15.

"Nutrition" [Polls]. *The American Enterprise*. March/April 1994, 94.

Paris, Peter J. "The Religious World of African Americans." *World Religions in America:
An Introduction*, ed. Jacob Neusner. Louisville, Ky.: Westminster/ John Knox Press,
1994.

Peterson, Peter. *Facing Up: How to Rescue the Economy from Crushing Debt and Restore
the American Dream*. New York: Simon & Schuster, 1993.

Popenoe, David. "The Family Condition of America: Cultural Change and Public Policy." *Values and Public Policy*, ed. Henry J. Aaron, Thomas E. Mann, and Timothy Taylor. Washington, D.C.: The Brookings Institution, 1994.

Potter, David M. *People of Plenty: Economic Abundance and the American Character*. Chicago: University of Chicago Press, 1969.

Quinn, Jane Bryant. "The Taxpayers vs. Higher Ed." *Newsweek*. 15 November 1993, 51.

"Rage of the [Black] Privileged." *Newsweek*. 15 November 1993, 56–63.

Reeves, Richard. *American Journey: Travelling with Tocqueville in Search of Democracy in America*. New York: Simon & Schuster, 1982.

Reich, Charles A. *The Greening of America*. New York: Random House, 1970.

Reich, Robert. *The Work of Nations: Preparing Ourselves for 21st-Century Capitalism*. New York: Alfred A. Knopf, 1991.

"A Rich Legacy of Preference: Alumni Kids Get a Big Break on Admissions." *Newsweek*. 24 June 1991, 59.

Riesman, David. *The Lonely Crowd: A Study on the Changing American Character*. New Haven: Yale University Press, 1950.

Riesman, David. *Individualism Reconsidered and Other Essays*. Glencoe, Ill.: The Free Press, 1954.

Roberts, Sam. *Who We Are: A Portrait of America Based on the Latest U.S. Census*. New York: Times Books, 1993.

Saad, Lydia, and Leslie McAneny. "Most Americans Think Religion Losing Clout in the 1990s: But Personal Faith Remains High." *The Gallup Poll Monthly*. April 1994, 2–4.

"Saving Youth from Violence." *Carnegie Quarterly*. Winter 1994, 1–15.

Scanzoni, John. *Opportunity and the Family*. New York: The Free Press, 1970.

Scanzoni, John. *Sex Roles, Lifestyles, and Childbearing: Changing Patterns in Marriage and the Family*. New York: The Free Press, 1975.

Schlesinger, Arthur M., Jr. *The Disuniting of America: Reflections on a Multicultural Society*. New York: W. W. Norton, 1992.

"Sexism in the Schoolhouse: A Report Charges That Schools Favor Boys Over Girls." *Newsweek*. 24 February 1992, 62.

"The Simple Life." *Time* Magazine. 8 April 1991, 58–63.

Solomon, Julie. "How Much Should We Be Paid?" *Newsweek*. 8 November 1993, 58.

Stampp, Kenneth. *The Peculiar Institution: Slavery in the Ante-Bellum South*. New York: Vintage Books, 1956.

Suro, Roberto. "Study of Immigrants Finds Asians at Top in Science and Medicine." *Washington Post*, 18 April 1994, 6(A).

Takaki, Ronald. *A Different Mirror: A History of Multicultural America*. Boston: Little, Brown, 1993.

Tauber, Peter. "A Free Country?" *Family Circle*. 3 September 1991, 130

Tocqueville, Alexis de. *Democracy in America*. New York: J. & H. G. Langley, 1845.

Toffler, Alvin. *Power Shift: Knowledge, Wealth, and Violence at the Edge of the 21st Century*. New York: Bantam Books, 1991.

"Trouble at the Top: A U.S. Survey Says a 'Glass Ceiling' Blocks Women from Corporate Heights." *U.S. News and World Report*. 17 June 1991, 40–48.

Turner, Frederick Jackson. *The Rise of the New West*. New York: Harper & Brothers, 1906.

Waldman, Steven. "Benefits 'R' Us." *Newsweek*. 10 August 1992, 56–58.

"The War for the West." *Newsweek*. 30 September 1991, 18–32.

Waters, Harry F. "On the Trail of Tears: Ted Turner's Massive, Compelling Chronicle of the Native American Order." *Newsweek*. 10 October 1994, 56–58.

Wattenberg, Ben J. *The Real America: A Surprising Examination of the State of the Union*. New York: Doubleday, 1974.

Wattenberg, Ben J. *The Good News Is the Bad News Is Wrong*. New York: Simon & Schuster, 1984.

Wattenberg, Ben J. *The First Universal Nation: Leading Indicators and Ideas about the Surge of America in the 1990s*. New York: The Free Press, 1991.

Wattenberg, Ben J. *Values Matter Most: How Republicans or Democrats or a Third Party Can Win and Renew the American Way of Life*. New York: The Free Press, 1995.

Weiss, Michael. *Latitudes & Attitudes: An Atlas of Tastes, Trends, Politics and Passions*. Boston: Little, Brown, 1994.

West, Cornel. "The '80s: Market Culture Run Amok." *Newsweek*. 3 January 1994, 48–49.

"When America Went to the Moon." *U.S. News & World Report*. 11 July 1994, 50–60.

Wilson, James Q. "Culture, Incentives, and the Underclass." *Values and Public Policy*, ed. Henry J. Aaron, Thomas E. Mann, and Timothy Taylor. Washington, D.C.: The Brookings Institution, 1994.

Woodward, Kenneth. "Dead End for the Mainline: The Mightiest Protestants Are Running Out of Money, Members and Meaning." *Newsweek*. 9 August 1993, 46–48.

Woodward, Kenneth. "Angels: Hark! America's Latest Search for Spiritual Meaning Has a Halo Effect." *Newsweek*. 27 December 1993, 52–57.

Woodward, Kenneth L. "What Is Virtue?" *Newsweek*. 13 June 1994, 38–39.

Yankelovich, Daniel. *New Rules: Searching for Self-Fulfillment in a World Turned Upside Down*. New York: Random House, 1981.

Yankelovich, Daniel. "How Changes in the Economy Are Reshaping American Values." In *Values and Public Policy*, ed. Henry J. Aaron, Thomas E. Mann, and Timothy Taylor. Washington, D.C.: The Brookings Institution, 1994.

New Word Index

The number after each word indicates the *page* in which the word was first introduced.

New Word Index **277**